Bill's Secrets

Belinda Probert

Belinda Probert grew up with her two brothers on the Pilgrims Way in Kent. She studied economics at University College London before doing a PhD on the Troubles in Northern Ireland. She then accepted a job at the newly opened Murdoch University in Western Australia to teach peace and conflict studies and social and political theory, but also to explore her Australian family connections. Moving to Melbourne she felt very much at home, making a career as an academic at Monash and RMIT universities. She is the author of books about Northern Ireland, gender equity, and working lives in Australia. Her most recent book *Imaginative Possession: Learning to Live in the Antipodes*, describes her attempts, as an immigrant, to understand the landscapes of Australia and the people who have shaped them. She lives in Melbourne in a family compound.

Belinda Probert

Bill's Secrets

Class, War and Ambition

UPSWELL

First published in Australia in 2025
by Upswell Publishing
Perth, Western Australia
upswellpublishing.com

Upswell operates in the city of Perth, on ancient country of the Whadjuk people of the Noongar nation who remain the spiritual and cultural custodians of this beautiful land. We acknowledge their continuing connection to country and express gratitude to elders past and present for their strength and creativity...Always was, always will be, Aboriginal land.

This book is copyright. Apart from any fair dealing for the purpose of private study, research, criticism or review, as permitted under the *Copyright Act 1968*, no part may be reproduced by any process without written permission. Enquiries should be made to the publisher.

Copyright © 2025 Belinda Probert

The moral right of the author has been asserted.

ISBN: 978-0-6459840-4-0

A catalogue record for this book is available from the National Library of Australia

Cover design by Chil3, Fremantle
Typeset in Foundry Origin by Lasertype
Printed by Lightning Source

Upswell Publishing is assisted by the State of Western Australia through its funding program for arts and culture.

For Colin and William

Contents

Introduction		11
Chapter 1	Coal is King: Born in the Rhondda	19
Chapter 2	The Education of Roy	41
Chapter 3	Roy's War: Secrecy and Bravery	65
Chapter 4	Never Going Back	99
Chapter 5	Love and Spying: From Vienna to Civvy Street	115
Chapter 6	Success: International Business and Life in the Stockbroker Belt	147
Chapter 7	Boredom and Frustration: From the City to the River Teifi	195
Chapter 8	France: Death and Discovery	215
Chapter 9	A Family Reconsidered	225
Chapter 10	Coda	235
Notes		249
Acknowledgements		263

As soon as we die, we enter into fiction. Just ask two different family members to tell you about someone recently gone, and you will see what I mean. Once we can no longer speak for ourselves, we are interpreted. When we remember—as psychologists so often tell us—we don't reproduce the past, we create it.

Hilary Mantel

Introduction

My father died on 8 April 1994 in the excellent heart clinic at Aressy, on the outskirts of Pau in the Béarn region of south-west France. He was seventy-eight years old, and his heart had been causing trouble for several years, though he had managed to continue playing golf and walking in the Pyrenees for most of this time. My brothers and I gathered from our respective homes in San Francisco, the Mayenne in north-western France and Melbourne to be with our mother for his funeral in the little church of St Faust de Haut, the village where they had lived for the last eleven years. The funeral was a small affair, partly because of the location, but also because Bill had no relatives apart from us: no brothers, no sisters, no nephews, no nieces and no cousins at any remove. His only brother, Colin—after whom Dad had wanted his first son to be named—had died a long time ago. William Royden Probert was buried in the village cemetery, on a gentle slope facing south towards the mountains, under a simple headstone made from local pink rock that left room for his wife Janet's name to be added.

The Bill we knew had been a successful businessman, always travelling overseas for work, speaking several languages fluently, cultured and well-read, a lover of all things French. He spoke the Queen's English in a way that meant no one asked him where he was from. We also knew him as Major W. R. Probert, DSO, who sometimes wore his parachute regiment tie, and who had done something brave during the liberation of France at the end of the Second World War. He always dressed well, and held himself upright, with his confident broad shoulders never edging forward. Bill was not an easy father, and his restlessness disrupted family life on several occasions; but I always thought his ability and willingness to try something completely new was admirable. It was as though he had managed to fit several lives into one, adding fly-fishing, house design and house building (twice) and sheep farming in Wales to the end of his international business career, and then following this up with the move to the Béarn.

Helping my mother sort through his finances before I returned to my life in Melbourne, I was impressed to see just how much money he had invested in bonds with Credit Suisse in Guernsey. I think I remember him telling me once that his aim was to leave us £1 million in that account.

*

About four months after Bill's funeral, Janet's favourite postman, Laurent, got out of his yellow van and handed over the gate an envelope addressed to Mr W. R. Probert. When Janet opened it, she found a lengthy handwritten letter from someone called Denzil Griffiths.

Brynhyfryd, Alexandria Rd, Brecon, Powys, Wales

Hello,

This letter will come as a surprise or maybe even an irritation.

The above address is surely the immediate give away, the name Denzil will confirm who I am.

How I have been able to find you is a long story, I'll just say that by complete chance it was through friends on holiday in the Pau area. This after many years of fruitless searching through military and official channels ...

Much has happened since those far off days in Ynyshir.

Denzil goes on to describe his wife and family and his career in Brecon, including being a local councillor for the past twenty-six years and mayor, and his pride in being selected as the Tory parliamentary candidate for Brecon and Radnor fifteen years earlier. He explains that his wife and children had arranged a special sixtieth birthday holiday for him in Pau, only twelve kilometres north of St Faust, so that he could surprise Bill with a visit. Sadly, Denzil had to send this letter instead, because the trip was delayed while he received hospital treatment of some kind. Denzil ends the letter by saying:

> I certainly want to meet with you personally again after all these years and perhaps simply learn of other members of your family.
>
> If there is no reply to this letter don't be too surprised if I arrive unannounced on your door-step from my hotel in Pau.

I do not have a copy of the letter Janet sent in reply to Denzil, but she must have told him that Bill had died recently, and that she had never heard of Ynyshir, nor indeed of Denzil and his family, and that she did not know who he was.

Denzil's response felt more like a depth charge than a bombshell.

> Dear Aunty Janet ... I am replying immediately to tell you all I know about Uncle Roy. I trust you won't mind me referring to him as such. This is the name the whole family addressed him by and I am so used to it now.

Denzil, it appears, was Bill's nephew, the son of a sister called Lily.

What Janet was about to discover was that Bill was born into a large mining family in the Rhondda, most of whom were still alive when she married him—including his mother, who lived for another seven years after this event, always in the same family house in Ynyshir. Ynyshir, we learn, is in one of the Rhondda valleys of South Wales.

According to Denzil, Roy simply disappeared from their life at the end of the Second World War. Unlike the rest of Roy's family, Denzil had subsequently spent decades looking for the war-hero uncle he so greatly admired.

Much warm correspondence was exchanged with our newly discovered relative—about Roy's Welsh-speaking father, his mother and Roy's many siblings; but nothing really seemed to explain why or how Roy from the Rhondda had at some point become Bill from Kent. There was no family story about an argument or conflict which might explain the rift, and Denzil had never heard anyone in the family speak ill of Roy. On the contrary, he had only heard warm words about him—albeit very few.

*

Janet lived on in the Béarn until her death in 2010, and from time to time I would become curious again about my father, imagining that Bill must have given something away during their long marriage. A few years before Janet died, I made the journey to Ynyshir myself, and stood outside the narrow terrace house where he had lived, and where his mother—it is hard to think of her as my grandmother—was still living when I was born. But Bill had never let anything slip and his four siblings, considerably older than him, were all dead, leaving nothing to go on apart from Denzil's information. Perhaps if I had lived in Britain, I would have made a serious effort to find Roy earlier, but from Australia it was all too hard. It had never been easy to be close to Bill, so it was more baffling than upsetting. The Bill we knew seemed such a strong and authoritative personality that there was little room for uneasy or troubling questions in our family background.

In 2022, almost thirty years after we were first confronted with this revelation about the identity of our father, my brothers and I made a serious effort to see each other. Living our whole adult lives on different continents, we have never been good at getting together, and we couldn't even meet by Zoom without one of us having to be in their pyjamas. However, the isolation imposed on each one of us by the Coronavirus pandemic (and our advancing years) made this get-together a priority. We agreed to spend two weeks in San Francisco, staying in the comfortable apartment on the bay belonging to Colin (the eldest) and his wife. It was the most time we had spent together since we were children and now, in our seventies, talk turned eventually to our mysterious father.

We began to think about the anomalies in our childhood that could have alerted us to his far-from-middle-class origins, such as his love of professional boxing and his enthusiasm for betting on the football pools. We argued about whether he could have been ashamed of his own family. We did not fancy ourselves as psychoanalysts, and whatever psychological bruises we might have incurred from Bill's periodic attacks on each of us, we were well beyond worrying about them now. I found myself thinking that I was mature enough to make a major effort to understand his life better, and that it was now or never. What appealed to me was the prospect of gathering every fact that I could about his life and re-assessing everything I thought I knew about him. We could try to work out how he managed to evolve from the son of a colliery blacksmith in the poverty-stricken Rhondda of the 1920s to the debonair man in the city, wearing his Moss Bros. double-breasted suits and driving a Jaguar. I said I would take this project on if they were as interested as I now was—which they were.

*

In discovering how Roy made his way out of the Rhondda, and how his wartime experiences gave him the opportunity to become Bill, I uncovered new secrets about his post-war life. As I went down a lot of rabbit holes, chasing the fragments of information I had, it suddenly became clear that his role with British intelligence had not ended with his last wartime mission in France. And in the middle of all my combing through historical archives, my brothers and I found a new relative—because someone else was also searching for the mysterious Major Bill Probert, DSO.

It had not occurred to us that a man so obviously good at keeping secrets might be hiding more than his working-class origins, but it should have crossed our minds that if we went searching, we might find something. I had never paid much attention to the growing world-wide enthusiasm for ancestry research, and programs like *Who Do You Think You Are?* but I now understand how one can become addicted to digging around on Ancestry.com or in military records. Almost everyone has a surprising ancestor somewhere—a criminal or a hero, a victim or a perpetrator—who will surface to nourish your hopes or fears.

But what if the focus of the hunt is your parent, who lived to a decent old age, and whom you thought you knew quite well? We are surely formed to some degree by our parents, whether this expresses itself by wanting to emulate them or reject them, so how will new discoveries about a parent make us feel?

Is it possible that I want to find out about my father's early history because this might make him more loveable? Or because it might make me feel differently about my experience of him? If I uncover more secrets, will they change my own past, or just briefly unsettle it? Will finding the 'truth' bring a parent closer, or might it have the opposite effect—because what you took for granted about that person becomes ambiguous; what seemed certain is replaced not by new certainties but by uncertainty.

While my brothers and I agreed that we should start with a fact-finding mission, in the end these facts would, I came to realise, have to be interpreted—inserted into a new story about our father. And if I am the one telling this new story, then the story will inevitably be coloured—if not shaped—by my memories, my experiences and my beliefs. I have spent most of my working life thinking about how societies function, how patterns of inequality are produced and reproduced and sometimes disrupted, and how families are shaped by economic and cultural forces. But alongside this analytical frame of mind, it is also true that I am a temperamental radical, better suited to the daily egalitarianism of Australia than the deferential traditions I grew up with in England. This may influence what I see and what I miss.

*

As more facts about Bill's life came into focus, his story seemed to map onto the major social transformations of Britain in the twentieth century. A mixture of luck and ability helped Roy navigate the collapse of the Welsh coal communities in the 1920s and the Depression years that followed, and his gift for languages and his courage (or it could have been foolhardiness) gave him extraordinary opportunities in the Second World War. He emerged as Bill, filled with ambition to make a good life and camouflaged to take full advantage of the economic boom years of the 1950s and 1960s. Perhaps his greatest stroke of luck was to find his wife, Janet. But this did not prevent him from keeping secrets from her, not only about his own family, but also his continued work in intelligence. It is a tribute to his extraordinary ability to keep secrets that none of us had any idea that his Welsh-ness went far beyond our Welsh family name. Until that letter arrived from Denzil, which in turn set us off on this belated project to understand how Roy became Bill, and what Bill did.

Chapter 1
Coal is King: Born in the Rhondda

Our newly discovered cousin Denzil gave us the address in Ynyshir where Roy's family lived from when he was a very small boy until his mother died in 1954. It was only by going there and talking to people on the street that I learned, thirty years later, that Ynyshir is pronounced Un-is-heer not Inisheer. Denzil also gave us the names of Roy's older brothers and sisters—or at least the ones who survived childhood. The history of the Rhondda was not completely new to me because an Australian friend had written a book about communism and working-class militancy in inter-war Britain, using a coal-mining town in the Rhondda as one of his case studies. I read the book when it was published in 1980 out of comradely spirit, but also because of my own enthusiasm for revolutionary moments in history. The town of Maerdy, the 'Little Moscow' in Wales that he had chosen to study, turned out to be only six miles further up the valley from where Roy was born. I had learned that my grandfather was a colliery blacksmith, and I had a book on my shelves with a three-page bibliographical survey about life in Maerdy and the Rhondda in the 1920s to get me started.

Getting to grips with the rest of my newly discovered aunts and uncles and grandparents required me to learn the dark arts of ancestry research. I signed up with Find My Past not long after I returned from San Francisco and wasted quite a lot of money over the next year doing inefficient searches for the names Denzil had provided us with back in 1994. I took out a modest-level subscription that gave me access to Welsh census data up until 1911. It took me a while to realise that I would have to pay extra for access to the 1921 census. This should now be 'freely' available as it is over one-hundred years since the information was gathered. But the cost of digitising the data led the National Archives to give the job to Find My Past in exchange for an exclusive licence to charge for access to it until 1925. So, for every household I wanted to check in the 1921 census I had to pay extra. Or take out a very expensive premium subscription for the year. I quite often found myself unable to resist the extra five dollars (payable with one keystroke as soon as you have subscribed) that will let you look at what you think might be a vital record, kept tantalisingly blurred out on your screen until you agree to cough up. It might just produce a thrilling discovery, or—more likely—turn out to be someone else's long-lost relative. It is a bit like playing the pokies: insert just one more token and three plums will line up, followed by a river of coins crashing into the tray.

Second-hand books about the history of South Wales began to arrive from World of Books in Goring-by-Sea, and the Probert family tree slowly took shape. An advertisement for the annual Hazel Rowley Literary Fellowship for Australian writers working on biography projects galvanised me into sharpening up vague ideas about turning the story into a book. The deadline for applications was a couple of months away, and applying would compel me to work out my aims for this project. It was also dawning on me that I would have to go to Wales to find the answers to some questions, and the thought of somebody else paying for my travel costs was understandably attractive. So now I had a serious incentive to start identifying archival sources that might shed light on how Roy managed to get from Ynyshir to King's College, London University (where he had told us he was a student). Being shortlisted for the fellowship as a rank amateur in the biography stakes was enough encouragement to make me start emailing archivists in Wales. I did not win the fellowship, but by the time this was announced I was well and truly hooked on the project.

*

My father, I learned, was born in his maternal grandparents' house on the corner of South and Wind streets in Ynyshir, just like his five older siblings. His parents, William and Minna, were living in the adjoining terrace house, identical to thousands of others that line the valleys of the Rhondda in South Wales. Ynyshir is a small town in the Rhondda Fach, one of the two main valleys that are often referred to collectively as 'the Rhondda'.

In 1915, when Roy appeared, the Rhondda was famous far beyond Wales for just one thing: its coal. For twenty years the Rhondda had been the most important steam coal exporting region in the world. Pit after pit had been opened along Roy's small valley, which in places was so narrow that there was barely room for the road and the railway lines to fit beside the river. Ynyshir's Standard Colliery shaft was sunk in 1876, and by 1915 it employed over 1300 men, including Roy's father. There were three large collieries in Ynyshir and neighbouring Wattstown, which between them employed not only Roy's father but his father's father (until his death in 1910), his mother's father, six of his uncles and three cousins. In the Rhondda as a whole, over 42,000 men were employed to dig out more than 9,600,000 tons of high-quality coal every year.

My father was christened William Royden Probert, but it seems he was always called Roy, perhaps because his father's name was also William. In the Probert family boys had, until then, always been named Richard, George, John or William. But Roy's parents broke with tradition—even if they ended up calling their children something different from the names they gave them at their christenings. Roy's oldest sister was christened Avarina in 1902, a medieval name appearing in mid-Wales in the nineteenth century. She was always called Rene. His oldest brother was christened Colenso in 1903 (probably after the tiny place in Cornwall near St Hilary's), but he answered to Colin. Roy's next sister was christened Lilian in 1905, but at least she was known as Lily. His third sister, Ada Violetta, died aged twelve months in 1907, and as far as I can tell, was never spoken about again; and his nearest brother was christened Ralph in 1908, but was always called Ron. There is then a seven-year gap before Roy arrives. This cavalier attitude to names made it unnecessarily difficult to track down these siblings on Find My Past when I set out to thoroughly excavate Roy's family.

It was Roy's paternal grandfather, a Welsh-speaking blacksmith, who moved his family in the 1880s from Aberystwyth on the west coast of Wales to Ynyshir in the Rhondda. Like everyone else in the valley, Richard Probert came for the work that was on offer. In his early forties when they arrived, he became a blacksmith at the colliery. By the time of the census of 1891, his oldest son William—Roy's father—was also a colliery blacksmith, and his second son, Richard, was a coal miner. Ten years later at the time of the next census, the third son, John, now aged sixteen, was old enough to be hewing coal, and the fourth son, George, was about to leave school and join his brothers as a miner.

Miners worked in a hierarchy of skills and rewards, and at the top was the collier, or hewer of coal. A collier worked in his own place at the coalface, bringing his knowledge and skills to the hewing work, and erecting his own pit props. He would teach these skills to his assistant, often a relative, who would then be able to find a place for himself at the coalface. Coal mining was an intensely family business in its own way and to be a collier was an occupation you usually inherited. Earnings peaked very early in life, and they also fluctuated sharply as the seam being worked changed along its length. Even though the money they could earn started to decline quite quickly, miners continued to work well into their old age if they were able. They also started young. Roy's uncles on his father's side were all working underground when they were fourteen years old.

The picture is almost identical on Roy's mother's side. Minna Knight's parents, James and Maria Knight, also arrived in Ynyshir in the 1880s. James was a coal miner just over the border in Gloucestershire before he moved his wife and seven of their eight children to the Rhondda. He was still hewing coal in 1901 when he was sixty-three years old. On this side of Roy's family there are three much older uncles who were all cutting coal in Ynyshir when he was born, and one of them (also James) already had two teenage sons, Roy's cousins Frederick and Sidney, working with him down the mine.

All this is to say that in the Rhondda coal was king; three-quarters of the men in work worked in a coal mine. Not surprisingly, the children of miners married into the families of other miners. So, by the time Roy started school, his oldest brother, Colin, had married a young woman called Ceinwen, the daughter of a below-ground 'coal miner timberman'. She grew up in South St, just round the corner from the Proberts' first home. By the time she married Colin, her brother Idris was hewing coal for Lewis Merthyr in the Lady Lewis pit in Ynyshir, while her father had become a colliery examiner.

It took me a while to find the right Ceinwen Rees and on several occasions I found myself paying the extra five dollars to see another 1921 census return for someone who looked as though they might later have married a Probert. Frustrating as this process is, I came to be grateful that the names Probert and Knight both originate from outside Glamorganshire. My searches would have been infinitely more tedious and unsuccessful if Roy had been born a Jones, Davies, Thomas or Williams. These are the names that dominate the Rhondda. Then again, at one level, it doesn't really matter as almost every family looks the same, with the men down the mine and the women at home, having babies, heating water for washing and bathing, and cleaning up the endless coal dust.

Both of Roy's grandfathers were part of an enormous influx of workers seeking employment in the Rhondda as the coal industry grew, all of whom needed housing. These valleys had been quiet, sparsely populated farmlands when the first shafts were sunk. Fifty years before Roy's parents got married, the total population of the Rhondda was less than one thousand. By the time they needed a house of their own, the population had grown to almost 114,000. Large families, often with one or two lodgers, lived in cramped spaces. Narrow terraces of two-up and two-down houses were constructed by speculative builders, often in rows of twenty or more, creating strips of housing along the floor of the valley to accommodate the influx of miners.

These strips of stone housing eventually met up with the houses from the next colliery, so that the whole valley became a winding ribbon of settlement, with each town marked off by its pit-head, its chapels and its hall.

At the end of the nineteenth century, these were not healthy places to live. In 'Counting the cost of coal: women's lives in the Rhondda 1881–1911', Dot Jones provides a grim summary:

> The overcrowding of large families into tiny houses, poor sanitary conditions and poverty contributed to one of the highest infant mortality rates in England and Wales and a high incidence of infectious diseases amongst young children ... [E]ach year through the 1890s, pneumonia, diarrhoea, measles, whooping cough, diphtheria, scarlet fever, convulsions, and other causes were killing one out of every twelve children under five years of age. Fifty-five per cent of all deaths were of children under five years old. It is not surprising that playing funerals was a popular childhood game.

The extreme hardship and crowded intensity of family life in industrial South Wales at this time lie behind two admired novels that bring these historical statistics to life. One of them is the story of Huw Morgan and his family, set in the Rhondda. *How Green Was My Valley* became one of the most widely read and beloved novels of the English-speaking world during World War Two, and was made into a Hollywood film directed by John Ford, as well as two British TV series in the 1960s and 70s. The other is the unsentimental story of another Morgan family, this time set in Merthyr. *Black Parade* by Jack Jones is a much grittier and often brutal narrative about the lives of Saran Morgan, her coal-miner husband, her daughter and her eight sons.

*

Married on Christmas Day, 1900, William and Minna Probert lived for more than fifteen years in their first house in Wind Street—the same house Minna's parents had occupied when they arrived in Ynyshir in the late 1880s. They had moved next door into the corner house, where Minna's enterprising mother was now a grocer. Wind Street is the oldest street in Ynyshir, close to the mine and the river. The ceilings in William and Minna's house were little higher than the doorways. It was here that their fourth child—the baby daughter Ada—died a particularly horrible death from 'Capillary Bronchitis and 5 days Convulsions'.

Just opposite them was a two-bedroom terrace house where one of Minna's older brothers lived. James and his wife, Jane, already had three sons and three daughters, and a boarder, Allen Lodge—an unmarried coal hewer from the Forest of Dean, who lodged with them for at least twenty years. He was probably an old friend of the family from their Gloucestershire days. By the time Roy arrived, they had three more children, and the three boys who were old enough were all hewing coal. While the two oldest girls had left home, six children and Allen Lodge were still living with James and Jane. As I endeavour to trace the lives of these cousins, I find that four-year-old Amy died at home from whooping cough and meningitis four years before Ada. On her death certificate her father has signed with an X—'the mark of James Bernard Knight'. His obviously unsuccessful schooling in England would have ended just as his parents moved the family to the Rhondda.

Not long after Roy was born, his family moved to 44 Gynor Place, the end house of a fairly recently built row of five terrace dwellings, three streets back from the pit, a little higher up the side of the valley. It had two small rooms downstairs and a lean-to outside toilet and coal store behind them, and two small bedrooms upstairs. At least some of the five children would have slept top and tailed. When I stood outside the house again with my brother William on our trip to look at the archives in Cardiff, we both lacked the nerve to knock on the door in the hope of seeing inside. Luckily for me, Malcolm Fisk, historian of housing in the Rhondda, went to look at the house on my behalf when I confessed my spinelessness, writing back to me that 'there would likely have been a coal-fired range in the "living room" with oven one side, hob on the other side, coal fire in grate in the middle (that heated the water). A tin bath would have surely been hanging from a hook on the back wall.' These details began to make this part of my father's history feel more real, but it was very hard indeed to imagine the Bill we knew in this tiny, overcrowded home.

Like most dwellings in the valley, his house is only a stone's throw from a Baptist, a Congregationalist, a Bethlehem Calvinistic Methodist and an Anglican chapel. There was also a Tabernacle chapel, and possibly others. One of the very few things I know about his mother, Minna, is that she was very religious and observed the Sabbath, seriously enough not even to lift her knitting needles. Denzil's widow confirmed that the Sunday dishes were left to be washed on Monday. My older brother would like to believe that our father deserted his Welsh family in part because of his mother's unusual and impossibly extreme faith. But I learned that observing the Sabbath was not uncommon in South Wales at that time. Even in 1962, the Bethel Baptist Church in the Rhondda objected strenuously to a proposal by the YMCA to run a fund-raising marathon on a Sunday, pointing out that some runners would feel unable to compete on 'The Lord's Day'.

In fact, the very first official recognition by the modern British state of the existence of a distinctive Welsh people was the Welsh Sunday Closing Act of 1881. Welsh people had demanded recognition of their Welsh identity and their enthusiastic embrace of Nonconformity, 'which had become almost as much of a national church to the Welsh as Catholicism had become to the Irish'. Which is not to say that Roy would have enjoyed 'The Welsh Sunday' as it became a by-word for gloomy piety, famous only for the number of pleasurable activities that were forbidden on the Sabbath.

The Welsh Sunday may have been the first political victory for Welsh nationalism, but at least its killjoy quality was rapidly offset by the emergence of an equally important—and longer lasting—national enthusiasm that combined singing and rugby. I have no way of knowing whether Roy and his brothers played rugby or sang in a male voice choir, but both these activities were immensely popular in the

Rhondda. By the turn of the century, there were thriving rugby teams in most South Wales towns.

Denzil and his wife told me that the Probert household was a musical one, and that when Minna died there was an organ and a piano in the front parlour to be disposed of. While we do remember our father's ability to whistle, and his good musical ear, my brothers and I have better memories of him taking us to the home of English rugby union at Twickenham. Bill may have been more willing to acknowledge his enthusiasm for rugby than male voice choirs because the kind of rugby played by the Welsh was, in England, an exclusively upper-class game. English rugby split into two camps at the end of the nineteenth century, with the working-class players from clubs in the north of England insisting they should be paid to play, provoking their better-off southern counterparts (the amateur gentlemen) to outlaw professionalism in any form. The rules of the professional game, governed by the new Northern Rugby Football Union, progressively moved away from those of the amateur game. The changes were specifically designed to produce faster and more entertaining play, more attractive to spectators, on whose willingness to pay the new organisation and its members depended.

The breakaway professional rugby league competition left the English rugby union team fatally weakened. While Welsh miners might have been expected to side with the rest of the British working class, a canny decision was made to stick with rugby union, a sport which they now stood a good chance of dominating. Between 1899 and 1909 Wales beat England ten times out of eleven, with the eleventh match ending in a draw. In Wales, not surprisingly, rugby became the most popular national sport precisely because they could beat the English, which the Welsh soccer team could not. And as a result, over one hundred years later, one of the smallest nations in the Rugby World Cup is still a regular favourite to reach the final.

Welsh national pride found a new form of overt expression around this sporting prowess as Welsh rugby fans began to sing 'Hen Wlad Fy Nhadau', or 'Land of my Fathers' as they watched their team consistently overcome teams from England, Scotland and Ireland. This rousing song was composed by a father and son from Pontypridd (just four miles south-east of Ynyshir) and it was originally known as Glan Rhondda—or Banks of the Rhondda. In 1905 the Welsh team defeated the visiting All Blacks from New Zealand, and the singing of the unofficial Welsh anthem at this event was an explicit and memorable celebration of nationhood. The New Zealanders, in the meantime, were administering a shocking series of defeats on the thirty-four other teams they played during their first tour of the northern hemisphere, and simultaneously sending a powerful message of cultural autonomy by performing the haka on each occasion.

The Welsh historian Gwyn Williams suggests that rugby was 'the only field where it was possible to be simultaneously Welsh and a gentleman (normally a difficult undertaking), where a doctor and lawyer could ruck happily shoulder to shoulder with miner and where Wales ... could hope to express its now self-confident identity in a continuous eisteddfod of Grand Slams and a continuous rugby-dinner chorus of God Bless the Prince of Wales'.

*

From 1891 onwards the UK census asked Welsh households to report what language was spoken by each person present for the census: Welsh only, English only or both. Roy's Welsh grandfather, Richard, reported that everyone in his family spoke both Welsh and English. In 1901, his son William (Roy's father) described himself as speaking both Welsh and English, and in 1911 he again confirmed that he spoke both Welsh and English. However, he marked English only for his wife Minna (who was born in England) and for his children. By 1921, when Roy first appeared in a census, his father reported that he and his wife spoke both Welsh and English, as did his oldest daughter Rene; but the youngest children, including Roy, were identified as only speaking English. The only thing that seems certain is that Roy's father—and his uncles and aunts on his father's side—grew up in a Welsh-speaking household.

When Roy was born, more than half the inhabitants of the Rhondda spoke Welsh. More and more English migrants arrived after 1880, like Minna's father, but they were easily counterbalanced by the Welsh-speaking Welshmen arriving from the depressed agricultural regions of West Wales. It was not, however, just a matter of numbers. The emerging culture of the valleys was strong enough to persuade many immigrants from England and even Spain to learn to speak Welsh. At the turn of the century, Welsh remained the dominant language of industrial as well as rural Rhondda, with Welsh being spoken at home, at chapel and in the pit. Kenneth Morgan suggests that in 1910 the native language was flourishing. The numbers speaking Welsh were increasing and 'they were using their language for a wider range of contemporary purposes, political and administrative as well as literary and academic'. An inspector's report on the Ynyshir boys' junior school in 1923, when Roy was a pupil, notes that the 'History of the locality and principality should receive more attention, and more ambitious work might well be attempted in the Welsh language'. In 1926 the Rhondda education committee unanimously agreed that Welsh should be the language of instruction in infants' schools and that all secondary schools should teach Welsh and, as far as possible, it should be used as the medium of instruction in other subjects. I am particularly struck by this clear evidence that my father would have been reading and speaking Welsh.

*

Whatever language they were speaking at home, Roy was born into a remarkably dense set of family networks, all centred around the mining of coal. I had no difficulty finding six uncles and three cousins, as well as both grandfathers, hewing coal or working as colliery blacksmiths, all within a mile or two of where he grew up. If I had put more money in the coin slot of Find My Past I would surely have found more mining relatives close by.

The discovery late in my life that I had a coal-mining grandfather produced what I confess was a slightly romantic workerist frisson.

Perhaps, like Australians who discover a convict ancestor, I felt it made me slightly more interesting. However, the more I learned about life in the Rhondda the more realistic my appreciation of family life became. Women are largely invisible from the most vivid accounts of life in the Rhondda, but Minna must have been struggling like almost every other housewife with the back-breaking nature of the most basic domestic tasks. When her sixth child Roy was born, less than two percent of the houses in the Rhondda had a bath, yet the housing shortage and widespread overcrowding meant that there were often many children and a lodger or two as well as the miners to be kept clean and fed. Minna would have always been boiling up large pans of water for washing both people and clothes. The harsh nature of women's lives, depicted so graphically in Jack Jones' novel, is reflected in the significantly higher death rate among the wives of miners compared to men in the years before the First World War—in all age groups. This is in direct contrast to the comparative death rates in the rest of Wales and England, where women lived longer than men. And it was the younger wives of workers at the coalface, those married to 'hewers and getters', who experienced the highest mortality rate of all.

Coal mining was itself an extraordinarily dangerous occupation. One-hundred-and-seventy-eight men and boys were killed by a pit explosion in Ferndale, four miles further up the Rhondda Fach in 1867, and another fifty-nine were killed two years later in the same pit. In 1896 another disaster at Tylorstown, between Ferndale and Ynyshir, killed fifty-seven men. Ten years before Roy was born there was a catastrophic explosion underground at Wattstown, on 11 July 1905. One-hundred-and-nineteen miners were killed in a pit adjacent to the one where Roy's father and grandfather were working. Of the dead, almost half (fifty-six) were not yet twenty years old. Eleven fathers died with their sons beside them. The story made the front page of the *New York Times*.

I had made many notes about this calamity before a member of the Glamorgan Family History Society, while helping me locate the first Probert house in Ynyshir, discovered that one of those who died that day was Roy's uncle, John Probert, aged nineteen. I had found him in the 1891 census and the 1901 census but had not been able to find him in the 1911 census—and now I knew why.

Every street in such a tight-knit community would have been affected in a personal way. Households just a few doors away from where Roy's family was living lost four men between them. The first of the funeral processions to bury the dead was four or five miles long, so that as it was entering Llethrddu (Trealaw) cemetery the end was only just leaving Wattstown. The entire length of the procession was lined with thousands of mourners. *The Rhondda Leader* (22 July 1905) devoted many pages to the sad story.

> The scenes at the gravesides were most pathetic, especially where two, or even three, members of the same family were buried at the same time. Young women wept for their sweethearts and husbands; mothers for their sons, and children for their fathers. In some cases the extent of the blow could be hardly realised. Relatives stood half-dazed, dry-eyed, looking at the shell which contained the mortal remains of their loved ones being lowered into the earth from which they sprung. Eyes could not weep those saving tears; but imprinted on many faces were furrows of grief in its most poignant form, with no warm spring of human tears to relieve the intense pain within.

The same newspaper report described how the 'work of exploring the mine, dangerous at all times, but a hundredfold more dangerous after a terrible and devastating explosion, has been carried out with such efficiency and expedition that even the three unfortunate victims whose remains yet remain a mystery cannot remain a mystery for much longer'.

> Science, indomitable pluck, and splendid endurance have penetrated the dark and formidable recesses of the tragic death-trap, and that which remained of those gallant men and boys, who went down into the gloom on Tuesday morning never to return alive, are to-day resting beneath a layer of earth in the little cemeteries on the hillsides.

I read the names of all the men and boys who were killed in this disaster, and it seems a miracle that I found no other Proberts or Knights working in the Wattstown colliery on that day. But in wondering about the lives of Roy's uncles I found the other threat to health from a life in or near these mines—diseases of the lungs. Young Alfred Knight, one of Minna's brothers who went down the mine at fourteen, died at only twenty years of age from phthisis—or miner's tuberculosis.

Fifteen years after the Wattstown catastrophe, when Roy was old enough to start at the infant school just next to his home, there were still 40,000 miners working in the Rhondda collieries, and one was killed every six hours, while another was badly injured every two minutes. It was perhaps some comfort to Roy's family that his father William worked 'above ground'. There were probably nine or ten forges in continuous use where he was employed, each one with a blacksmith and his assistant. They were engaged in a huge range of work, making and maintaining machinery and equipment as well as making horseshoes.

Working above ground did not, however, protect the family from economic insecurity as lock-outs and strikes (as well as inevitable variations in the demand for coal) affected almost everyone, including those employed in shops and trades in the valleys. In the years that followed the arrival of Roy's grandparents in the Rhondda, regular periods of unemployment had cancelled out much of the short-term gains from bursts of high wages. But in the years from 1900, when Roy's parents got married, up to the First World War, wages rose, and employment was more constant.

The distinctive culture that developed in the communities of the Rhondda reflected the domination of one industry and the shared experience of work, where the mine hooter regulated the tempo of everyday life. The dense nature of settlement along the valleys, and the absence of coal owners from the social life of the valleys, meant that the workers were left to develop their own Nonconformist, occasionally evangelical society, shaped by the traditions of Welsh dissent. Across the Rhondda there were 151 Nonconformist chapels which could seat over 85,000 people, supporting choirs and bands; music, literature and the tradition of the eisteddfod were the main cultural interests in the valleys. In Dai Smith's words, it was a 'one-class, one-industry-dominated, geographically isolated area, full of mass actions, collective institutions and self-confidence'.

*

This world into which Roy was born had changed dramatically for the worse by the time he finished his primary schooling. The Rhondda reached its economic peak in 1913, with a population of more than 160,000. By the end of 1925, the 'good times which were the hallmark of Edwardian Rhondda, when front rooms of terraced houses had been decked with family photographs and doily-covered pianos, the objects of pride and prosperity and status, were over.'

During the First World War the British government had taken control of the mines and given in to union demands for improved pay and conditions for miners to ensure essential wartime coal supplies. As Roy started his schooling at Ynyshir infants, control of the mines was returned to the owners, who immediately went on the attack. On the day of 'decontrol', 31 March 1921, the miners were locked out unless they accepted the reduced pay levels being offered. In reaction to the lock-out tactics, the miners in Ynyshir chose to stop the pumps and flood the pits, to prevent any blackleg workers from operating the mine. After three months, the Ynyshir stoppage had to be called off when the organisers failed to persuade the railway and transport workers to come out in support. Predictably, the mine owners continued with their offensive, and over the next few years there were regular disputes, strikes and lock-outs, all involving loss of income for families like the Proberts and the Knights.

The close communities that had evolved around work, chapel, rugby, singing and Sabbath observance re-organised themselves around trade unionism, the Labour Party, and defiant resistance, led by the Communist Party. Arthur Horner, one of the most important

Communist organisers in the Rhondda, lived in Ynyshir. The South Wales Miners Federation, 'the Fed', wanted the national union of miners to affiliate to the Red International of Trade Unions. Mickhail Borodin, the Bolshevik revolutionary himself, fresh from the Comintern in Moscow, 'is said to have consulted the Ynyshir Unofficial Reform Committee which controlled the Rhondda district of the Fed'. 'South Wales became the 'semi-mythical Red Belt of the British Working Class'.

It is entirely possible that the Probert and Knight families did not agree about the best way to protect their livelihoods. As in the Morgan family from *How Green Was My Valley*, there may have been harsh words between the generations. Saran Morgan in *Black Parade* has no time for the strikes and political militancy that attract her sons. As an above-ground worker on a day wage, Roy's father may have considered the militancy of the below-ground workers to be foolish or damaging to the industry. But as a member of the Fed, he would have been on strike with everyone else, including his coal hewing cousins and nephews, and he may have been as militant as the next man.

In 1926 the industrial war being waged in the Rhondda reached its climax as the British Trade Union Congress (TUC) called a general strike, designed to prevent further attacks on the wages and conditions of Britain's coal miners. When the TUC called off this historic national strike after nine days, the miners decided to fight on alone, only surrendering after another six months of defiance. This meant six months with no income for families with few resources. They had to rely on union strike funds, credit from the local co-op or shopkeeper, and communal kitchens, as well as collecting coal from seams lying close to the surface of the ground.

A few months after the miners capitulated, Roy's father came home from his work at the National United colliery, sat down in a chair to remove his boots, and died suddenly, from apoplexy (or a massive stroke as we would now describe it). It was not a good time to lose the family's main breadwinner. His death certificate tells me that Roy's oldest brother, Colin, was in the house when his father died, though he had recently moved into his wife's family home, an almost identical terrace house, a ten-minute walk away. Colin had a respectable job as a shop assistant at the Ynyshir co-op, but it did not pay well. It is hard to work out where Rene was since women were not recorded in the electoral register until they were thirty years old. Rene would have been twenty-six, and four years later she married a hotel cook in Aberystwyth, suggesting that she had probably gone into domestic service or something similar on the west coast. Lily had left home several years before, at sixteen, and gone into service as a cook in a big house in Brecon. I have no evidence about what Ron was doing in 1927, except that he was living at home. He left Ynyshir boys' school in 1921, shortly after his thirteenth birthday—because he was old enough to do so. He would have been working since then, almost certainly as a miner. The family story that has survived about him is that he 'went down the mine' when his father died, in order to ensure that Roy could stay at school, and presumably to support his mother, Minna. But he was probably there already, as there were really no alternatives.

Roy was only eleven years old. On that Wednesday he would most likely have come home from school, a five-minute walk away, in time to witness his father's sudden death—something Bill never ever spoke about. By this time, they were a small family living in Gynor Place, just William and Minna with Ron and Roy. The strikes and lock-outs would have meant more time together, even if less money. Did William take his sons fishing or shooting rabbits to put food on the table like so many other Rhondda families? It is not hard to imagine that Roy might have been profoundly affected by his father's death and that this event might have contributed to his later decision to leave the Rhondda behind.

The town of Ynyshir existed only as a community of miners. It was expected that a boy from Ynyshir 'would go into the pits when he reached his fourteenth birthday and stay there for the rest of his life'. Wilf Jones, from a mile or so further up the valley, was born two years after Roy. Writing when he was in his eighties, he remembers 'The Coal Strike' and how during those months he would 'go up the tip with my father to dig for coal. The tops were like anthills with me and the boys digging.' Coal stealing was half of all recorded indictable crime in the neighbouring Cynon valley in the 1920s. Wilf's father managed to get an allotment which meant they were guaranteed some food at least. But in a family of seven children, Wilf's wage was needed when he turned fourteen. 'Come 1931, on 31 March I was a schoolboy; next day, 1 April, I was a "man". I started work in the local colliery, up at 5.30 am with excitement running high.'

*

The first decade of Roy's life was, in many respects, the same as that of nearly every other working-class boy in the Rhondda at that time, shaped by the close family networks of the coal communities, the cramped living conditions, and shared economic difficulties. He would have been unmistakably Welsh. It is, however, impossible to say what kind of family they were. Denzil's widow told me that her mother-in-law, Lily—ten years older than Roy—never talked about her childhood in Ynyshir nor her family. She was, it seems, a rather rigid and sad person who did not show affection. Roy was perhaps an unexpected sixth child, born seven years after his nearest sibling, when Minna was forty years old. It is tempting to imagine that Roy was able to cut himself off from her in later life because she too did not show affection. But there is no clear evidence to support this idea.

There is, however, good reason to think that Roy loved his oldest brother Colin, the only sibling he ever admitted to having. Denzil's widow gave me a formal studio portrait of Colin, in tie and wing collar, aged in his mid-thirties perhaps, when he would already have suffered the devastating loss of his wife, Ceinwen, and his son Glanville. It is hard not to feel drawn to him, though he bears little if any physical resemblance to Roy. When their father died, perhaps it was Colin, then in his early twenties, who stepped in to fill the hole this left in his much younger brother's life. Ceinwen's brother named his son, born in 1935, Colin—which suggests to me much affection for Roy's oldest brother. Colin is not a traditional or common Welsh name.

In all of this, Roy's life is not unusual for the time and place. Indeed, his family may have been relatively fortunate. None of the Proberts or Knights that I have added to the family tree died or were injured as soldiers in the First World War, unlike Saran's sons in *Black Parade*. But it is still somehow astonishing that Bill could so totally eradicate from his later life all references to his childhood—the poverty, the coal mining, the strikes, the speaking of Welsh and performing at eisteddfods, the drawing of leeks and the piano in the parlour.

As for his mother and father, apart from the facts of their birth and death and their place in their own families, I have unearthed little that sheds light on their personalities. Minna's strict observance of the Sabbath might seem distinctive, especially if she hung on to it all her life. But it is William Edward's creation of a miniature train that is remembered by every member of the Knight or Probert families who visited 44 Gynor Place. The first thing Denzil told us about Bill's father was that 'he was an extremely clever craftsman in metal work. He built items such as railway engines and carriages etc to scale, capable of running on railway tracks.' Almost thirty years later, Denzil's widow wrote to me:

> The train that was in Ynyshir had been made by your grandfather—there were also rail tracks in the garden and it worked by steam. Apparently children were able to ride on it, and that was why Denzil was quite upset when it never came to him certainly after he had children of his own.

As I finished writing this book, I discovered an elderly second cousin—through an Ynyshir community Facebook group—who now lives at the other end of Gynor Place. Gaynor can only recall one thing from visiting Aunty Probert at No 44 in the early 1950s—'when I was very young and can remember a train in a large glass case in the living room'.

I was looking for any memories at all about Minna, but all I got was the train. My new-found cousin kindly followed up, reporting that:

> I have phoned my only remaining cousin on the Knight side, Desmond Cooper, born 1928—my late Aunty Ethel's son, he remembers going to visit Aunty Probert in Gynor Place, he said that he was told that the train could pull 10 men.

This train is memorable, unforgettable—even if the stories about it became exaggerated. Everyone seems to have known about it. I want to think that it embodies William Edward's love for his children, and his youngest son in particular. How could Roy leave it behind literally and figuratively? And what did his brother Ron do with it when Minna died in 1954?

*

As I was finalising the text for this book, I began looking for photos of Ynyshir's coal mines. By this time, I knew where Roy's father and grandfather had been employed and could search archives more productively. But I was nonetheless elated when I found myself looking at a formal photograph entitled 'Standard Colliery Craftsmen 1890' (Itcm 1202 out of 2056 in the Rhondda Cynon Taf photography archive). I could tell that there was more than one colliery blacksmith among the twenty-four or so men and boys in the photo, and I felt almost certain that Richard and William Edward Probert, aged fifty and nineteen respectively, were looking out at me. A curator at the Big Pit National Coal Museum in Wales was able to explain that the men are probably all blacksmiths or their assistants (the latter holding their smaller hammers to attention). Could I learn anything about their characters if I manage to identify Richard and William? It was easy to feel the thrill of the ancestry chase, but I think I am hoping for some sense of real connection to these men from whom I am descended.

The scale of the imaginative challenge presented by this photograph is, of course, a function of my total ignorance about my father's origins. Everyone who has heard Bill's story wants to know why we never asked him about his family, finding it hard to believe our lack of curiosity and our mother's ignorance. I don't have any memory of Bill signalling that his early life was off-limits, that we should avoid the subject. After some fruitless soul-searching about our lack of interest, I now wonder if there is anything so unusual about this—at least in an era before ancestor-hunting became so popular and so easy.

My children have never asked me questions about my family (which has not prevented me from telling them things). Nor do I recall being particularly curious about my mother's family. We knew about it not because we had asked, but because there were relatives who had to be explained and who behaved as though we were connected. As we grew older, and Janet found she had American, French and Australian grandchildren, she decided—with admirable foresight—to write family histories for them so that they might understand their lineage better. She had interesting material to work with on both sides of her family, but these histories were written after Bill had died. Before his death and the uncovering of his secrets, I think we probably assumed that his silence meant that Bill did not have any particularly interesting stories to tell. And he was no longer around to ask. I find I have many friends my age who regret not asking their parents more about their lives.

Chapter 2
The Education of Roy

My brothers and I had always thought our father was a university student at King's College, London before the war. We cannot recall him ever talking about his university experience, but we would have taken it for granted, like our mother's Oxford degree. The premise of my new project, however, was to take nothing for granted, so it seemed prudent to check on the straightforward question of his enrolment. It did not take long to confirm that Roy did indeed graduate from King's College in 1938 with a B.A. Honours degree, and that he majored in French and Spanish.

Finding the record of students who graduated from the University of London in that year turned out to be encouragingly straightforward, so I moved on to the obvious next question about his education. Given what we now know about his family's circumstances, what made it possible for Roy to stay at school long enough to pass the 'higher' exams that were required for matriculation and access to a university? And why did he go to King's College when ninety percent of Welsh students who managed to pass their 'higher' exams went to the University of Wales at Aberystwyth, Cardiff and Bangor—colleges that had been established in the 1870s and 1880s. And who was paying for all this?

Apart from Roy, it seems that all the Probert and Knight boys were at work by the time they were fourteen, almost all of them hewing coal. The minimum school-leaving age was increased from twelve to fourteen only in 1918. His sisters also left school by the time they were fourteen, but with few work opportunities. In 1921 Rene and Lily were both still living at home, aged nineteen and sixteen, with no employment. For Roy to stay out of the mine, let alone finish his secondary schooling, his two older brothers would have had to support him as well as provide for their widowed mother, Minna. Colin, the eldest, had avoided coal mining, probably because his health had been compromised by childhood rheumatic fever. His whole working life was spent with the co-op in Ynyshir, and he did eventually rise to the position of manager in gents outfitting. But in the early 1920s, as a shop assistant, he would only have been earning about £2 5 shillings a week. Around this time, the men employed by the Treorchy co-op in the neighbouring Rhondda Fawr valley had written to their co-op committee, respectfully requesting a twenty percent increase in their pay, drawing attention to their 'low wages in comparison to all other classes of labour'. Married at the age of twenty-two, Colin was unlikely to have had any spare capacity. As for Roy's nearest brother, Ron, it has turned out to be frustratingly difficult to know anything but the bare outlines of his life. It is almost as though he avoided registering for anything but the census. But when their father died, we know that Ron was still living at home and, we can assume, he was working—at least when the valley was not on strike. He would have joined the workforce in 1921, between the major industrial shutdowns in the Rhondda of 1921 and 1926.

Wherever they ended their schooling, Roy and his four older surviving siblings all started at the infants' school for girls and boys in Ynyshir, an imposing stone three-storey building on the steep hillside, right beside the family home in Gynor Place. His sisters could stay in that building once girls and boys were separated after the infant years, and they would have completed their schooling there. Roy and his brothers moved from the infants' school to the boys' school just down the hill, in the centre of Ynyshir. This much I can learn from the other side of the world, with the invaluable help of the Pontypridd and Rhondda branch of the Glamorgan Family History Society.

In order to apply for the literary fellowship that I didn't get, I identified archives in Cardiff that contain records from the Rhondda schools that Roy would probably have attended. In December 2022, I discovered that Qantas had suddenly made available that rarest of gifts: a Qantas frequent flyer return trip to London in mid-May 2023. I snapped it up and in late May I was doing my first proper archival research in the Glamorgan archives, not really understanding what was in the files I had requested. At least I managed to avoid embarrassing myself by sitting on the cushion that had been provided on my allocated table—realising just in time that it was for the documents I was to receive, not my bottom.

Bent over my spot in the archive—which closes for lunch and doesn't open on Mondays and Fridays even if you have come from Australia—I learned that the headmaster of Ynyshir infants, like all headmasters, was required to keep a logbook or diary in which he noted any absences of teachers and the reasons for these, any half holidays granted or special events, as well as regular reports on the attendance rates of his pupils.

The logbooks from the first two decades of the last century, which cover the years when Rene, Colin, Lily and Ron would have been pupils, provide unexpected insights into the poverty and ill-health that characterised children's lives in the Rhondda. Throughout the year 1909, for example, the headmaster comments on the low attendance rates for most months in the first half of the year, noting that significant numbers of children were absent because of whooping cough and measles. On 28 July there were still '117 absent [out of about 270] through measles and scarlet fever'. One of these may well have been Colin, as his rheumatic fever would almost certainly have been caused by scarlet fever. In September measles and scarlet fever were still affecting a lot of children. By December the headmaster reports that there was 'still very low attendance because of sickness'. The pattern is repeated every year, with diphtheria and chicken pox as well as flu and eczema also taking a regular toll on the numbers. In 1921, when Roy would have just started, the school was closed for ten days because of a 'flu epidemic'—perhaps the last wave of the global Spanish flu pandemic.

In this coal community, it was not just illness that kept children away. In 1905 the infants' school was closed on 7 July and 14 July for the funerals of those killed in the Wattstown explosion, like Roy's Uncle John, who would, in all likelihood, have attended the same school.

The incidence of ill-health in the terribly over-crowded and ill-housed communities of the Rhondda has been well documented, and the direct effects of poverty on educational success are also clearly manifested in these logbooks. I was initially puzzled by the regularity with which the headmasters noted bad or inclement weather or rain, accompanied by very poor school attendance. On one April day in 1905, only 165 children out of 295 were present because of rain; in early October that year there was again bad weather and low numbers, with an average attendance that week of only sixty-five percent. The following year, on one occasion heavy rain was reported with only 104 students making it to school. And in 1907 almost every school month is characterised as having days of very poor attendance because of rain or stormy weather. It was the archivist who pointed out to me that this was not because families were happy to let their children stay home in bad weather; but rather, it was because many of these small children did not have shoes, let alone raincoats. (Roy had no excuse, living next door to the school.) When Roy was old enough to have moved down the hill to the boys' school, there is a note in that logbook about a week of good attendance in the month of May. 'With the exception of a few boys who have no boots, the number of boys absent without any reasonable excuse is very small.'

On rare occasions, the Ynyshir schools were closed with the permission of the director of education so that children could participate in Welsh cultural events, such as an eisteddfod. On 1 March 1922, St David's day, the logbook for the boys' school notes that 'the Ordinary Time Table was dispensed with this morning' and instead the first half hour of the day was devoted to singing Welsh hymns, 'with reference to most eminent Welsh Hymnologists and translation of Bible into

Welsh'. To recognise St David's Day (celebrated in Wales since the twelfth century), this was followed by an hour devoted to patriotism, with reference 'to the men who have made Wales famous, in different spheres'. The next hour was to be spent drawing leeks or daffodils and discussing the Legend of the Leek—which I confess sounds like a Monty Python skit to me. But some believe that in the sixth century, St David convinced Welsh soldiers to wear leeks on their helmets during a battle against the Saxons so they would know friend from foe. Centuries later, at the Battle of Crécy in 1346, loyal and brave Welsh archers feature, fighting in a field of more leeks. To complete the celebrations, before lunch there was singing of 'Welsh Airs, Welsh Recitations, Folklore and Legends.' And while St David's Day is not a public holiday in Wales, the director of education instructed that the school should close for the afternoon.

*

For Roy's four brothers and sisters and his ten cousins still living in Ynyshir, their formal education ended as they turned thirteen or fourteen and compulsory schooling came to an end. However, in 1928, at age twelve, Roy left Ynyshir boys' and started at the Rhondda intermediate school (later known as Porth County Boys School), which was just over a mile back down the valley, in the town of Porth. As was his degree from King's College, London University, Roy's attendance at this school was noted in his army service record, which is how I knew which school files to check in the Glamorgan archives. According to his nephew Denzil, it seems that the young Roy, alongside an impish sense of humour and penchant for practical jokes, showed an unusual amount of academic talent—enough to make his family agree that he should stay in school, even though they faced increasingly insecure employment as the Rhondda economy collapsed. This was Roy's first big break.

In the 1920s in England and Wales, only a very small proportion of young people over fourteen years of age were enrolled in state schools, and even fewer of those over sixteen years of age. Wales was, nonetheless, already recognised in the late-nineteenth century as a region with a particularly strong belief in the importance of education. The Welsh Intermediate Act of 1889 was a significant piece of legislation that gave Welsh students many advantages over English students, creating a system of publicly funded intermediate (selective secondary) schools in Wales. These new schools were to be divided between first grade schools (twenty percent of the total) which would educate children to the age of eighteen, and second grade schools (the other eighty percent) which were to educate children to the age of sixteen, with a focus on local white collar or engineering employment.

Even within this stratified framework, Porth County—a first grade school established in 1896—was a most unlikely kind of institution for its overwhelmingly working-class locale, with a curriculum completely focused on preparing its pupils for further education and university. Porth is a small town in the Rhondda, standing where the two main valleys, the Rhondda Fawr and the Rhondda Fach, meet. The Lewis Merthyr colliery, with its pits on both sides of the Rhondda River, dominated the town, employing between two- and three-thousand men in the first two decades of the twentieth century. The school, however, drew its pupils from the top to the bottom of both Rhondda valleys. Unlike any other secondary school, its catchment area was enormous, with a population of over 88,000 (compared to about 8000 for all other school districts). Students competed for a place, and some had to travel long distances on foot to get there if they were successful. The school's goal of successful matriculation for its students completely determined what was taught and the way the school was organised. And to support this goal, unlike other Rhondda schools, it recruited its teachers from all over Britain.

So distinctive was the school's history that its last headmaster, appointed in 1961, wrote a book about it, providing rich insights into what it was like in the 1920s and 30s when Roy was there. Owen Vernon Hughes describes 'a highly selective, competitive, achievement-orientated grammar school', which from the beginning charged fees. The first headmaster, Mr Evan Samuel, was a 'thunderous presence' wearing ribboned pince-nez and gown, and a mortar board.

He even introduced Saturday lessons, believing that any obstacles to academic success were only there to be overcome.

Expert opinion was sceptical about the school's chances of success, arguing that 'where one industry is predominant, such as a mining village, the possibility that a son can do other than follow his father is remote'. Many of these sons were also living in a state of extreme overcrowding, in houses that had been officially described as not fit for human habitation, with unfenced scavenging tips dangerously near to them, 'giving rise to foul gases and unbearable stench'. Colonies of pigs ranged the riverbanks, and the rare water closets 'flushed directly into the rivers.' Jack Jones in his novel *Black Parade* describes the view from Saran's front door on the Morlais Brook in Merthyr. 'Butchers and fishmongers, once anything began to niff a bit, would fling it over the back wall into the brook. Splosh, and out the rats would rush to investigate it.'

The reaction of the assistant headmaster at Porth County Boys in the 1920s to this squalor was to design a green-and-yellow cap which was to be worn in and out of school, especially in the most impoverished part of the town, which, according to him, 'needed a few Public School overtones ... as badly as it needed anti-rickets vitamins.'

The extreme nature of the industrial concentration along the Rhondda valleys at that time limited not only the horizons but also the lives of many children. At the same time, it produced social and cultural institutions that focused strongly on education as the key to any upward social movement, something that was valued precisely because of the dangerous and insecure nature of mining work. 'The prominence of chapel in community life, and non-conformity as a political force, the unifying effect of the Welsh language ... and the growth of unionism merged to foster an atmosphere in which a collective sense of altruism and mutual support was mobilised in the cause of education as a basis for social mobility.' Headmaster Owen Vernon Hughes suggests that 'Close proximity and the ever-present threats to survival also resulted in an aggressive competitiveness' which was expressed in things like the eisteddfodau, solo and choir singing competitions, champion boxing matches, and a similarly competitive attitude to academic achievement. One of the school's most famous graduates, the writer Gwyn Thomas, said that 'once a boy got into secondary school, if he had any sense at all, he really set himself to winning the scholarships that would take him out of the valley into another place.'

The appearance of widespread and equal access to the newly created intermediate schools was maintained by having a straightforwardly competitive process of selection—a sort of precursor to the eleven-plus exams. 'Every pupil in an elementary school was given the opportunity to sit the scholarship examination for the intermediate schools (a decade before this was the case in England) and Scholarship provision ... was far higher than over the border.' As Gwyn Williams describes it, 'During the depression ... family after family, aided by sympathetic Labour local authorities, tried to get their children out of the pits via the examination obstacle race.'

The first headmaster of the new Porth County school led the institution for almost thirty years, finally retiring in 1925 just before Roy won a place there. The school initially accepted girls as well as boys but was divided into two separate schools in 1915. Mr Samuel did not believe that school should be an easy place for any boy, and the focus was relentlessly on exam performance. Teacher–pupil relations were 'professionally formal, unsentimental and unsympathetic'. Streaming determined everything, with each form subdivided into a higher and lower, A and B stream. The school set its own scholarship examination for entry (on thick white paper, unlike the flimsy pink and green paper used by the other secondary schools) and streamed the successful boys on the day they began; movement between the streams was almost impossible after the first year. Boys in the A stream of the top form were being prepared for matriculation and university. Their teachers were gowned graduates of English universities teaching only their specialist subjects. The curriculum included Latin, Greek, the Welsh and English languages, European modern languages, maths and natural sciences.

Leaving aside the incongruous nature of this curriculum in a town like Porth, it seems completely illogical that a grammar school for the Rhondda should not only charge fees but require boys to pay for a school cap (which cost half a crown) as well as their textbooks. Everything I learned about the Probert family in the 1920s suggests that Roy would never have been able to attend Porth County without some external financial assistance. I hoped that a file in the Glamorgan archives called 'Porth County School Scholarships and Bursaries Account Book 1899-1937' would tell me how he did it.

When the archivists brought me the book, I began with the pages that covered the mid-1920s, since I was not sure which year Roy had started at the school. Each page has two columns of names in copperplate writing, organised by form and stream. I saw that there were several different kinds of awards that a boy might receive, and as I turned the pages, I realised I was holding my breath. I confess now to a fist-pump and shouting (quietly) 'Yes!' when I spotted Roy, down in the bottom right-hand corner of the page for the school year ending in July 1929. He was the recipient of a 'Governor's Entrance Scholarship', and he was in Form 1A not 1B. I felt some kind of reflected glory—perhaps because I am an eleven-plus girl myself. Then I found him in the book each year after that, working his way up the school, always in receipt of the Governor's Entrance Scholarship, and always in the A stream. I have been unable, as yet, to determine the difference between the scholarships offered, and how a boy won a Governor's Entrance Scholarship. Perhaps I want to know that, like Gwyn Thomas, he was top of the Rhondda, when really it is irrelevant to Bill's story. The important point is that he was able to go to this school.

Denzil provided us with a photocopy of a battered old photograph under which he pencilled 'Uncle Roy (Bill) as a young student'. Initially I thought he had a made a mistake as this dapper, slim figure in a tie, V-necked jumper and jacket, with 1920s baggy pants and two-tone shoes, did not resemble my father at all. I now see that it is indeed him, only his face is yet to fully mature. I was slow to recognise him because I had never seen a picture of Bill before he was well into his twenties. I emailed Denzil's widow hoping that the original might still be somewhere in her house, but it can't be found. With so little to go on, I keep looking into this grainy photograph as though my father might suddenly make himself visible. He was emerging as a snappy dresser, and that is already something. Was teenage Roy imagining life beyond the Rhondda?

*

At the Treorchy public library a little further up the other Rhondda valley—the Rhondda Fawr—I looked at the electoral registers for the 1920s and 1930s which informed me who was living in the Probert house at 44 Gynor Place while Roy was at school (apart from women under the age of thirty, who were ineligible to register). It seems that his mother, Minna, needed to take in a lodger after his father died, to share the already cramped accommodation. As well as the lodger there was Roy's older brother Ron still living at home, and from 1932 they were re-joined by Colin and his very young son, Glanville, who may already have been showing symptoms of tuberculosis. Roy would presumably have shared a bedroom with his brothers and his nephew, and probably the lodger as well. He must have done his homework in the front parlour.

The years that Roy spent as a student at Porth County Boys were years during which most Rhondda families suffered serious deprivation. During the 1920s power shifted rapidly away from the miners towards the coal owners who took full advantage of the new environment. Wages were cut, hours were extended, and working conditions deteriorated. Roy's uncle James Knight, from Wind Street, was employed in the Lewis Merthyr colliery, but he is recorded as being 'Out of Work' in the 1921 census, as is his youngest son, a fifteen-year-old colliery assistant, just starting out beside his father. Roy's youngest uncle, Ernest George Probert, had married into a family who ran a grocery in Porth before the war. By the census of 1921, Ernest's father-in-law had been reduced to a colliery labourer who was now on strike, and his two brothers-in-law were also on strike—both coal hewers employed at the same colliery as the Knights. The militancy of the mining communities was extraordinary, but also doomed. Not only were coal export markets declining, but there had never been any investment in mechanical coal-cutting which might have improved mine productivity. Profits had been too easy for the owners for too long. Now that the market was more challenging, the owners went on the attack. Inefficient pits closed, collieries were amalgamated, and men were laid off in their thousands.

By 1931 the mining workforce had been cut in half. Unemployment in Glamorgan rose to forty-one percent in 1932. Unemployment was worse in the Rhondda Fach (where the Proberts lived) than the Rhondda Fawr, with roughly one-third of all Rhondda families living on unemployment benefit in 1936. This 'benefit' was only allocated after brutal means-testing, with the result that families experienced malnutrition. Children suffered from rickets, diphtheria and pneumonia. Babies were even contracting rickets in their mother's womb. Not surprisingly, maternal death rates rose in the 1920s, and by the 1930s young women in South Wales were dying from tuberculosis at a rate seventy percent higher than the average for England and Wales. In Merthyr Tydfil it was 250 percent higher.

The Proberts were not immune. Roy's young sister-in-law, Ceinwen, died from tuberculosis in 1931, and his nephew Glanville died in the Glan Ely sanitorium four years later. Six years after the death of his son, Colin died from heart problems caused by rheumatic fever. It seems a miracle that Roy did not become ill. What he could not avoid, however, was watching his young nephew's slow decline.

While Roy was at school in Porth, 65,000 inhabitants of the coalfields died 'avoidable deaths' caused by the impact of poverty on their health. By the time he finished school in the summer of 1934, one-fifth of the Rhondda's population had left the valleys, most of them under thirty years of age, heading to the new industrial towns like Oxford, Coventry, Watford and Slough, as well as London and Birmingham. A government commission into the problems of unemployment in South Wales could only come up with a proposal for large-scale emigration. As Saran's son Benny describes it at the end of *Black Parade*, 'what the commissioner recommends is the transference of all surplus labour of men and boys under forty-five years old to more prosperous districts'.

*

The writing was on the wall for the Rhondda by the time of the general strike, when Roy was still at school in Ynyshir. The people of Porth responded to the continuing industrial warfare by holding the first major Porth carnival in July 1927, while the pit wheels were silent and the air clear of smoke. Thousands of people came to see an exhibition game of baseball by two visiting teams from Cardiff, with carnival contests between marching jazz bands—'men, women and children dressed up in often outlandish home-made costumes, tea cosies on their heads, with their music played on marching drums and the gazooka.' Over the next two months larger and larger crowds came to watch new events, including a competition in which sixty bands participated. The purpose of all this activity was to raise money for the community's distress fund. Each township in the Rhondda had a fund, and this resource paid for the food and drink at communal soup kitchens, and for the supplies to sustain the boot repair centres. It also paid for children's clothes and other essential items, and kept debt and rent collectors at bay—at least for a time.

Porth County school, meanwhile, seems to have ignored the industrial action despite its distressing impact on the whole of the school's catchment area. The focus remained resolutely on academic achievement. The second headmaster, E. T. Griffiths (called E. T. by everyone) presided for most of the time Roy was there. He came from very modest origins himself, securing the money for his own books by competing in 'every eisteddfod for miles around'. Like many others in similar circumstances, he found a way up the educational ladder by becoming a pupil teacher. After he managed a 'brilliant first in French', he did an M.A. in Geneva, where he also completed his licentiate. He was ambitious, energetic, and dictatorial according to Owen Vernon Hughes. After seven years at Porth County he left to become an entrepreneur, owning a macaroni factory during the war. He was clearly a man who knew how to make things happen.

E. T.'s obsession with foreign languages, and his goal of making Porth County Boys the best place to learn them, opened a route out of the Rhondda for Roy and, to a large extent, determined the kind of war he would have. In a speech E. T. gave in 1926, there is no mention of the general strike, only his determination to get his boys into higher status branches of the civil service. The problem was the 'total lack of attention paid to modern languages in our Welsh schools. In a school of this kind it is an untold loss that only one modern language should be taught'. Winning the support of the school's governors to employ another language teacher, E. T. persuaded a Swiss intellectual called Georges Rochat—whom he had met while studying in Geneva—to take a teaching position at Porth Boys. This remarkable linguist then extended language teaching to Spanish, Italian, German and Greek. The boys already faced Latin in Form IIA, not just because Horace and Cicero were good for them, but because Latin was essential for entry to the best of England's universities.

Almost immediately some Porth boys began to win scholarships to those institutions. Perhaps the most well-known of them is Gwyn Thomas, whose 'autobiography of sorts', *A Few Selected Exits*, was made into a film by the BBC, starring Anthony Hopkins. (In the Wikipedia entry for Porth, there is a list of its most notable citizens. Gwyn Thomas is one, together with J. Gwyn Griffiths, an Egyptologist and poet. The others are two boxing champions, a captain of the Welsh international rugby team and a girl evangelist.)

Gwyn Thomas was born in 1913, the youngest of twelve children. His father was employed tending pit ponies and his mother died when he was only six years old. In his memoir he writes with his trademark black humour that living in Porth, he and his siblings 'were so deprived we lacked even the sense of being deprived. We were lucky that way.' Gwyn sat the competitive entrance exam three years before Roy, 'coming seventh in the all-Rhondda race for a scholarship—the golden ticket out of the mines.'

Heading into the A stream at Porth County, Gwyn found himself in language classes being taught by the newly appointed Georges Rochat. The teacher from Switzerland spoke little English on arrival but was nonetheless given the job of getting the first group of students through the equivalent of Spanish O level in just ten months. Five years later Gwyn became the first pupil in Wales to take Higher Spanish, getting perfect grades and topping the Higher Certificate examinations. Winning three different financial awards, he was offered a place at Oxford in 1931—one of the few universities in Britain where he could continue to study Spanish.

It was not just his obvious intellectual abilities that got Gwyn to Oxford. On one occasion when caught smoking and telling jokes in the school cellar, E. T. beat him with a walking stick. Later in his life Gwyn recognised how he had been singled out for help, even if of a rather brutal kind. E. T. 'watched me closely after that. Every time I turned up late I was clobbered. I was often late.' E. T. would wait for him in the morning at the top of the school drive, watch in hand, 'determined to put the disordered fragments of my life into something like shape. Sometimes he would wait for a few more laggards to fall into the net, but most often I was the end of the procession.' When Gwyn's final examination results were known, E. T. invited him to have tea at his large and imposing home ('a piece of old Versailles against the general architectural background of the valley'). Gwyn listened to him describe all the men he knew who started out in villas and homes 'twice as crouched' as Gwyn's, but who went to Oxford and on to 'golden careers'. On a more practical note, E. T. gave him £25, as a loan to be repaid after Oxford, saying, 'You know I've watched out for you over the years.'

As Roy moved up the school behind Gwyn, Spanish was becoming increasingly popular, mainly because Georges Rochat was a remarkably gifted teacher of languages. His talents are reflected in the sheer volume of prizes won by his pupils, and the number who ended up as professors of Spanish in later years. It is impossible to know if Roy needed to be kept on the straight and narrow or whether that was already his instinct. What we do know is that he was given the opportunity to learn French and Spanish by an inspiring teacher and, like Gwyn Thomas, he found that he had a natural facility. He was always able to sound like a native speaker in whatever language he tried but French, in particular, gave him access to a culture that he admired and enjoyed for the rest of his life. In this way Porth County Boys provided Roy with a passport out of the Rhondda and into Europe.

*

To continue studying Spanish, Roy—like Gwyn—had to leave Wales. We know that he accepted a place at King's College, London, in 1934 to do a Bachelor of Arts. But once again there is the question of how he could have afforded to go to university, let alone in London. In his early descriptions of the Probert family before the war, Roy's nephew Denzil tells us that Roy's brother Ron 'was working all hours to help support him', believing that Ron was working in the mine like his father before him. Sadly, Ron has turned out to be the most elusive of Roy's family, and I can find no record of his employment in the Rhondda. Indeed, it is hard to know what employment Ron could have had in Ynyshir as the coal industry collapsed over these years. What I do know is that 1934 is the last year Ron is living in the family home. Not long after Roy starts university, Ron moves to Coventry to stay with a Knight cousin, finding work as a 'wood machinist', and later as a car paint-sprayer. He stays there, living in his cousin's small house in Guphill Avenue—even after he marries a girl from the Rhondda—for the rest of his working life. But no matter where Ron managed to find work, it is difficult to understand how Roy's family could have had enough money to send him to London.

The excellent King's College archives turn out to have detailed material about individual student enrolments from the 1930s, kept in registry slip books. They can tell me exactly what subjects Roy took each year. He began with Latin, French and Spanish, as well as ethics—offered by the philosophy department. Latin included classes on language, composition and Roman history. In his second year he took honours classes in French and Spanish, which included prescribed medieval texts and literature, as well as classes on Balzac, Hugo and the nineteenth century. I know he enjoyed Balzac in particular, as he warmly encouraged me to read books from Balzac's famous *La Comédie Humaine* when I was doing A level French at school, even though I don't think they were on the syllabus. I remember discussing Stendhal's *Le Rouge et le Noir* with him. It is tempting, with hindsight, to link Roy's interest in both Balzac and Stendhal to the topic of some of their greatest writing—the fate of 'arriviste' young men, clever, cynical and ambitious, trying to make their way in the most snobbish and class-conscious periods of French history. It is because of his university experience that I can still recite parts of Lamartine's great poem, 'Le Lac', by heart. To my educational benefit, he also made me 'choose' Latin when my school divided us up at age twelve into the domestic science stream and the Latin stream. I had been set on the cookery class after learning to make a white sauce.

King's College in 1934 would not, however, have felt at all familiar. At Oxford, Gwyn Thomas never felt comfortable, longing to get back to the valleys at the end of each term. Apart from anything else he found the height of the other undergraduates disconcerting. In the Rhondda, he claimed, the average height of 'our men was about five feet six … The abundance of men over six feet in height at Oxford, all serene with health and strength, startled me.' King's College was not quite Oxford and Roy was perhaps taller than the average Rhondda man (though well under six foot). But King's was still very much the preserve of students from upper- and middle-class backgrounds. A large survey of university students who graduated in the 1930s from English universities tells us a lot about the social class of this cohort. Almost half of those who went to King's were from professional or managerial/executive families. Another quarter were from higher non-manual families. No one came from an unskilled manual household, and only eleven percent came from any kind of manual working-class background. In this socio-economic pattern, King's College was more like Oxbridge than the newer universities such as Nottingham. (In the 1930s there were still only eleven English universities, including Oxford and Cambridge, and five university colleges.) Roy's academic preparation at Porth County would have been as good if not better than anyone else's it seems, but there is no evidence that he had ever moved in anything but working-class social circles, or even left the Rhondda, before coming to London at the age of eighteen. Some might have found this daunting.

As far as we know Roy made just one good friend while at university, a friendship that was sustained by shared experiences during the Second World War, and then carried over into peace time—which is the only reason I know about it. I found his friend's name a couple of pages before Roy's in the 1938 list of graduates from London University. The King's College archivist confirmed for me that Roy and Richard Lawrence Flynn took almost identical subjects, both completing their honours degrees in French in 1938. Dicky, as we always knew him, was also something of an outsider in this environment. I learned this when I finally managed to make contact with the youngest of his daughters, in the hope that Dicky might have been more forthcoming about this friendship than Roy ever was.

We email back and forth about our fathers, and when I describe what I have learned about Roy's childhood, Dymphna tells me that Dicky knew him as Roy, and knew he came from Wales. Dicky's background was Irish. His father had come from a farm in Cork to join the police force in London, rising to become a police inspector. Dicky's older brother John, like Roy's brother Colin, spent his working life in retailing, in his case in menswear, specifically hosiery. In both cases this employment seems to have been determined by their ill-health. John suffered badly with asthma, finally dying from an asthma-induced heart attack at the age of sixty-five. Dymphna tells me that Dicky won a scholarship to a private school with strong links to French-speaking Belgium, which is where he got his start in languages.

Before he met Georges Rochat at Porth County Boys, Roy was already living in a bilingual house, with his father and his Probert uncles all growing up speaking Welsh. For a moment I wondered if Dicky too had grown up in a bilingual house, but it turns out his parents were not Irish speakers (though Dicky married an Irish speaker at the end of the war).

It seems that both young men arrived at King's thanks to scholarships they had won to good schools, where they were able to develop their language skills. Probably both were particularly cognisant of the way accent, language and class constrained social life in England. Dymphna and I think that the significant friendship between Roy and Dicky began with their shared outsider status at King's College. Dicky, Dymphna tells me, 'was really well spoken with an English accent ... in fact he had a beautiful voice'. Roy too, had an attractive voice, and perhaps Dicky was his first model of the right kind of English accent to develop as well as showing how it could be done.

Neither would have had any incentive to draw attention to their parents' origins by sounding Welsh or Irish. Dicky lived at home with his parents in Hounslow while studying, at a time when there was widespread anti-Irish sentiment in England. J. B. Priestly, in his 1934 travelogue, *English Journey* writes:

> ... if we do have an Irish Republic as our neighbour, and it is found possible to return her exiled citizens, what a grand clearance there will be in all the western ports, from the Clyde to Cardiff, what a fine exit of ignorance and dirt and drunkenness and disease.

As late as the 1950s and 60s it was common for English landlords to operate a 'No Irish and No Coloureds' policy.

At the same time, the Great Depression caused such economic misery in Wales that there was mass migration to England in the 1920s and 30s. Welsh immigrants often learned to speak without any Welsh accent in case it might disadvantage them. So, while Roy and Dicky came from the occupational extremes of coal mining and agriculture, they might have seen themselves as similarly placed in relation to most of the English undergraduates at King's. They also shared a love of linguistics—a love of words and languages—which Dicky parlayed into a life-long career as an admired teacher of modern languages in

London. Sharing photos with Dymphna, I can see that Dicky was a tall, very good-looking young man, exuding confidence, and an air of mischief. Roy wasn't tall, but he was certainly attractive, and it is not difficult to imagine his confidence, and what his nephew described as 'impishness'. I am getting a picture of Roy's life as a student and I think he was enjoying himself. Thinking of the two of them together makes me smile.

Dicky could live with his parents as a university student, but what made it possible for Roy to study in London? The King's College archivist tells me that they have no record of him holding a scholarship or studentship. Yet the fees alone were between £32 and £36 a year, before accommodation and living costs were added on. There were no part-time jobs for students in the 1930s, and not many for anyone else come to that. Wondering where he might have lived during term time at least, it finally occurs to me to ask if there is an address for Roy in the King's archives. The answer is immediate: Roy lived at 26 Angell Rd, Brixton, and then at 7 Dempster Rd, Wandsworth. Both were likely to have been large villas converted into boarding houses in the first half of the twentieth century, before being demolished in the 1960s and 1970s to make way for council housing. So, like many other students from all kinds of backgrounds, Roy spent his second and final years as a student in London living in one or other South London boarding house. This did not, however, help explain how he could afford this.

At this point in my research, I discovered that mining communities historically had very strong scholarship funds for miners and their families. I found a recent MPhil. thesis on something called the Miners Welfare Fund, and its role in 'improving the social and working conditions of miners 1920–1946'. The fund had a substantial scholarship scheme, with a large endowment to support tertiary education, and it seems that the number of applicants from South Wales in the mid-1930s was consistently high. I eventually find the recipients' names on the website of the Durham Mining Museum, under 'The Science and Art of Mining'. I see Gwyn Thomas is there for 1932, the year he went to Oxford (having been offered three different kinds of scholarship). But there is no sign of Roy.

*

While emailing back and forth with the helpful archivist at King's College I discover that both Roy and Dicky interrupted their studies for a year, with no record kept at the college about what they were doing during this time. Our family had always been under the impression that Bill spent some time at the Sorbonne before the war, but now we know about his childhood, the question of who could have paid for that, on top of everything else, becomes even more curious. I know from my mother that both Roy and Dicky were immediately assigned to the field security police (who were to become the Intelligence Corps) when they enlisted in 1939, so I now went down another badly illuminated rabbit hole trying to work out if Roy at least, and possibly Dicky, had been 'picked up' while at university by a British War Office that was increasingly desperate to find linguists to support the army in the coming war. From my enquiries it appears that this is not an unrealistic suggestion, and that the university education of some potential army linguists was indeed paid for by the War Office. What is more, their initial hunting grounds for language students were Oxbridge and the University of London. I open a file on spying and secrecy.

As well as the year taken off in the middle of his university studies, there is also a missing year after Roy completes his B.A. in 1938. My mother has always said that he was in Yugoslavia when Britain declared war on Germany. I admit I am drawn to the idea that Bill's secret life might somehow be explained by his long-term loyalty to British intelligence, starting before the war and going on long after he returned to civilian life in 1947. What was he doing in Yugoslavia in September 1939? Having a holiday as Janet believed? It seems so improbable. Who would have been paying for any of his expenses over the previous five years, let alone a 'holiday' in what would then have been a relatively exotic place?

In the end it was Dymphna who provided the clue to these missing years. What Roy was doing turned out to be disappointingly mundane compared to intelligence, though it again illustrates the limited options faced by working-class boys in the 1930s. Dicky, Dymphna tells me, spent the academic year 1936–37 as a teaching assistant at a lycée in the Dôme region of central France. This was a requirement for any student who was doing honours in a modern language with a view to teaching it in a secondary school. Such students were required to spend 'at least six months in study abroad under approved conditions before beginning the course of professional training [as a teacher].' An email to the historical records section of the Institute of Education (IoE) in London, asking whether they have any records for Dicky and Roy, brought confirmation that they were both enrolled in the Diploma of Education in 1938/9, and both had spent the missing year in the middle of their undergraduate studies as teaching assistants in France. I was sent copies of their enrolment cards at the IoE which confirmed they had met the undergraduate requirements for studying abroad, and showed that Dicky had undertaken teaching practice at Tiffin School—a grammar school in Kingston Upon Thames—for which he received the grade of B; while Roy had undertaken teaching practice not far away, at Wandsworth School—a selective grammar school in South London—for which he received the unpromising grade of C+/B-.

My romantic thoughts of pre-war Roy at the Sorbonne, then doing mysterious things in Yugoslavia, disappeared in the face of this humdrum discovery. But at least I now knew how he could afford King's. By applying for the Institute of Education's four-year course not only would Roy's university fees be paid, but he would also receive a maintenance grant. Unfortunately, this arrangement involved a Faustian bargain. He would also have to commit to several years working as a schoolteacher on graduation. Admission to this four-year course was, not surprisingly, very competitive. It was almost the only way someone as poor as Roy could get to university at all. The IoE booklet specifies the amount of the annual maintenance grant that would be paid each year, depending on whether the student resided in a 'recognised hostel' (£43) or somewhere else (£26); and it includes a table showing how these grants would be means-tested, according to the parents' annual income and how many dependent children they had.

Now that I knew where to look, I put in a request to the Glamorgan archives in Cardiff before my visit, asking to see the item called 'Rhondda Education Authority Scholarship records 1917–1936'. When I get there, I find it is a large book with a separate page for every successful student over those twenty years. This records the school they went to, the tertiary institution at which they were offered a place, and the exact amount of money awarded both for fees and living allowance. There are about 150 entries, bound in no chronological or alphabetical order, so it is a question of working through the record page by page, feeling increasingly disappointed as Roy fails to appear. The vast majority of the students in this book gained places at either Cardiff or Aberystwyth universities, or Treforest School of Mines. In the 1930s only one student was going to Bristol University, one to Imperial College and two to King's College, London. I admit to more fist-pumping and muted cries of 'Yes!' when I find Roy towards the back of the book. There is a record of his annual fees being paid (of between £31 and £35), as well as his living allowance for each term. He got the maximum grant. Each year, only seven such scholarships were awarded by the Rhondda Education Authority.

From her invaluable survey of students who completed a university degree in the 1930s, Carol Dyhouse explains:

> It is clear from the sample as a whole that the sons of families lower down the social scale who were dependent upon these Board of Education scholarships were in the main those who were least clear about their vocational goals. The 'pledge' to teach was often made out of strategic compliance, since there appeared to be no other way of obtaining financial support for study.

It is not surprising then that during the Depression Wales became notorious for its over-production of schoolteachers. Dyhouse points out that of the men in her sample, a sizeable number got out of teaching as soon as they could, and 'a number did so gratefully with the outbreak of war'. That sounds like Roy to me. I think it is reasonable to conclude that he never wanted or intended to be a teacher (unlike Dicky, whose family had to pay his university and diploma fees).

I think Roy may have been planning another escape route from school teaching before the war broke out. When he persuaded Janet to marry him she believed that 'but for the war, he'd probably have been a lecturer in modern languages now'. Decades later he told me that he 'had a scholarship to do a doctorate in Paris in 1939', which would have postponed any requirement to start teaching. He added, looking back, that 'the war saved me from an academic career, for which I was truly grateful'.

*

Roy's way out of the Rhondda was made possible by the enthusiasm with which the Welsh promoted school education beyond the compulsory years, but more particularly by the peculiarities of Porth County Boys School. However, not every young man who was given this opportunity chose to stay away forever. Gwyn Thomas, whose path out was in many ways so like Roy's—from an impoverished Welsh mining household to Oxford—always wanted to return. Much later he wrote that while at Oxford, 'The vacations were sweet. Each term's end seemed to bring a drift of sanity back into my days.' When he got home, 'the hills around the valley brought solace'. Not fit enough for war service, Gwyn taught French and Spanish for two decades at a grammar school in Cardigan, in West Wales. In his memoir he describes returning to Llanwonno, just over the hill from Ynyshir. Sitting alone in a familiar pub, he finds himself surrounded by the Pendyrus Male Voice Choir—'singers of matchless passion from the Little Rhondda'. As they sang, he writes, 'I was home, at my earth's warm centre. The scared monkey was back in the branches of his best-loved tree. I've never had any truly passionate wish to be elsewhere.' And I have no doubt that listening to a Welsh male voice choir could easily do this for you.

Others of the same generation had the opposite reaction to their Welsh origins.

> Wales is a very small country where everyone seems to know everyone else and interests are often parochial, hermetic and suffocating. There is frequently a yearning for occasional and sometimes permanent escape, a feeling that could lead one college principal to say that coming home to Wales was like going back into jail, and led Dylan Thomas to tell his Fathers what they could do with their Land.

For Roy, it seems that there was no looking back. He would have arrived at King's as a very Welsh young man, with a dense family network of uncles, aunts and cousins living in and around the collapsing economy of Ynyshir. It is not just that he was given an education which was as good as any and which could take him out of the valleys. He was given a particular education about Europe through the remarkable teaching he experienced with Georges Rochat at Porth County Boys. The intensity of the school's focus on French and Spanish languages took him to London (and France) where he lived for five formative undergraduate years. He was able to experience and to imagine a much wider world in a way that played to his intellectual strengths. Roy's university education was not just a passport to professional employment. His absorption of France's history and culture and his growing admiration for that country helped shape the man he chose to become. The outbreak of the Second World War cut across everything as he finished his studies, but his experience of that war was also profoundly shaped by the education he had received, and the aptitudes it had revealed.

Chapter 3
Roy's War: Secrecy and Bravery

As a child growing up in the 1950s on the North Downs in Kent, I was drawn to tales of British heroism in the Second World War. My brothers and I loved reading our little black-and-white comics about the scrambling of Spitfires from Biggin Hill (not far from where we lived), and the desperate dog fights that happened between our planes and German Messerschmitts during the Battle of Britain in the summer and autumn of 1940. Like thousands of other British and Commonwealth children, we read Paul Brickhill's book *Reach for the Sky*, about the legless flying officer Douglas Bader, who insisted on re-joining the Royal Air Force at this moment of crisis, finally being shot down over France in 1941. We knew about the danger of the enemy coming from out of the sun, believed in the aerial superiority of the Spitfire, understood how pilots were summoned to their planes for take-off, and appreciated the terrible loss of lives in the air. Stories of ground combat left fewer impressions, except that German soldiers would shout 'Achtung!' or 'Befehl ist befehl!' (Orders are orders) as they were about to do something brutal, while Japanese soldiers were hiding everywhere in the jungles of the far east. We read about Colditz and German prisoner of war camps where British soldiers used extraordinary ingenuity to dig their way out to freedom.

By contrast, I have no recollection of my father ever talking about the war. Nor anyone else, come to that. But his high lace-up parachute boots were always in the boot room, and occasionally we would use them for dress-ups. We knew that's what they were. Bill would wear them, with his old military jacket, when he worked in the garden. He also kept his khaki great coat when he was de-mobbed. In the bottom of an elegant antique chest of drawers in our parents' bedroom were his medals which we would occasionally get out of their boxes to look at. We had no idea what they were for, only that they represented something good. My brothers tell me that they each remember Bill taking out a dagger from the high cupboard above the larder to show them, and William thinks Bill explained to him how you would kill someone with it. When I follow up William's description of it, I realise it is a Fairburn-Sykes fighting knife, made famous during World War Two when it was issued to British commandos, the Special Air Service (SAS) and many other units. With its acutely tapered, sharply pointed long blade, it is often described as a 'stiletto'. I am sure Bill never showed it to me as I would have remembered its sinister shape. There are many online descriptions of how it was to be used. It was probably issued to Bill as part of his training with Special Operations Executive (SOE) for parachuting into France in 1944.

Bill's silence about the war is partially offset by the large amount of documentation that I am able to find about his participation in the Allied liberation of the Ariège region of south-west France towards the end of the war in Europe. In fact, even now, almost eighty years after the event, I discover that his name continues to crop up in books about the British Intelligence Corps, or SOE. For the start of Bill's war, five years earlier, I have my mother's account of his enlistment in 1939 with the Royal Warwickshire Regiment and his immediate transfer to Mytchett in Hampshire, for training with the Field Security Police—the units that were to become part of the new Intelligence Corps six months later. There are some wartime photos in my mother's album, taken mostly in Egypt and Madagascar, including one where Bill is wearing army shorts and a slouch hat turned up in the Australian military style, under which she has written 'King's Own African Rifles?'. She thinks he was in Kenya with this regiment. In the summary she wrote for me of Bill's war, it is not surprising that my mother found it all slightly confusing: 'I can't work out all his changes of unit at all.'

I can find almost nothing on any official war records sites apart from confirmation that he enlisted in the Royal Warwicks and was later with the Intelligence Corps. I realise I will have to do some serious work if we are to know more about his war, and how his experiences during those years might have encouraged or helped Welsh Roy to become English Bill.

*

When Britain declared war on Germany on 3 September 1939, Bill was in Yugoslavia. My mother believed he was on holiday in Dubrovnik, though now that I know he'd spent the previous five years living on a tiny grant, it is hard to understand how he could have afforded such a luxury. He had just completed the Diploma of Education, with his less-than-stellar grade for teaching practice. Adding mystery to this is the existence of a studio photograph of Bill and a young woman, taken in Yugoslavia in 1939. The photograph somehow found its way to his sister Lily, in Brecon, and ended up in the hands of her son Denzil. In fact, it has ended up in my hands, passed on to me by Denzil's widow, Audrey. Denzil sent a copy of this photograph to Janet when endeavouring to share with her everything he knew about his uncle's life, noting only that the woman's identity is 'unknown' but they thought she was an aristocrat of some kind. The photograph was not a total surprise, since after the war Bill told Janet that he had been engaged to a young Jewish woman in Yugoslavia, but that the engagement was a ruse, suggested by a mutual friend, to help her get out of the country. The photograph does not intimate any romantic attachment, but rather an air of parallel artlessness and youthful charm. But whatever the story behind the photo, Britain's declaration of war meant Bill had to abandon any holiday or marriage plans and immediately return to England. When I asked my mother about this photograph, she told me that after the war Bill was able to make contact with the woman and was reassured to discover that she did in fact get away safely, to the USA. Eighty percent of the Jewish community in Yugoslavia was murdered after the Axis powers invaded in April 1941.

On 29 September 1939, less than four weeks after war was declared, every member of the civilian population in England and Wales was required to fill in a survey in preparation for the introduction of identity cards and rationing. While the register is not the same as a census, it means we know where Bill was. It is an invaluable source of information for any family researcher because all the 1931 census data was destroyed by fire in 1942, possibly caused by an employee's discarded cigarette. (Future family historians will curse that careless employee as we approach 2031 and the theoretical public release of the data from that census.) From the register I can see that Bill was staying with his cousin, George Alfred Knight (occupation 'motor works policeman') in Coventry. Alfred, as he was known, was the son of Minna's oldest brother Sidney Knight, a collier who left Ynyshir to find work in the Derbyshire coal mines at the turn of the century. Born twenty years before Bill, Alfred started work with his father in the same mine, as a 'colly lamp examiner', but in the 1920s he moved to Coventry where he lived in the same modest terrace house for the next forty years. Also living there was Bill's brother Ron (occupation 'wood machinist').

Bill was now qualified to teach modern languages in a British secondary school, and this is the occupation he gave in the 1939 register. His holiday in Yugoslavia, if that is what it was, suggests he had no teaching position lined up for the new school year. His friend Dicky Flynn, who unlike Bill was keen to teach, had also failed to find a position. In any case, on that survey night they would both have known that they would shortly have to present themselves for military service. Parliament had already passed the National Service (Armed Forces) Act imposing conscription on all males aged between eighteen and forty-one. Those medically unfit were exempted, as were others in key industries and jobs such as baking, farming, medicine and engineering. Being a baker would have exempted Bill's brother-in-law in Brecon. His brother Colin would have failed on medical grounds. His brother Ron also managed to avoid being called up, perhaps because he was the factory fireman at his workplace.

Those aged between twenty and twenty-three had to register by 21 October. Bill enlisted in Coventry on 30 November, becoming part of the second batch, just a couple of months after his twenty-fourth birthday. He gave his address as that of his cousin Alfred in Coventry. As next of kin he nominated his mother, Mrs Maria Probert, but instead of her Ynyshir address he again used his cousin's address in Coventry. Perhaps he had already begun to disconnect—or be disconnected from—his mother, and to erase his ties to Wales?

Meanwhile, in Isleworth, one hundred miles south of Coventry, Dicky was also enlisting. Like Bill, he was immediately shipped to Mytchett, along with another language student from King's College. By 1 December Bill and Dicky were reunited in this unlikely spot. There is a disarming posed formal photograph of Bill and Dicky in their uniforms—riding breeches, puttees, peaked caps, and tunics with high collars and brass buttons—taken in January 1940. They are smiling broadly to camera as though they have just won something, though the photograph was probably taken to acknowledge their graduation from the short training course. Bill is a little plump in the face. The photograph of the two of them is stuck into my mother's photo album next to separate portraits of them, taken in Cairo probably very early in 1944. The contrast between the cheerful boyishness of January 1940 and the experienced, manly faces of 1944 is poignant.

*

My first ill-informed internet searches for information about Bill's war, using the words Roy, Royden, Bill, Probert, Intelligence, SOE, DSO, and Royal Warwickshire in various combinations, took me only to stories about his role in the liberation of the Ariège region of France. But they also took me to a resource I was somehow surprised to find: a Military Intelligence Museum (MIM). It exists to tell the story of British military intelligence from the Boer War onwards, promising to share the secrets of 'the shadowy world of intelligence, security, espionage and other military intelligence disciplines, telling the stories that you will not hear in any other museum in the United Kingdom'. The museum's website even has an archival research enquiries page, where I was able to lodge a question, asking if they have any information about William R. Probert and Richard Lawrence Flynn.

Living in Melbourne I was rarely at my desk at the same time as the people I was trying to contact in England or Wales. As a result, some of my most rewarding emails were there in my inbox when I woke up in the morning, giving a fillip to my spirits. On this occasion I woke up next day to a reply from the admirable Intelligence Corps historian, Fred Judge, telling me that the museum has all the publicly available material about Bill's deployment in France with SOE towards the end of the war, and the citation for his DSO (Distinguished Service Order). 'He was undoubtedly a very brave officer.' Another email arrived a few hours later with the information that Bill's SOE personal file 'no longer exists'. It appears it might have been destroyed after the war, but more likely was retained by the Secret Intelligence Service (SIS) because of wartime links to them.

It seemed remarkable to have such an expert at the other end of the email, and he endured—with good grace—many further requests for information from me over the next few weeks. For Dicky they could only find a record of his commission in 1942. Nothing else. The absence of any other records, I was told, suggests that Dicky had been recruited by the Secret Intelligence Service. As with my father's personal file, the disappearance of Dicky's file could be blamed on SIS (also known as MI6). In cases like theirs, Fred warned me, where any work had been undertaken for the Secret Service, a personal file would not be released until at least a hundred years after the event. 'It will then go to the National Archives where, assuming TNA don't add another half century to it, you will be able to see it.'

While the museum was unable to tell me anything much that I did not know already about Bill, my request for information about Dicky produced the lead that eventually connected me to Dicky's youngest daughter Dymphna—who helped me uncover Bill's brush with teacher training and the facts about his missing university year. Fred informed me that Dicky's son had been in touch with them a few years earlier, on a similar mission to my own. For a moment I let myself imagine finding this son and discovering that he had already worked out what our fathers were up to in North Africa.

The museum would not, however, give me any contact details for Dicky's son, not even his first name; nor would they pass on a message from me. I turned to my mother's photo album looking for clues and found an old photograph under which she had pencilled 'With Dickie Flynn's children. 1957'. (These pencil notes are from much later, when the spelling of Dicky was of no great importance to her.) There is the son, with a younger sister, standing with me and my brothers on the sunny front porch of our house in Kent. I am seven years old, and Dicky's children look about the same age as us. Dicky must have brought them with him from North London on one of his rare Saturday visits to see Bill. I have a faint memory of driving to the Thames at Woolwich to collect him from the ferry on one occasion. My mother failed, however, to write the names of the visiting children.

Looking at the photograph inspired me to do some more pleading with the museum, and I was eventually rewarded with the son's first name. Now all I had to do was find someone called Patrick Flynn, probably aged about seventy, and possibly living in London. For some reason my mother's address book did not contain Dicky's last address before he died, which would at least have given me somewhere to start.

The thought of finding Patrick began to obsess me. I could suddenly see that Dicky was the only person who knew Roy as he emerged from the Rhondda, knew him as a lover of French poetry at King's College, shared a tent with him in Cairo as lance corporals, as well as the experience of riding motorcycles back and forth across Egypt and Libya for the Intelligence Corps (another memory of my mother's). He then stayed in touch with Bill the successful family man in the 1950s. The rest of us only knew Bill as post-war Bill, while his nephew Denzil only knew him as pre-war Roy. Indeed, Denzil keeps apologising to us for calling him Uncle Roy, explaining that is the only man he knew.

My mother certainly spoke to Dicky by telephone after Bill died, telling him about our astonishment at learning of Bill's Welsh origins and his early life as Roy. If Dicky was less secretive with his family than Bill was with us, then it was entirely possible that Patrick would know more than I did about important parts of Bill's life. And he was way ahead of me researching Dicky's war, which would certainly shed light on Bill's.

*

But how was I going to find Patrick Flynn? Just for fun, I put his name and his likely date of birth plus or minus a couple of years into the Find My Past data base, using England as the location. That gave me 123,145 possible results. I was clearly going to need a more targeted approach. After a bit of effort, I was fairly confident that I had found Dicky in the death notices for England and Wales, since I had good intelligence about his likely year of birth and year of death. But I could find no funeral notice for him—which I had hoped might give me some way of contacting his children. As a novice family history researcher, I was extremely ignorant and inefficient.

It was a random lunch with a constitutional researcher from the British House of Commons visiting Melbourne that alerted me to the fact I could request Dicky's actual death certificate from the British government. Not only would this give the occupation of the deceased and the cause of death, but it would include the name and address of the 'informant'—usually the next of kin. For a mere £11, I could have a copy of the death certificate posted out to me within four working days. Too impatient to wait for such an important piece of paper to reach Australia, I requested that it to be sent to a friend in Oxford, asking her to copy it to me by email without delay.

When it arrived, and I read the name Patrick Flynn as the informant on the death certificate, and saw a North London address for him, I think I probably let out a whoop of excitement. I refused to let the fact that this address was now twenty years old worry me. I couldn't send an email or make a phone call, but I could write a letter, reconnecting with someone who had stood next to me in the sunshine over sixty years before.

I wrote immediately, including a copy of the photograph of us together. As I was sticking the stamp on the envelope, I checked the postcode once more because the street address was offering me two different London postcodes on Google maps. To establish the right one, I googled Patrick Flynn and South Woodford, and the first page that came up gave me his handsome smiling face—sitting above a funeral notice. He had died just nine months earlier.

I felt not only a sharp pang of disappointment, but also real sadness. Patrick looked out from my screen with such good humour and intelligence. I think I felt deprived of our shared project—something that had looked so promising and potentially so enjoyable.

A day or two later it occurred to me that Patrick might have shared his research with his family, so I went back to the funeral notice. It included the name of his widow, Roberta, and the names of four younger siblings: Siobhan, Nuala, Eamonn and Dymphna. With low expectations I searched for 'Roberta Flynn South Woodford' and came up with a local paper notice about an illustrated lecture on Vincent Van Gogh, to be given by the art historian Roberta Flynn in a South Woodford church. Despite the event having occurred thirteen years earlier, I emailed the address given for further information, explaining my mission and asking if a 'letter' could be forwarded to this Roberta Flynn, should there be any reason to believe she had been married to someone called Patrick.

People researching their family history must all experience the same all-too-frequent dead-ends and the very occasional stroke of good fortune. My stroke of good fortune was the church organiser at the other end of my email who not only got on the case immediately, but then printed off my 'letter' and arranged for it to be delivered to Roberta Flynn by hand. Within a week I had an email from Patrick's youngest sister, Dymphna who not only had the notes Patrick had made from his work on Dicky's war before he became ill, but also the ones he had made about his father's friend, Roy.

Patrick's second email to his siblings reporting on his research into their father's war, sent on 9 October 2015, begins:

> Dear Sisters and Brother
> Here is the rest of the stuff on Dad's pal.
> I thought my notes would be shortish, but turn out to be longish, not for the first time. Blame Roy's comrade in arms, Commander 'Bruno' who turns out to be one of the most important figures in 20th century French military history, though not a particularly pleasant personality.
> However, he and Roy played a big part in liberating a whole French Département from the Nazis, no mean feat.
> Read all about it –
> How do one million elephants enter the story?
> How does Genghis Khan figure in a tale of the South of France?
> See the nice 'photo' of the 20th Century Three Musketeers!!! [Roy, Commander Bruno and the leader of the Spanish maquis, Royo.]
> Major Probert's recommendation form for his DSO reads like an item from a 1950s boys war comic or indeed the famous 'Boys Own' magazine. [He attaches the form]
> You will be relieved to hear this will be the last despatch on military matters for some time from the Stanley Road Bunker [his home].
> I'm off for a stroll through the Epping Forest maquis.
> Love
> Patrick

Patrick's search for more information about his father's war was cut short by his fast-moving dementia. The last email to his siblings about 'Dick's Deeds in the Desert' was sent in March 2016. His notes are full of dry humour and wit about the years 1940–42. And they provide me with new leads to follow about Bill, even though we have clearly been traipsing around many of the same resources. Had Patrick lived I think we would have enjoyed the shared pursuit of our fathers through North Africa, where they seem to have spent a lot of time riding motorbikes and relishing being in the desert.

**

Britain was singularly ill-prepared for this war, despite having introduced a measure of limited conscription in May 1939, which required young men to undertake six months' military training. Some 240,000 registered for service as a result, but intelligence had become a military backwater after the end of the First World War, and little attention was paid to it in 1938–39. It was only in September 1939 that a separate Directorate of Military Intelligence (DMI) was created in the War Office. Plans were largely the same as for the 1914–18 war; a 1931 plan for a small Intelligence Corps to accompany any British Expeditionary Force (BEF) relied on the rapid mobilisation of suitable people identified in peacetime. Revised in 1938 it became the basis of the ad hoc Intelligence Corps which would support the Expeditionary Force sent to France in September 1939. But for Major (later Field Marshall Sir Gerald) Templer, there would have been no intelligence organisation at all on the outbreak of war. He oversaw the identification of suitable officers to receive intelligence and security training, and in 1938 the Field Security Police (FSP) was created.

The FSP was based at the Corps of Military Police Depot at Mytchett, which provided a suitable administrative structure and 'cover', albeit the Field Security recruits were later keen to demonstrate they were not military policemen. Two sections of a hut were put aside for a fourteen-day course of training that initially involved interrogation techniques, the need to maintain morale through security awareness and propaganda, and the importance of uncovering the deployment of Germany's forces. Their eventual role was, according to Captain Sir Basil Bartlett (one of the first Field Security officers) to 'thwart enemy attempts at espionage, sabotage and propaganda'. In the early stages of the war, thirty-one small Field Security sections were raised to accompany the British Expeditionary Force into France to carry out both intelligence and security duties. These recruits needed to be fluent in French (and Italian if they were to be monitoring the Italian workers who were still building French fortifications near the border with Belgium).

Such was the shortage of people with relevant language skills for intelligence work that the War Office was obliged to advertise on the BBC and in the national press for linguist volunteers to undertake 'special work in the Army'. Patrick told his siblings that he was 'pretty sure one of these adverts prompted Dad to join up'. He sent them a copy of a story he had found in the *Derby Daily Telegraph* of late September 1939 as an example of what might have caught Dicky's eye, telling them to note 'the emphases on "Personality" and the promise of quick promotion'. Apart from needing to be proficient in at least one European language, these recruits were required to have 'Character, intelligence and personality—with special emphasis on personality'. A retired senior intelligence officer sent me another example of this recruiting strategy, from a Yorkshire newspaper, running the same story in early October 1939 with the headline 'ARMY OPENING: A Chance for Linguists'. Pay was to be two shillings a day, plus a shilling Corps pay. Suddenly it seems obvious to me that Bill and Dicky telephoned each other or wrote to each other about these 'ads' and co-ordinated their attendance at their respective enlistment centres with the objective of joining the Field Security Police. This is more plausible than seeing their simultaneous arrival in Aldershot as a fluke.

Patrick's notes take me to Malcolm Muggeridge, the English journalist and satirist, who was one of the five hundred volunteers who stepped forward.* He kept detailed diaries for much of his life and used them in his *Chronicles of Wasted Time* to create an amusing and sardonic picture of his experiences with the emerging intelligence force. In Aldershot the tensions between the Military Police and the Field

---

* Muggeridge is best known for having gone to work, enthusiastically, in the Soviet Union in the 1930s. What he saw turned him into an anti-communist, and he moved to work as a journalist in India. When war broke out, he immediately tried to volunteer. Dicky certainly met him at Mytchett, and almost certainly Roy did as well.

Security recruits were well known. As Muggeridge describes it, the FSP were an alien element at Mytchett.

> An advertisement for linguists such as brought us together there, was calculated to assemble as sorry a company in their eyes as could possibly be imagined; ranging from carpet-sellers from Baghdad and modern language teachers in grammar schools and colleges, with a stray expert on Bengali or Sanskrit, or pimp from Marseilles or Beirut; as well as tourist agency men, unfrocked priests who had lived irregularly in Venice and Rome, and contraceptive salesmen who had roamed the world.

The Red Caps (the real Military Police) 'looked with ill-concealed distaste and disdain at we Field Security men'.

Many of the FSP recruits were equally keen to distance themselves from the Military Police, with whom they were easily confused. Some filed the words 'Corps of Military Police' from their cap badges, and Dicky reminisced with my mother decades later about how he and Bill 'lurked about off-duty, trying to hide their insignia. At least they didn't have to wear red bands, as proper military police did.'

In January 1940 the new recruits underwent their two-week Field Security course that included mastering Norton 500s, BSA 350s and Matchless motorcycles as well as firing off a few rounds from .38 Webley revolvers. Muggeridge suggests the 'intelligence' element of the training he received was based exclusively on World War One practice, and hopelessly out of date. Examples included tapping garrulous barbers and taxi drivers for information, and a playlet where an agent's ballpoint pen with invisible ink was found in his toilet accessories.

Some FSP sections were deployed immediately to France, attached to different military divisions, only to be evacuated after the army was forced to withdraw from France in the middle of the year, as Hitler invaded. Bill and Dicky, however, were sent directly to the Middle East. For the British, their greatest fear in 1940 was that the Italians— from their African colonies—would seize Egypt and the Suez Canal.

Cairo became a vital training ground for all elements of intelligence including Political Warfare (PWE) and SOE. Many Egyptians were sympathetic to the Axis powers, and Cairo was a great cosmopolitan city, 'tailor made for espionage and subversion'. In Tripoli and Benghazi Italians made up between thirty and forty percent of the population and Dicky, who had learned Italian somewhere along the way, would have been useful before Italy joined the war, picking up political gossip if nothing else.

It is highly likely that Bill and Dicky travelled in a small group with another recruit—an insurance agent from London—whose deployment is described in a recent book about the Intelligence Corps by Nicholas van der Bijl. They went by troop train to Marseilles, and then embarked on the troopship *Lancashire* which was on its way to India. The FSP recruits disembarked at Port Said on 29 January, and from there travelled by train to Cairo, to become the first identifiable intelligence group under British military command in the Middle East.

Just as I was finishing this book, Dicky's daughter Dymphna unearthed three photographs of Roy (as Dicky calls him on the back of the photos) and Dicky, taken outside the famous Shepheard Hotel in Cairo in the summer of 1940. They are dressed to kill, larking about with a third member of their FSP section, Geoff Barnes. 'Lance Corporals in plain clothes' or 'Spycatchers' as Dicky jokingly describes them. In these photos it seems they are using Roy's camera (he is holding an empty camera case in one of them) and having fun. Roy is the dandy (or Hollywood gangster), wearing a black short-sleeved shirt with a white (or very pale) wide tie, and baggy trousers falling to turn-ups that sit perfectly on his immaculate two-tone shoes. In a second photograph he is grinning beside Dicky, who has his arm around Roy's shoulder. They are both wearing white or cream jackets, but Roy's is double-breasted. In the third photograph, the three of them are hiding behind a palm tree, with just their heads poking out on one side, from shortest (Roy) to tallest (Dicky).

These photos, like the blurry one of the younger Roy, are the only evidence I have of my father's character as a young man. Colin and I both take pleasure in his apparent 'dapper roguishness'. The other two surviving photographs from the period are formally posed—one with his Yugoslavian 'fiancée' and the other as he graduates from Mytchett. Neither gives much away. But here in Cairo I can see that he is not looking like a middle-class man nor a university man. Is he modelling himself on James Cagney? American movies were enormously popular in the cinemas of the Rhondda in the 1920s and 1930s, especially among schoolboys. Walter Hadyn Davies, a little older than Roy, grew up in a mining family near Merthyr Tydfil. Writing about his childhood he describes how kids walked two or three miles to villages that had 'picture halls'.

> Although the early films were crudely projected, their stories nevertheless seemed wonderful to our boyhood eyes ... They carried us into a world of wonder, of excitement and anticipation, where fun and games were of life, and where even the most dire perils were safely overcome if one was a 'hero'... an association which was always mentally invigorating ... Out of a wider world came the wiles, the glories and the romance of wonderful gods and goddesses, touching each yearning boy's heart and transmogrifying him from puny dwarf to romantic giant, from collier boy to knight errant.

Bill is, in any case, a man full of optimism who seems to have chosen with great care how he wishes to look, and who is showing the broad chest and held-back shoulders he kept all his life. He is with a friend who knows him well, and they look like they are on holiday together, beaming to camera. I know that by the end of the war, when Roy has become Bill, he is dressing differently, but always with the same care for his appearance and bearing.

*

In June 1940, Italy did indeed declare war on Britain, threatening Egypt from its colonial bases in Libya. In September Italy invaded Egypt, pausing just over the border, at Sidi Barani, on the Mediterranean. Bill's French would have been put to work gathering intelligence about Vichy plans, as it was far from clear how the French in Algeria would align themselves in the lengthy campaigns that were to be fought for control of North Africa.

In January 1941, General O'Connor captured Tobruk after pushing the Italian army back across the desert, taking a total of 130,000 prisoners. Dicky may well have been very busy interrogating the Italian prisoners of war interned in detention camps after the Italian army in North Africa was defeated. My mother wrote to me:

> [Bill] was certainly with the army in the Libyan desert when Wavell drove the Italians back from Egypt. I remember Bill describing his amazement at the luxurious baggage, including silk pyjamas, left behind by the Italian officers. He also told me what a wonderful experience living and sleeping in the desert had been.

Hitler was not, however, going to accept this loss of territory. In February 1941, Rommel was appointed commander of the new Afrika Tank Korps and despatched to re-take North Africa. There were Axis landings in Tripoli from mid-February 1941, and the Allies were pushed back again, retreating eastward, leaving Rommel to retake Benghazi in early April, followed by a move to surround Tobruk before pressing on to the Egyptian border. During this long campaign to control North Africa, Bill's army service file (when I finally managed to extract it from the Ministry of Defence) shows him to have been attached to a number of different units: 5th and 11th Indian Brigades; 19th Australian Brigade; HQ 7th; Armoured Division Advance HQ and 9th Australian Division HQ in Tobruk. I am not at all surprised that my mother found Bill's service history confusing. The FSP units were always attached to one or other military division, though often moved between subordinate brigades, depending on planned operations. This makes it hard to follow an individual's trajectory. Nor is it at all clear what Bill was actually doing with these units.

It does seem probable that both Bill and Dicky were caught in the siege of Tobruk. The 11th Indian Brigade was captured at Tobruk, and we know that Bill spent enough time with the Australians who were left to defend the city for them to introduce him to 'Aussie beer'. The unique experience of being trapped with Australians, the Rats of Tobruk, may well have set him up to respect his Australian mother-in-law after the war. She was formidable, if not loveable. From Dymphna I learn that Dicky had told his younger son Eamonn that 'the nearest he came to danger/death during the war was at Tobruk'. He, too, was attached to a military unit, perhaps as an interpreter, but he was evacuated early on. The ships involved in the evacuation were attacked by German bombers, and Dicky saw the ship sailing just before his 'blasted'.

By November of that year, 1941, Dicky had been made a sergeant and so had Bill. My mother wrote that Bill had told her 'it was the proudest moment of his life, walking into the sergeant's mess!' The exclamation mark seems to reflect my mother's surprise at Bill's reaction. But perhaps her surprise is more an illustration of her total ignorance about Bill's origins. How could she have known what this meant in his life up to that point if he had told her nothing about it? For a young man who had been something of an outsider, the move into the sergeant's mess meant, unequivocally, that he was on an equal footing with everyone there. (Becoming a commissioned officer later did, of course, require more remodelling of Roy, and he was probably already observing what joining the higher ranks would require.)

At this point in the war there were about 140,000 Allied troops based in and around Cairo. Artemis Cooper provides a vivid picture of wartime life in Cairo, from the military campaigns to the nightlife. Men were lodged in camps around the city, made up of row after row of square tents with one window where men slept on the ground using their boots as a pillow. Bill and Dicky certainly slept in the same tent at certain points. But once promoted, officers like Bill and Dicky were permitted to rent flats. Between campaigns Cairo was a city full of English-speaking young people only there to win the war. 'It gave their world a glamorous, magazine feature quality'. Their days ended with dinner and dancing and night clubs. Dicky found time to form a relationship with an actress called Doreen Lawrence, performing in Cairo with ENSA—the Entertainments National Service Association, established to entertain British armed forces wherever they were stationed. Doreen is best known for then marrying the famous actor Jack Hawkins, but there is a photograph of her with Dicky in Cairo in 1943, possibly taken by Bill. She later wrote a book called *Drury Lane to Dimapur: Wartime adventures of an actress*, providing an insight into the lives of the units of the Eighth Army that had been left behind in the desert to deal with the debris and destruction of the earlier battles. 'The men we performed to felt isolated or abandoned, either waiting for leave in Cairo or just returning from it, bored and lonely.'

*

The Intelligence Corps was now a large organisation, with Field Security teams active on every front of the war as the Allies' campaign moved from North Africa to southern Europe. There were teams deployed from Burma to Greece, and from Palestine to Ethiopia. In Africa, the eastern seaboard and its offshore islands were part of an extensive network of sea lanes needing security provision, stretching across the Indian Ocean to the Persian Gulf and the Bay of Bengal. There were FS units working in East Africa, trying to locate Germans in the area, and working with Ethiopian guerrillas behind the Italian lines. It was here that Bill spent most of 1942 and the first six months of 1943, first in Italian Somaliland and then in Mombasa—a prized asset. What exactly Bill (or Dicky) was doing it is impossible to know. But by May 1942 Bill was working for the Political Warfare Executive (PWE) and was a lieutenant, attached to the East Africa Intelligence Corps.

PWE was one of the nine British secret services of the Second World War. Among the other services were MI5, MI6, SOE and the Government Code and Cipher School. From Goring-by-Sea I order up a second-hand copy of *The Secret History of PWE* by David Garnett. This book, I discover, was so 'uninhibited and honest' that it was classified 'Secret—For Official Use Only' for over half a century, and only finally appeared in 2002. The introduction, written by Andrew Roberts—an eminent historian of the Second World War—claims that

PWE was an extraordinary body that recruited some of the most exceptional, unusual and talented people of any of the nine secret organisations. It was an organisation devoted to secrecy and security—the ideal training ground for anyone who might have their own secrets they wished to keep.

In August 1942, Bill joined the British and African brigades that were brought together (in Force 121) to occupy Madagascar, where he would work on propaganda, making effective use of his French. This was when he may have been attached to the King's Africa Rifles, a regiment forming part of the Allied invasion force. The island was in Vichy hands, and the Allies were unprepared for the level of resistance they met. There was good reason to fear that the staunchly pro-Vichy governor would offer the island's facilities and ports to Japanese and Axis warships. Intelligence experts worked to identify Gaullists being held in prison who were to be released; carried out surveillance of the Vichy authorities, moving any with a record of collaborating out of their positions; and screening and detaining crews of German merchant ships and numerous Italian seamen. PWE prepared propaganda leaflets in French, inviting the French garrison to surrender, and a broadcasting service was set up to counter pro-Vichy propaganda still being broadcast from the unoccupied area. Bill had made friends with another good linguist in the Royal Marines, Michael Wormald, who ran the radio station set up by the Allies in Diego Suarez.

Bill spent enough time with the Allied invasion force, and then the British and Allied Islands Area Command headquarters that was subsequently established in Madagascar, to fall in love with the island. My mother wrote to me that at the end of the war, Bill and Michael 'seemed to talk of little else'. We also know that he became restless enough to volunteer for a one-man mission to the Comoro Islands—500 kms from the coast of Madagascar—to check whether Japanese submarines were refuelling there. He went by dhow, with a Malagasy crew, a compass and a radio, arriving badly sunburnt to a warm welcome from the French authority. He could find no trace of Japanese submarines. But this episode suggests Bill knew he could handle new and unforeseen circumstances. He was 'in command' now. By May 1943 Bill had been promoted to temporary captain.

Early in 1944, Bill was back in Cairo, where he is recorded as having undertaken a Political Warfare course. Searching for more information about PWE, I find a wonderful grainy fifteen-minute documentary on YouTube—a promotional video describing the British training camp for Political Warfare just outside Cairo. Like an old Pathé newsreel, an American voice describes how men are selected for the training, shows their transport to the camp by jeep, including film of such a jeep passing the pyramids and a sandbagged sphinx, and then taking us past the camp's tents and sheds. On this occasion men are being prepared for the campaign in the Balkans. They are trained in 'calisthenics, history, geography, language, radio broadcasting and monitoring, propaganda leaflet composition, portable printing press operation, interrogation techniques, and vehicle operation and maintenance'. I find myself peering into the screen looking for Bill. He claimed 'experience' in Yugoslavia according to the 'special qualifications' noted in his service record, which I can only assume reflects his pre-war holiday there, and his languages now include a 'smattering of Yugoslav, Arabic, Swahili and some German'.

*

Once I start looking seriously, I discover that the last part of Bill's war is very well documented indeed. In the box of family papers that I inherited, I find his original typewritten reports—faded, detailed and signed—on the 'Activities of the mission "Aube" in the Ariège Department'. From these I can see that whatever Bill had been doing he must have gained experience as a fighter, quite apart from his intelligence work. Without this, he would not have been accepted when he volunteered in May 1944 for an SOE mission to parachute into occupied south-west France in order to 'train, organise and coordinate "Maquis" groups' in the Ariège region. In one lengthy report, he ends by writing that it 'is absolutely essential for any officer going into the maquis to have a thorough military training and what is more important experience in actual warfare.'

Special Operations Executive (SOE) was a secret organisation, established in July 1940, 'to coordinate all action, by way of subversion and sabotage, against the enemy overseas'. A major focus of its work was to aid local resistance movements, and to coordinate the activities of resistance fighters with the military priorities of the Allies. The mission for which Bill volunteered was similar to the so-called Jedburgh missions. These were three-man teams that were parachuted into France, generally at night, to support the Allied landings in Normandy and southern France by linking up with local resistance groups and organising airdrops of arms and ammunition. They were armed and uniformed military personnel who had to be fluent in the language of the European country where they would be dropped. One of the officers would be British or American while the other would be a native of the target country. The third would be a radio operator, of any nationality. For Bill's mission there was also a junior officer, 'Casanova', who was from the region that was to be liberated from the Germans.

These SOE missions relied on volunteers since if anyone was captured, they would not be treated as prisoners of war and would have no protection under the Geneva Conventions. Hitler had issued his Kommandobefehl (Commando Order) in 1942, ordering that all captured Allied commandos, in or out of uniform, should be summarily executed without trial, even if they had surrendered. Any German officer who failed to carry out this execution order would be punished. You did not volunteer for such a mission if your primary objective was to survive the war.

Fifteen of these Jedburgh teams were sent to Algiers to prepare to parachute into southern France. The experience of one of these teams is recounted by Fred Bailey to Sean Rayment for his book *Tales from the Special Forces Club: The Untold Stories of Britain's Elite WWII Warriors*. Fred describes in detail their training in Britain and his subsequent drop into Provence. Bill's mission was slightly different, however. He was selected for one of the twenty-six Inter-Allied Missions (IAMs) dropped into France. These had a similar role to the Jedburghs but worked broadly at the next level of command, coordinating all resistance forces in a 'Département', and working to overcome the conflicting political interests of different groups that might undermine a unified resistance effort. In the event, circumstances in the Ariège meant that Bill and Bigeard needed to take a direct role in combat.

The selection of Bill's IAM to lead the liberation of the Ariège region, and their parallel intensive training at 'Massingham' in Algeria, is also well documented. 'Massingham' was the codename for the joint SOE and American Office of Strategic Services (OSS) base in Algiers, also known as the Special Projects Operation Centre (SPOC). Alongside the formal reports submitted to SOE after the successful mission, there are the books written by and about the French member of this mission, Marcel Bigeard, who went on to become one of France's most famous and decorated generals. He was a French commander in Vietnam at the battle of Dien Bien Phu and then was sent to lead the French forces fighting the National Liberation Front in Algeria. In his autobiography, *De la Brousse à la Jungle*, Bigeard describes the three months 'rigorous training program' he underwent at the Club des Pins, an ultra-secret spot on the Algerian coast controlled by the English. In those three months he was 'going to learn a lot: parachute jumping, handling explosives, how to tail someone, how to escape being tailed, walking between 50 and 80 kms, learning hand to hand combat, climbing a cliff'. The three-men teams were trained together so they knew and understood each other perfectly, and all English parachutists into France had to be fluent French speakers. One admiring academic account of Bigeard's life describes how he willingly 'travelled to freed Algiers' for this training. 'No Anglophobe, he was particularly inspired by a man named Bill Probert, a veteran of Tobruk.'

Since Bill never talked to us about this mission, it is disconcerting to read so many accounts by other people (mostly written decades later) that emphasise the camaraderie and bravery of the team, and Bigeard's respect and affection for him. I feel I need a more objective contemporary account of this period, like the extremely succinct official reports made about each team member as they underwent this training. I do not have Bill's personal SOE file, but by a small miracle I have Bigeard's which includes his superiors' reports on his training progress, set out like a school report, using headings like 'General intelligence', 'Character', 'Weapons training' and 'Interrogations'. On 22 May 1944 Captain Cox notes that Bigeard is 'fit, strong and very good at close combat'. Map reading is 'good', and weapons training is 'very good'. Bigeard is also deemed good at 'demolitions' and 'fieldcraft'. Under 'practical exercises' Captain Cox concludes that he is 'not very inspiring as a leader' (which is ironic given his post-war fame as a leader and motivator of his troops). Under the 'Instructor's remarks' Bigeard is described as having good knowledge of all his subjects 'but spoils himself by being rather conceited'. After another month of arduous training, Captain Douglas Delves scores Bigeard as 'good' for general intelligence, imagination and initiative. As to his character he is 'strong determined forceful and resourceful'. He is 'very good' at interrogations but his 'attitude is far too aggressive'. He is 'quite capable of organising a region' and generally 'easily the best student in his group'.

What was written on Bill's report card, I wonder? All I have to go on is Bigeard's own description of Bill at the time, written in his inimical staccato style.

> Bill Probert, my English major, 30 years old, 'une gueule d'amour',* had done Tobruk, Ethiopia, Tanganyika, Madagascar, and was supposed to be re-joining Tito's forces when he was picked to jump into France. A beautiful visiting card.

On the night of 8 August, the Allied mission took off from Blida airfield, near Algiers, with a portable radio, secret codes and 500,000 francs plus 50,000 francs in pieces of gold. Their Halifax plane had

---

* The phrase has no English equivalent. Perhaps heart-throb, a face to which people are drawn, a beautiful face. A French film from 1937 entitled *Gueule d'Amour* was released in English as *Lady Killer*.

a round trapdoor beside which they sat as they flew over the Mediterranean. A biographer of Bigeard, describing this flight, claims that Bill, 'unconcerned, has closed his eyes and is dozing, tired no doubt from his latest amorous exploits around El-Biar'—'a seasoned fighter [un vieux baroudeur] who had hung his parachute boots out in the most unlikely corners of a world at war'. Perhaps this description is as revealing as a training supervisor's report, but it is a trifle unsettling, and who knows how much weight to give it? Should I start to think of my father as some kind of wartime Lothario? It does not resonate with the Bill I knew, but wartime is different.

I have had a copy of Bigeard's autobiography since it was published. It is inscribed 'Belinda with love from Mum. September 1994', the year it was published (a few months after Bill's death). In this book there is a full-page photograph of Bill, Bigeard and John Deller* (the Canadian radio operator), Bigeard with his arms around the others' shoulders, all looking straight to camera with their parachute wings bright against their khaki uniforms and the sombre, curtained background. I have had the same photograph on my family pictures wall for years, with Bill's faint smile and Bigeard's self-assurance on display. But I did not read the parts of the book that describe their mission until quite recently. While I am wary of Bigeard's self-regard and his desire to project a vision of a France that is 'propre, forte et généreuse', it is hard to beat the immediacy of his narrative.

In his account, the trap door is opened at 1 am.

> We look good, all of four of us, sitting, legs hanging into the void. I am number one, Probert two, Deller three, Casanova 4. Go! I leave, followed by my team members. Beneath me, the three fires lit by members of the resistance. Swaying/swinging above the French soil, in this inky night, bracing air, tension has made all tiredness disappear. The fires get closer. I wait for the shock of landing.

---

* His name is in fact John Dehler but Bigeard and other writers consistently misspell it as Deller.

There is no shock as Bigeard's parachute has caught in a tree, from where he can hear men talking loudly in a foreign language. For Bill there is a considerable shock from a hard landing on his backside.

The voices Bigeard has heard are those of the Spanish resistance fighters who will provide the manpower to take on the German troops in the region. Bill's language skills are going to be critical. The Spanish maquis in the Ariège are part of the Agrupaçion de Guerilleros, whose aim is to destroy Franco's dictatorship. They are all veterans of the Spanish civil war who have taken refuge in France after the Republican defeat. Bill reports that they are 'extremely well organised and disciplined' unlike the local French resistance which he describes as being 'ill-armed, undisciplined, untrained', and also corrupt. The local Free French resistance were, he believed, only interested in receiving arms to support their take-over of power once the Germans had been defeated. They would happily have let the enemy forces 'wend their tranquil way to Toulouse and thence back to Germany'.

This, Bill wrote, was not good enough for the mission, 'nor, let it be said to their everlasting credit, was it good enough for the Spaniards'. However, the Spanish fighters numbered only 225. Radio messages were sent to Algiers to organise multiple arms drops to support a campaign of guerrilla warfare. It became 'literally a question of taking the arms from the containers, giving a ten-minute course of instruction to the maquisards, and then sending them off immediately to ambush Jerry convoys on the roads.'

On 18 August, Bigeard, Bill and Pascual Gimeno Rufino, the chief of the Spanish maquis (called Royo by everyone), despite being seriously outnumbered, decided to attack the German garrison in Foix, the administrative centre of the Ariège. For his role in the liberation of the Ariège, Bill was awarded the Distinguished Service Order (DSO), the second-highest award (after the Victoria Cross) available to officers for gallantry under fire. The citation reads:

This officer volunteered for a mission to train, organise and coordinate 'Maquis' groups in France and he was parachuted into ARIEGE on the 8th of August 1944.

In the absence of competent leaders among the Maquis forces in the area, Major PROBERT took over [in conjunction with Commandant Marcel Bigeard] the active command of the troops and directed the main operations against the enemy.

On the 19 August 1944, Major Probert led an attack on Foix with fifty Spanish Maquis troops. The Germans, with two well-sited machine guns, covered the bridge leading into the town, and held up the advance of the Maquis force. Selecting a party of four, Major Probert forded the river, taking the Germans in the rear. In the fierce street fighting which followed, Major Probert's gallantry and leadership were largely responsible for the withdrawal of the Germans to a block of buildings in the centre of the town.

Learning of the imminent arrival of a train-load of German reinforcements, Major Probert entered the buildings alone and succeeded in obtaining the surrender of 25 officers and one hundred and twenty men, together with ten lorries and important material.

With captured German equipment Major Probert was able to build up his forces, and when the Department was finally liberated more than two thousand Germans had been accounted for.

Recommended by Major General Gubbins, Special Operations Executive, 18 February 1945.

By the end of August, 245 Germans had been killed or wounded, and 1400 prisoners were taken including thirty officers. The mission had suffered losses totalling forty killed or wounded. Both Bill and Bigeard were also awarded the French Croix de Guerre avec Etoile de Vermeil. When this award was finally presented to him, two years later, the citation concludes: 'Le Major Probert sous le nom de Bill est devenu pendant les journées de libération de l'Ariège, un héro légendaire dont le renom a dépassé les frontières du département.'

For now, however, Bill and Bigeard were already experiencing accolades from the newly liberated citizens of the Ariège and celebrating their victory. Bigeard was obliged to collect invoices to account for the mission's expenditures while they remained in Foix, and I can look at them in his SOE file. They include everything from hotel bills to 28 kgs of chicken and 264 eggs which were probably for the 'Soirée de Gala' that the three of them organised to raise money for the rebuilding of the nearby town of Rimont. The Germans had been in the process of 'destroying every house with dynamite and incendiaries' when Bill, Bigeard and Royo launched their attack. This also probably explains the invoice for seventy bottles of Blanquette and sixty bottles of other wines, spirits and champagne, together with the hire of four wine racks and fifty-seven bowls.

The celebratory evening, which the regional newspaper of the FFI called 'Une soirée inoubliable', was held in the Château de Lauquié—previously the home of the Gestapo. Requisitioned in February 1943, over one hundred suspected members of the resistance had been imprisoned there, interrogated and tortured before being transferred to prison or concentration camp. Two bodies were found in the garden shortly before the celebratory evening. It is not surprising that the local community was ready to party and express their gratitude.

The long newspaper article describes the events of the evening, with the presentation of the 'brave men of the maquis' to the assembled guests, reporting that attempts to get them to talk about their exploits fail because of their modesty. This is followed by the introduction of the 'exuberant' Royo, the French heroes from the FFI, and finally the Allied mission team. First to be presented is the 'belle figure' of Bigeard, and then 'our other allies'. The British Major Probert is asked about his impressions when he touched down on French ground. 'It is quite firm,' he replies, with a certain humour—'for I am still carrying the scar—on my backside.' Then the Canadian Deller is presented, 'un demi-français en somme', a giant blond from Ottowa, who is 'incredibly shy'. 'It doesn't matter, we make up for it by vigorously shaking hands with him and saying thank you!'

At the gala, according to Bigeard, all three of them were 'assailed by the so-called weaker sex. Bill has noticed a small blonde woman, very pretty. My tall Canadian flutters between the brunette and the redhead with ease, regretting that so many pretty girls had had their heads shaved.' Bigeard himself was already a devoted married man, watching on with amusement. Keith Lowe has written perceptively about the way the British and American press regularly featured stories of male heroes being kissed or otherwise worshipped by women during and after the war. The pictures were not, he argues, mere propaganda. They 'reflected the experience of many ordinary British and American soldiers, who were often overwhelmed by the outpourings of gratitude they received.'

The evening was a success beyond expectations, with an orchestra, dancing until dawn and, above all, the 'American auction' which included two of the parachutes, one red and one blue, which had been used to turn the ceilings of the two 'salles' into immense, magnificent canopies. The auctions raised a total of 300,000 francs, calling on the hearts of all those gathered to show their solidarity with the devastated community of Rimont. Bigeard's parachute alone sold for the very large sum of 40,000 francs.

A week later the trio left Foix, re-joining the Special Projects Operation Center (SPOC) in Avignon on 23 September. Along with their written reports on the mission, Bigeard and Bill undertook a verbal de-briefing on the 28th. The report on this in Bigeard's SOE file notes that he was now volunteering for any kind of work and 'awaits directive' about his future after he has taken fourteen days leave. Bill was proceeding to London with Deller to report to SOE, and was expected there on 5 October 1944, a few days after his twenty-ninth birthday. He had written in his own report that 'For the future I would like to return to England for leave (I have almost completed five years consecutive service abroad). On the termination of [it] I shall place myself at the disposal of S.O.E.' In the event, this marks the end of Bill's military engagement in the war—though not his work in intelligence.

In the meantime, Bill, Bigeard and Deller headed to Paris in a coveted convertible Mercedes Coupe that they liberated from the Germans. Bill left behind the classic Citroen Traction Avant he had managed to pick up—the black car with front-opening front doors that features in every film about France in the Second World War. Bigeard writes that 'in our combat outfits, with our Para berets, we are stars'[vedettes]. They arrived only five weeks after General de Gaulle finally made his entry into the liberated city, creating an extraordinary atmosphere of relief and celebration. Keith Lowe writes that, 'Sometimes the passion of the crowd, and particularly of the women in the crowd, was like some kind of erotic frenzy.' Alan Moorehead describes the 'hysteria' he witnessed during the liberation of Paris as a kind of patriotic fervour. 'Women were lifting their babies to be kissed. Old men were embracing. Others were sitting weeping in the gutters. Others again just standing and crying aloud with joy.'

It was the first time Bigeard had seen Paris. 'After squaring the account of my mission, returning the funds that had been placed at my disposal, we move into Claridges, Champs Elysées'. 'On ne se refuse rien!!!'. With Bill he went out to dine in black market restaurants where you could have anything, you just needed to pay. 'Life is beautiful, too beautiful, unreal.' One evening they were in a nightclub and found themselves sitting next to Raimu (a very famous French actor), Marie Bell, a classical actress who worked for the resistance in Paris, and Edith Piaf. A captain from the French para regiment appeared, accusing Raimu of being 'bourgeois, du profiteur'. Bigeard felt obliged to intervene, assuring Raimu of his total admiration. And he then danced with Piaf, the little lady who only came up to his waist. Bill may well have followed suit.

*

These last six months in 1944 are the most well-documented of Bill's life, and some of the events still stir up political passions even eighty years later. There are four different plaques in and around Foix commemorating the liberation of the Ariège region. Since 2003 there has been a blue plaque in the garden of the farmhouse where the three Allied parachutists were hidden after they were dropped. Not far away, by the roadside, there is another plaque which reminds passers-by that in August 1944 'le Cdt M. Bigeard', 'le Major anglais B. Probert' and 'le Radio canadien J. Deller' organised parachute drops of arms in this area to support 'la resistance ariègoise'. In August 2021 the mayor of Foix decided to install another plaque in the town of Foix, outside the hotel where the Allied mission based itself after the liberation. This plaque only featured Bigeard, asserting that he led the Spanish maquis and obtained the surrender of the German forces.

The new plaque and the mayor's decision to focus only on Bigeard provoked outrage and criticism from the national president of the association of former guerrilla fighters in France, as well as local demonstrations. The mayor's plaque mysteriously disappeared shortly afterwards and was replaced by a very similar plaque, but this time it featured a photograph with the Spanish hero Royo in the centre, with his 'brothers in arms', Bill and Bigeard, on either side of him. No one seemed to know who was responsible. But not long after the new plaque appeared the mayor had it removed and replaced with a copy of his original homage to Bigeard.

The regional association for commemorating cross-frontier resistance in the Ariège denounced this: 'Unfortunately the mayor has taken down the plaque and replaced it with a shameful and historically incorrect one using the bravery of the guérilleros to excessively honour a soldier whose reputation, unfortunately, was called into question over allegations of torture during the war in Algeria.' (Royo, who returned to Spain in October to fight for the republic, was murdered by the Stalinist leadership of the Spanish Communist Party in 1945.)

One result of this ongoing political conflict is that someone hunting for information about Bill's war has only to enter Probert and Foix into a search engine to find photos and stories about this brief period of his life.

*

As anyone who has done any kind of family history research knows, a stroke of luck is worth months of dedicated work. Despite being told by everyone that Bill's SOE file will never be released (well, not until after I am well and truly dead), I do have a summary, taken from that file over twenty years ago by the SOE advisor in the British Foreign and Commonwealth Office. Two unlikely coincidences were needed for this summary to end up in my hands. The first involves a Captain Probert, a member of the Intelligence Corps in 2000, who came across a reference to Bill in the history of the Intelligence Corps called *Forearmed*, published in 1993. Probert is a common enough name in Wales, but not so much in the British army, so Captain Probert set out to find out more about this other Probert, and to see if he was related in some way. He was able, without difficulty, to arrange to see extracts from Bill's personal file—extracts that cannot be seen by anyone else. The second coincidence ensured that Janet received copies of these extracts before Captain Probert realised that he was not, in fact, related. The SOE advisor who released these file elements to him had, 'by an amazing coincidence', just met 'Major PROBERT's widow in France the other day. I am sending her a copy of this letter and she has agreed that I may let you have her address in case you wish to write to her to attempt to discover whether or not you are related to Major PROBERT.'

The SOE advisor, Duncan Stuart, had been brought together with my mother over the recent discovery of the grave of a British RAF pilot whose plane went down when on a reconnaissance mission in south-west France in November 1943. The plane crashed after developing mechanical difficulties and then running into terrible weather as twenty-eight-year-old Wing Commander Walker attempted to fly south across the Pyrenees to safety. His body was taken by shepherds from the Navarre to the now depopulated village of Torre de Peña, where it was buried among their own.

Fifty years later Monsieur Piot, a keen local historian from Pau, rediscovered this lost village and the grave and talked to Bill and Janet, now living in the foothills of the Pyrenees, about how the history of this grave might be uncovered. It was Duncan Stuart who was able to extract a report on the mission and the crash from the Ministry of Defence and forward it to M. Piot in early 1999. Janet had by now also made the long walk up into the 'secret' village, and M. Piot was consulting her about his plan to hold some kind of memorial ceremony for the dead pilot in Torre de Peña.*

Duncan Stuart met M. Piot and Janet in Pau, just as he was opening Bill's SOE file for Captain Probert, Intelligence Corps. An amazing coincidence indeed. Sadly, Captain Probert discovered that we are not in any way related, and therefore abandoned his research into Bill's war—research that would have been a great deal more fruitful than mine, given his privileged access to military records as a current member of the Intelligence Corps.

The brief extracts that reached us from Bill's SOE file are, nonetheless, useful confirmation about some hunches. They also contain a small but deliberate inaccuracy where his formal education is recorded. 'B.A. from King's College, London University (Modern Languages: French and Spanish) 1933–39 including 1 year at the Sorbonne'. What I now know, of course, is that he did not spend a year at the Sorbonne. Instead, he spent most of that year as a teaching assistant in a French lycée. Bill did not allow this teaching detour to become part of his recorded history.

*

Bill's silence about the war was not, I think, in any way unusual. Nor did it reflect, as far as I can tell, any particular trauma. On the

---

* The small ceremony finally took place on 11 November 2007, at the graveside in Torre de Peña, exactly 64 years after the crash. By this time Janet was too frail to make the journey, but her closest friends went in her place.

contrary, I think in many ways Bill enjoyed much of his war, and it gave him extraordinary opportunities to enlarge his knowledge of the world. Some of his experiences in the North African desert and the time he spent in Madagascar seem to have given him great pleasure, even if he never talked to us about Africa afterwards. His capacity to find enjoyment in these experiences must, in turn, have rested on a strong sense of self-confidence, both physical and psychological.

When I got in touch with my first serious boyfriend to ask him what he remembered most clearly about Bill, fifty years later, John wrote back: 'I only have a few memories of Bill, but I notice they are quite vivid. I thought of him as powerful with a touch of charisma.' He then told me about a brief conversation they had had about his SOE mission.

> He talked about how the training made them fit and aggressive. He was involved in a night attack on a German occupied village in France. He said, 'I remember lying on top of the wall with my dagger at the ready just itching for someone to come along so I could stick it into him.'

I think Bill liked John (and John liked him) which may explain this rather extraordinary disclosure. It was certainly not made in my presence.

It pleases me to discover that my father had 'a good war'. At the same time, knowing so much more about this part of his life makes him somehow less recognisable, or less familiar. For a while I was tempted by the idea of visiting Foix, as though this might make me feel closer to him, better able to understand some fundamental aspect of his character. But on reflection, I concluded that it was a rather bad idea. While Bill emerges as a hero from these events, I know that it was not, in reality, a Boys' Own Adventure. I am not sure that I want to let those events come to life in my imagination. I also realise that I am partly attracted to the notion because of the reflected glory I might experience. Most important though, Bill would hate me visiting Foix. He stayed away deliberately.

*

By the time Bill enlisted in the British army at the start of the Second World War, he had already spent five years living away from the Rhondda, mostly in London. Those years of study seem to have had a profound effect on his intellectual development and created an attachment to French life and culture that lasted his whole life. By the time he returned to London in October 1944, as the war in Europe was ending, he had been away from Ynyshir for a decade; he had spent much of his military service speaking French and working in Europe's African colonies. It is perhaps not surprising that he no longer felt close to Roy from the Rhondda, the boy he once was.

Chapter 4
Never Going Back

An intelligent and ambitious working-class young man could not fail to be acutely aware of the way English society revolved around distinctions of social class, even if until now he had been able to observe this from the safety of a well-regarded university. The British army was one of the most class-divided institutions of all. All armies must, of course, distinguish between officers and men, but in the British army this division was heavily reinforced by difference in class. At the outset of the war, eighty-five percent of trained officers came from private schools, and the majority of these had been educated in the most prestigious of private boarding schools. This statistic is even more startling given the tiny proportion of students (about eight percent) who went to a private school at this time.

After conscription was introduced in 1939, it became readily apparent that there was an acute shortage of officers. In an attempt to increase the selection of officers from the ranks of ordinary soldiers in order to address this shortage, officer cadet training schools were established. After a mandatory period in the ranks, men could be recommended by their commanding officers as potential officer material, and they would then appear before a regimental panel.

During the first years of the war, it was evident, however, that most of the men on these panels believed that 'family background, school, accent and social skill counted much more than intelligence, temperament or capacity for leadership'. By the end of 1940, those who had been to the right kind of school were still fourteen times more likely to become an infantry officer than those educated in the state system.

This class divide undoubtedly reduced the talent pool for army officers, but it was also made manifest in almost every aspect of military life. Officers ate different food, had far better accommodation, access to reserved bars, as well as pensions and rail permits. There was also a much-resented practice among officers of commandeering military vehicles for 'recreational travel'—something which it would seem Bill exploited once he became an officer himself. If you were captured, being an officer was still a huge advantage since an officer prisoner of war could not be put to work for the Reich. Not only that, but every captured officer was entitled to have an orderly under the Geneva Convention. I was shocked to discover, while reading about class in the British army, how my childhood hero Douglas Bader treated his 'servant' when he was imprisoned in Colditz. Ben Macintyre tells the story of Bader's non-combatant medical orderly Jock Ross, who was entitled to be repatriated from Colditz. When he happily informed Bader that he was going home, Bader replied, 'No, you're bloody not ... you came here as my lackey and you will stay with me as my lackey until we are both liberated. That's that.' Even in Colditz the school you went to mapped perfectly onto the internal divisions among prisoners

Bill was perhaps lucky that his attachment to the Royal Warwickshire Regiment—a regiment that dates back to 1673—was largely a formality. Even though he continued to wear their regimental insignia for much of the war, he never served with the regiment. With all Field Security personnel, he was transferred to the Intelligence Corps in July 1940, and then commissioned into the Corps.

Whether it was good fortune or conscious planning, his selection for what became the Intelligence Corps probably protected him from some archaic regimental traditions and prejudices—though he would have had plenty of opportunity to witness them first-hand in North Africa. His particular war experiences involved him in small FSP teams, attached to a confusing array of military units, landing him finally with SOE. And as the recruiting advertisements insisted, what the early Field Security Police were looking for was language skills and 'personality'. Though at this distance it is hard to know how 'personality' was supposed to express itself, or how it was distinguished from accent and social skills.

When Bill returned to London in October 1944, after five years in uniform overseas, he was given a month's 'disembarkation leave', with Free Travelling Warrant. I do not know what he did with this time, which any other returned soldier would surely have used to be reunited with their family after such long and dangerous service abroad. According to Denzil, Bill did not visit his mother in Ynyshir, nor his brother Colin's grave, nor his sisters in Brecon and Aberystwyth, nor his surviving brother Ron, who was still living in the same house with their cousin Alfred Knight, in Coventry. This was Bill's residential address for the duration of the war, but it seemed he was not going to collect any mail. As far as we know, none of his family ever saw him again. Why this break occurred is the most tantalising question that we, Bill's children, want to understand. But Denzil was unable to shed any light on it, remarking that he never heard his mother, Lily, or other members of the family speak critically of Roy. There is almost nothing to go on.

Even though I have known about this family fracture for three decades now, I am still shocked when I finally see a copy of the Last Will and Testament drawn up by Bill's mother, Minna, a week before she died in 1954. I had no idea until my recent trip to Wales that one can order a copy of any probate record and will made since 1857 for a mere £1.50 (and have ordered up quite a lot of wills now I know how easy it is). Witnessed by her son Ron—on a visit from Coventry—and a neighbour, it is a hand-written, strangely detailed and carefully worded document designed to ensure no one can mistake her intent.

> I direct that the Agent continue to collect the rents of my four Houses, No 13/14 Witherdine Road, Stanleytown, 15 Ynyshir Street, Ynyshir, and No 33 Llanwonno Rd, Ynyshir, and all Rates and expenses to be paid out of them, after which all the Profits to be equally divided

between my Three children, namely Averina Nettell of Aberystwyth, Lily Griffiths of Brecon and Ralph Ronald Probert of Coventry. The profit to be paid to them every 3 months. Should either of my Houses become vacant or suitable price offered, the same can be sold at the convenience of my Executors, and the proceeds of each House again divided between my Three Children, Averina Nettel of Aberystwyth, Lily Griffiths of Brecon and Ralph Ronald Probert of Coventry. In the event of the death of Ralph Ronald Probert, his portion in this Will shall pass equally divided to my two daughters, Averina Nettell of Aberystwyth and Lily Griffiths of Brecon, and in the event of death of Averina Nettell or Lily Griffiths, their portion in this will shall pass to their respective children.

Minna could not have been more explicit. It is not just that Roy was not to receive anything, but Minna did not even recognise the existence of her youngest child. My instinctive reaction is to think ill of her and perhaps protective of my father. He had no need of any inheritance, but this denial of his existence by his mother—even as she is dying—is very hard to swallow. What could he have done to warrant this? Nothing that I have learned about him suggests that he was capable of wounding her so severely.

Alongside this bracing clarity about her wishes, is the equally confronting fact that the widowed Minna had somehow come to own four terrace houses, not to mention the longstanding family home in Gynor Place. How she managed to achieve this is, thus far, beyond my sleuthing capabilities, but it suggests a very ambitious and disciplined character. There is also a new question mark about Ron, since Denzil's widow has no recollection that her mother-in-law, Lily, ever received anything from the sale of these houses. Ron not only disposed of the much-loved train, but as executor of Minna's will may well have exploited the tenuous links between his siblings. It is as though he has taken care to leave minimal traces of his life—never appearing on an electoral register after he leaves the Rhondda, never living in his own house until he retires back in the Rhondda next to his mother-in-law (in what might have been a house owned by wife's family) and leaving no will. What was he really like?

There is little to go on, but I go back to Find My Past to take another look at Minna's family, especially her siblings, in an attempt to understand a little more about her. With the help of the reference and local studies librarian from Treorchy, I discover that some of Minna's seven siblings did well for themselves. Their father, James Knight, was still working as a coal hewer in his sixties, but it seems that his wife, the grocer, may have been a bigger influence on the children. Minna's two oldest brothers remained coal miners all their lives, but her other four brothers followed in their mother Maria's footsteps, becoming grocers or, in one case, a draper with his own business. The most successful of them, the draper William Knight, even started to call himself Trigg-Knight in his census returns from 1911, adding his mother's maiden name to his father's. He had one child, and this son was the only one of Bill's many cousins who also made it to university, studying chemistry at the University of Wales in Cardiff.

But perhaps the closest I get to understanding these houses is when I use Facebook to tell my newly discovered second cousin in Ynyshir about them. Gaynor's grandfather, Allen Knight, started out as a grocer, but in middle age he became a Christian Spiritualist Minister in Ynyshir. I do not know how much religious faith he shared with his sister Minna, but they both seem to have invested in houses. Gaynor writes that Allen left houses to his children, but 'when my Dad went to check the one that was left to him only a small deposit had been paid and at the time my Dad couldn't afford to buy it. He thought it was because he wouldn't follow his father into the ministry, so he ended up with an umbrella.' It seems entirely possible that Minna's houses were also heavily mortgaged, and equally that she may have been unwilling to leave anything to her atheist son, Roy.

This belated discovery of Minna's will changes the way I think about the transformation of Roy into Bill. For a mother to deny the existence of the son who had been sent into war as a young man, and who survived five years in North and East Africa, returning as something of a war hero, seems brutal. What would it take for a mother to do this? In trying to understand what might have happened, and with no way of knowing why, it is hard to know what to call it. A rupture?

A rift? Or a slow separation resulting from the clash of two uncompromising personalities over many years? Minna's reaction seems to suggest something steely and unforgiving. Her will not only denied Roy's existence, but also failed to acknowledge Ron's wife of fifteen years, and tried to ensure that her daughters' husbands were also disqualified from any benefit.

*

Unable to make any progress on the why question, I decide to focus on anything that might point to when the definitive break occurred. Bill enlisted in the army from his cousin's house in Coventry, where his brother Ron was also living, so the whole family would have known how Bill's war started. When I finally receive a large, photocopied package of Bill's service file from the Ministry of Defence (not the same thing as a 'personal file'), it comes with a very small blue notebook called 'Officer's Record of Service: Army Book 439'. One of these, I learn, was issued to every serving officer. In it they were to note their next of kin, their vaccinations, their promotions, any courses taken, and then the units in which they served (with an injunction that they must not show the one in which they are 'at present serving'). They were also to write the full name and address of their next of kin 'in pencil'.

Bill had been making entries in this book up until the end of 1946 when he was demobbed, and at this point he wrote his wife's name and address in ink in the spot for next of kin. Curiously, there is nothing in this book to link him to Ynyshir or Wales. On the final page an official has written that Bill has been issued with 'special clothing coupons' (and 'Duty free labels'). The instructions state that the army book then had to be handed to the War Office 'for disposal'.

At the back of this little book are two pages on which the officer can elect to fill out a 'Form of Will'. One page is to be used by any officer 'desirous of leaving the whole of his Property and Effects to one person'; the next page is for officers 'desirous of leaving legacies to some one or more persons, and the residue to another or others'. There is space for the officer to nominate an executor and then two individuals to whom 'particular articles or money' are to be given. This is followed by a space for one name and address, to whom the rest of the officer's 'Estate and Effects and everything that I can give or dispose of' is bequeathed.

Bill chose the second option. He nominated as executor, Mr Howard Drew, whom I locate with ease on Find My Past. He was an assistant superintendent with the Prudential Association in Coventry, so Bill was thinking ahead. The first person Bill wished to leave money to was Lt. R. L. Flynn. I am very touched to see that he made a special bequest to Dicky—such a clear indication of his real affection for this friend from university days. The second special bequest was to his cousin Alfred Knight, in Coventry. I assume that this reflects some kind of gratitude or respect. Alfred looms as someone who might have been able to shed light on Bill's secret life, but he died in 1976 and had no children of his own. Why did he and his wife share their Coventry house with Bill's brother Ron and Ron's wife from the Rhondda for two decades? The fact that neither couple had any children cuts off this line of enquiry, though it does not stop me coming back to it again and again.

Turning to the space where Bill needed to identify who was to receive the rest of his estate, it is possible to make out that he nominated his mother and wrote the first number of the house at 44 Gynor Place as the start to filling in her address. But that was all he wrote—just '4'. His mother's name has been vigorously inked out, and it is only discernible if you know what you are looking for. The rest of this page, which is allocated to signing the will, and getting two people to witness his signature, had not been filled in.

It is only the third or fourth time I look through this little blue army book that I notice the page for making a will required Bill to fill in his rank. Because the will was not signed there is no date on it, but he did note his rank as T/Maj. He'd been carrying this document around for over four years, adding small details from time to time, but it dawns on me that he must only have got round to filling out the will in July 1944, since he was not promoted to major until the end of June in that year. In other words, he filled it out while at the training camp in Algiers, preparing for the mission to the Ariège. Did he fill it out at this point because, for the first time in his war, he was taking seriously the possibility that he might not survive? It seems entirely plausible that in the intensity of their preparations to be parachuted into France, the voluntary nature of the mission caused Bill to think about the consequences of his choice, leading him to start filling out these pages of his army book. But why, when he started to fill out his mother's details, did he abruptly stop? And why did he then ink out her name so it cannot be read? (It is hard to see why anyone else would have done this.)

When I try to make sense of this document, together with the fact that we know he never saw his mother again (not, of course, because he was killed), there is only one scenario that seems at all logical. Is it possible, as he sat down prudently to write his will in 1944, that his will to live—and to live a good life—simply overwhelmed him? My mother told me that Bill never ever wanted to see a doctor, let alone confront his own mortality even when his heart began to let him down, and she found this strange since he must have known, at some level, that he was lucky to have survived the war.

The moment of looming real danger may well have focused his mind, first on the idea of dying, and then on the importance of not only surviving but making a great life for himself after the war. He would have seen enough of the way English society worked to realise his origins were always going to count against him. It was ten years since he had left the Rhondda and as the war was coming to an end, he would surely have begun to imagine the future. He had no money and no expectation of inheriting any, but this never seemed to hold him back. What would hold him back, however, was being a working-class Welshman from the Rhondda.

Bill removed his mother from his will, and he also crossed out in a censor's black lines the sums he wanted to leave to Dicky and Alfred (though I think I can make out the words 'one hundred pounds' for each of them). He did, however, leave their names and their addresses and those of his executor untouched. It is tempting to think that after he abandoned the idea of leaving his estate to his mother, he then wondered about how much money he might leave to Dicky and Alfred, before giving up on completing the will altogether.

It is almost as though Bill had been reading Jean-Paul Sartre who, at the same time, was writing about what he noticed during the liberation of Paris—the longing for freedom and the fear of what this would bring with it. In his philosophy of existentialism, as he most famously puts it, 'man first of all exists, encounters himself, surges up in the world—and defines himself afterwards'. I think Bill was more likely to have encountered Sartre's ideas than those of Erich Fromm in *The Fear of Freedom* (1942), but both were describing the difficulty individuals face in embracing freedom. Most people are unable to confront the implications of their freedom and will abandon their responsibility for themselves to some other higher power. This might be religion, society, our social class or our family, the nation or belief in some form of world government. Keith Lowe gives his book about the longer-term impact of the Second World War the title *Freedom and Fear* because he sees these as the two forces playing out all over the globe in the succeeding decades. Individuals will clutch at an 'ideology that gives us a sense of belonging ... because anything is easier to bear than the responsibility and agony of freedom'. Whether he had read anything or not, Bill is a rare example of someone who seemed willing to confront his freedom and define himself.

My brother Colin loves this way of understanding Bill, and I am drawn to it too. It is almost heroic. It is also somehow incompatible with my younger brother William's sense that Bill was ashamed of his origins, telling small lies to hide them and then finding it too hard ever to admit to them.

*

To narrow down the timeframe within which the break between Bill and his family occurred, I try to work out the last time he returned to Ynyshir. I start out with two conflicting propositions from Denzil and Janet. When Denzil first told us everything he knew about the Probert family, he wrote that his Uncle Roy was able to get home at least once to visit his mother during the war, when he was convalescing 'from being wounded in North Africa'. He believed that Roy also kept in touch with his oldest sister, Rene, while he was overseas. Denzil, who would have been about eight years old at the time, told us that he remembered 'Granma [Minna] very proudly displaying a handbag and a pair of shoes, made from crocodile skin, that Uncle Roy had given her on a quick visit.' Janet, when she heard this story after Bill's death, insisted that he would never have been able to get back during the war—and there is certainly no formal record of any such trip. Of course, he would in any case have hidden it from her. His mother was supposed to be dead. One of the first things Bill told Janet about himself when they met was that both his parents had died. Informing her mother of her engagement, Janet wrote that the man she planned to marry 'has no family to speak of'.

Denzil was not to be put off by Janet's contention, and on a visit to the Probert family home in Ynyshir after he had shared this information with her, he spoke to the Evans family who had always lived next door to Minna and been her close friends. Mrs Evans' daughter, apparently, 'knew Uncle Roy very well and for good reason remembered him regularly visiting his mother whenever possible during the war. Uncle Roy was, she said, emphatic that no one know of his visits, swearing his mother and the Evans family to secrecy'.

My mother's track record on Bill's life before she met him is not totally reliable, so I am prepared to believe she got this wrong. The idea of 'regular' visits is certainly a misremembering, perhaps simply because the event would have been thrilling and unforgettable. But, on reflection, the story of the crocodile handbag and shoes is too good to have been made up, and these gifts are perfectly plausible from North Africa. So far, I am with Denzil, but the story is rather vague.

It is only when trawling through Bill's record of service for the third or fourth time—with the sixteen pages of advice beside me on how to interpret all the acronyms and abbreviations used—that I work out what probably happened. I can see that Bill was hospitalised for up to two weeks on several occasions during the war, and I know from Janet's account that at least once this was with dysentery. But I can find no record of him ever being wounded. He did, however, have a very serious accident of some kind in January 1942 while stationed in Somalia, which landed him in hospital for three weeks. His file notes that he sustained 'concussion. Severe injury, but not likely to interfere with future efficiency as an officer'. The decision of the General Officer Commanding is that it was a 'Motor Accident'. Bill was 'not on duty, partly to blame'.

The injuries were serious enough for him to be granted twenty-one days' sick leave after his discharge from hospital in February. This was when he probably managed to hitch a plane ride back to the UK and went to see his mother. Not a war wound, but more likely the result of his enthusiasm for driving fast. I want to believe that Bill was smart enough to wangle a trip back to the Rhondda, bearing glamorous gifts. Serving officers did occasionally manage to hitch a lift home, so it is perfectly possible. Was he looking for respect and affection which Minna was withholding? Or was he coming to see his brother, Colin, who was struggling with an incurable and fatal heart condition, caused by his childhood rheumatic fever? Whatever his motives, I can well imagine that Bill let his family believe his injuries were war wounds rather than the more mundane reality of a motorcycle or jeep accident. The war wound story may also have helped him get the ride.

If there is disagreement about the war years, everyone at least agrees that after Bill returned from France in October 1944, the family, including his mother, never saw or heard of him again. Bill cut all ties to his mother, and his siblings, Rene, Lily and Ron, and to the place where he grew up, and the name they knew him by. There is no record of any falling out or family conflict. A sudden rift would surely have been talked about. Bill's sister Lily, would, when pressed by her son, say a few words about him. According to Denzil, 'she was obviously very fond of Roy and spoke of him in kind terms—never really critical'. But when Rene, then living in Aberystwyth, sent her sister a cutting from *The Times* newspaper announcing Bill's marriage in December 1945, Lily made Denzil promise not to go looking for him—'at least during her lifetime'. This strongly suggests Bill did not want to be found.

The willingness of Roy's whole family to just let him go seems, in some ways, more unfathomable than his decision to abandon them. We only have Denzil's account of the family's response, and his much later conclusion that Roy's disappearance is somehow connected to his ongoing involvement with the secret service.* But Denzil was certainly baffled that Roy's family seemed to show no interest in what became of him. Is this Minna's baleful influence? If so, her power extended well beyond the grave.

*

It is clear that I am running up against Bill's extraordinary ability to keep secrets—an ability that his wartime training in intelligence would certainly have cultivated. This training in secrecy is something that Germaine Greer writes about with great perception when she sets out to uncover the truth about her own father's life. Published in 1989, I am reasonably certain I read *Daddy, We Hardly Knew You* before my father was sprung by his nephew. I think I was drawn to the book by its title because I too suspected that I did not really know my father. Perhaps because I now lived on the other side of the world, I was contemplating Bill with some new detachment and curiosity?

---

* 'He was mysterious alright. Even his wife didn't know where he was half the time. When he was with the Foreign Office he would go off on assignments to South America or elsewhere and be gone for months or even a year at a time. It's possible was doing something secret for the government.' Denzil Griffiths, quoted in 'Hero who took town back from Nazis single-handed', Catherine Norton, *The Western Mail*, 4 March 1996.

I remember thinking that some of the peculiarities of her father's behaviour felt familiar to me. At the beginning of the book Greer tells us that 'Daddy's life was an exercise in forgetting. He never referred to any kin, neither father nor mother nor sisters nor brothers nor aunts nor uncles, not even in a chance anecdote. He was a man without a past.' This was certainly a shared starting point. While searching for any documentation that might support the claims her father made about his war experiences, Germaine Greer suddenly wonders 'why Reg Greer never came to any of our speech days or speech nights. We three children all supposed that it was because he was too busy or too tired.' Or that he was 'his own boss' and just did not have to put up with sitting in a school hall listening to 'interminable speeches and watching other people's children singing badly and dancing even worse'. This was another of her observations that immediately struck a chord.

As I re-read her book now, conscious of my own father's secrets, I am struck by more affinities. Germaine asks herself:

> What if Daddy's dignified, standoffish manner was all invented, modelled on some movie hero, some member of the royal family, or the Saint by Leslie Charteris?... What if he pretended to be upper crust, top drawer, and invented the kind of past for himself that could never be checked? ... If Daddy had ever claimed an ancestry or hinted at a claim, I would find it easier to believe that he was a phoney. He said nothing after all. He wore no old school tie. He made no attempt at social climbing.

I am filled with admiration for the extraordinary lengths to which she went to track him down. Her search is dogged by many more empty rabbit holes than mine. As she discovers, 'In the missing persons game there is no substitute for luck. Even Philip Marlowe and Lord Peter Wimsey have to have luck. It never occurred to me in setting out on the father hunt that I would be dogged by super-bad luck.'

I have the advantage of starting my project knowing Bill had a past that he hid from us, and with enough clues to be able to trace his family of birth and his early life—especially because it was embedded in such a well-researched industrial community. Greer, on the other hand, knows nothing about her father's early days except that he too invented his adult identity. She eventually discovers that he changed his name from Eric Greeney to Reg Greer, throwing his daughter completely off the scent and sending her on a fruitless year of ancestry searching for Greers. About his wartime experiences as Reg Greer, she gets hold of as many military records about her father as she can find, all without the extraordinary advantage of powerful internet search engines. She initially misses 'one obvious untruth' in the record. Reg Greer was not a manager when he enlisted, as he claimed. 'He was not a manager until shortly before his retirement, nearly twenty years after the war was over.' By the time I re-read her book I had learned where Bill had left his own, relatively small, 'untruths'.

Reg Greer was an unwilling volunteer in the Second World War, with his active service beginning two years after Bill's, in January 1942. Greer thinks her father was 'frightened and revolted' by his relatively brief stays in Aden, Cairo and Alexandria, while Bill seems to have relished the heat and the desert and perhaps the mayhem as well. As a thirty-seven-year-old Australian working for British intelligence on cyphers and codes, Reg was somewhat socially isolated, and found his transfer to Malta unbearable. He arrived there in time for the last great German air assault on the island, before being invalided out with an 'anxiety neurosis' in April 1943. But while Bill and Reg had very different wars, they shared being trained in secrecy, and then successfully hiding their origins for the rest of their lives.

Greer wonders whether her father was already a 'deception person' or whether his trainers made him one. In her attempt to answer this question, Greer goes to great lengths to learn about the pressures placed on anyone working in intelligence to keep secrets. She contacts Fred Winterbotham, a senior officer with MI6 during the war, responsible for recruiting, training and distributing men to the various commands, and then ensuring 'absolute security' afterwards. She concludes that men like her father, in signals, 'were forbidden to fraternise or confide. They were true to their word: they held their peace. Most, including

F[lying]/O[fficer] Greer, died with their mouths still shut.' She realises that her attempts to get closer to her father by studying how to crack code probably drove them further apart. As she wryly reports, when 'Commander Edward Travis was awarded a knighthood for his work at Bletchley during the war, his wife could not imagine what it was for. If she had shown any real interest, he would have had to deceive her or avoid her.'

Greer is unforgiving of her father's lies about his identity, but serious and sympathetic about the nature of his 'anxiety' and the corrosive effect of keeping secrets. 'Lies are vile things, with a horrible life of their own. They contaminate the truth that surrounds them.'

> Every member of the Secret Service catches the disease. They all live as if the right hand was not to be trusted to know what the left hand is doing. Once the initial breach has been made in the self, once a man has learned to live a double life, it is a simple matter to live a treble or a quadruple life.

This is brilliantly illustrated in the story of Marcus Pym, John le Carré's most famous creation, in his most autobiographical book, *A Perfect Spy*.

I realise that I have been discomforted by the discovery of Bill's lies about his year at the Sorbonne and the occupation of his father. They suggest an insecurity that is totally inconsistent with my experience of him, and possibly something that I do not want to associate with him. But the lie about having no family does not discomfit me, simply because I do not know why he told it. In fact, Bill told very few lies. His great ability was to remain silent about so much. It is possible that keeping secrets had some serious side-effects, but it is not at all clear what they might have been, and I would not describe them as 'corrosive'. They probably made it hard for us to understand him better or to be closer to him. However, without them he simply would not have been the Bill he was, and this Bill was no mean achievement. It is hard for me to wish it otherwise.

When I ask the Corps historian at the Military Intelligence Museum about the kind of training Bill might have undergone, he too writes about the emphasis on secrecy and how Bill would have been monitored by his 'training personnel and conducting officers to make sure his languages were up to scratch, and that he did not risk his and others' security (very often without his knowledge)'. He also warns against assuming I will find out very much more, because of the 'utter security mindedness of those involved in these operations and which they held true to right up into their dotage. Stories of husbands and wives not sharing with each other details of their individual wartime exploits are not fairy stories.'

*

When exactly Roy became Bill is hard to tell, but I think it is safe to assume that by the end of 1944 he was Bill, and he had removed all trace of his Welsh accent. He'd had ample opportunity to study accents over the previous ten years, and he had an excellent ear for them. He had also successfully adapted to the world of commissioned army officers as he was promoted, leaving France with the authentic air of a decorated major in the British army. He remained with SOE in England, probably undergoing various kinds of refresher courses with the possibility of being deployed to Burma in the ongoing war against Japan, until he was selected to join the Allied Control Commission for Austria in early 1945. Unlike his friend Dicky, he obviously had no intention of finally making use of his training to be a schoolteacher. As we've seen, his proudest moment was walking into the sergeants' mess, not getting a good degree. He was also a gifted linguist with substantial knowledge of North and East Africa. The question for Bill was what to do with his talents and his freedom.

Chapter 5
Love and Spying: From Vienna to Civvy Street

By the middle of 1945 Bill had persuaded a beautiful, young upper-class Englishwoman to marry him. The gulf between their social backgrounds would have rendered any meeting unlikely were it not for the war. But as the war came to an end in Europe, their paths crossed in circumstances that were perfectly designed for falling in love.

In late March 1945 they were both on a ship that was carrying a group of British men and women from Liverpool to Naples, on their way to establishing the British section of the Allied Control Commission for Austria. Control commissions were the form through which the Allies—Britain, France, the US and USSR—took control of defeated countries.

A couple of weeks after the British staff arrived in Naples, the Soviet army wrested Vienna from German control, and unilaterally installed a new socialist government for Austria, causing tensions with the British, American and French governments. Before any other Allied representatives were allowed entry into Vienna, the Russians insisted there must be agreement on how the city was to be partitioned into four occupation zones. It was not until July that agreement was reached about how Austria and its capital were to be divided up. As well as the different zones in Vienna, an international zone was to be marked out, with sovereignty over this shared zone to alternate at regular intervals between the four powers. The British Control Commission for Austria finally got its base in the city.

Roy was now Major Bill Probert, DSO and Croix de Guerre, speaking English with what was once called 'public school pronunciation' (or later the Queen's English), detached from any connection to place or region. Bill had, ostensibly, been recruited to run the British interpreters' pool for the commission. Janet Russell had been recruited from the Ministry of Food to work in the commission secretariat. She had spent most of the war as the assistant private secretary to Lord Woolton, one of the most effective and successful wartime ministers in Britain. According to Janet, she and Bill were both recruited to the commission by the same man, Michael Wormald, who knew Bill from the campaign to take Madagascar from Vichy hands in 1942. In the letter to her mother announcing her engagement, Janet describes her first, inauspicious encounter with Bill. They find themselves together in Wormald's office in Hammersmith. 'I thought he was altogether too like a tough character out of one of Hemingway's novels, and he thought I was tiresomely clever and "Bloomsbury"!'.

Janet believed Wormald persuaded Bill that this would be a 'cushy' way to see out the rest of the war, unlike volunteering with SOE for Burma. As I learn more about Bill's war, I realise that yet again Janet has not got the whole picture.

Michael was a close enough friend to both of them that he accepted the role of godfather to their first child, but I can find no record of his military career apart from a reference to a Lt Wormald RN in an account of political warfare in Madagascar. I have a photograph of him in my mother's photo album, so he did exist—even if for some reason he never enacted his role as godfather. Bill certainly never mentioned him to us, and Colin was surprised to hear, from me, that he had this mysterious godfather, about whom he knows absolutely nothing.

The mystery was resolved with some expert help from a retired colonel in the Intelligence Corps who worked out that Michael Wormald was in fact Avison Wormald, a French-speaking Royal Marine (not Royal Navy) involved in the Madagascar campaign, where he did indeed make friends with Bill. My hunt for him had been deflected by his decision to call himself Michael, and the typographical error about the navy—RM not RN. It appears that Avison spent most of his postwar life working in South America, which explains his disappearance from our lives. But most importantly, he is responsible for introducing Bill to Janet, or vice versa. The photograph I have of him is taken in Venice where the three of them are sitting out in the square in front of Saint Mark's Basilica, and Janet has agreed to marry Bill.

While the Allies wrangled over the carving up of Austria and Vienna, the staff of the British contingent to the Austrian Control Commission were obliged to spend several months in Italy waiting for the boundaries to be agreed. A temporary office was set up in the centre of Rome, in the Ministerio dell'Aeronautica, an imposing pallazio built for the Royal Italian Airforce by Mussolini, designed to project the power of his fascist regime. The takeover of this particular building by the commission may explain my mother's blurry photograph of four flying officers in front of a warplane's fuselage, under which she has written: 'Savoia bomber crew who let me fly her!!'. The Savoia Marchetti was the most important Italian bomber of World War Two, with a reputation that contrasted with most Italian weapons of the day. This idea is enough to strike fear into her children who know that she was never really safe on the roads, let alone in the air. This rather unkind judgment is backed up when I discover a letter in the family documents box from Janet's cousin Pamela to her sister Marjorie during the war. It reports that Janet was feeling around for a job, 'because she is bored with an office stool and wants to lead a life of action. She wants to take to the air, but as she cannot drive a car, one hopes that her sporting intentions will be frustrated.' But a lovely, gregarious young woman in Rome was going to get a lot of such offers from Allied servicemen.

In the photos that have survived, Bill is always in uniform, the distinctive parachute wings worn over the left breast of his shirt or jacket pocket, above the strip of medal ribbons. It was only when I began seriously looking into his war experiences that I learned the significance of their placement. During World War Two only 'paras' who had served, normally meaning they had been dropped by parachute behind enemy lines, could move their wings from the right shoulder to the left breast. It was, apparently, a coveted distinction. Learning this reminded me of an experience I had as a young teenager, when Bill took me to Wimbledon (a rare and therefore memorable experience, like going to Twickenham with him). I think we might have got the tickets through our village tennis club lottery. In between matches, we were outside the courts, eating the obligatory strawberries and cream, when a stranger approached us. I don't know why I remember this, but I could tell the man did so with deference, and that he recognised the tie Bill was wearing—his parachute regiment tie, the maroon one with the 'jump wings'. This was twenty years after the war had ended.

The significance of regimental ties in the early post-war years is nicely captured by John le Carré's *A Perfect Spy*, when the double agent Marcus Pym reflects on the powerful class signals they send, provided you know the language. He is recalling how he was recruited to MI6 by Jack Brotherhood.

> Do you know what else you wore apart from your good brown suit? Your Airborne tie. Prancing silver winged horses and crowned Britannias on a maroon field, congratulations. You never told me where you had been for it, but the reality as I now know it is no less impressive than my imaginings: with the partisans in Yugoslavia and the resistance in Czechoslovakia, behind the lines with the Long Range Desert Group in Africa and even, if I remember right, Crete ... I remember as if it were yesterday how, as Pym grasped your great dry hand, that Airborne tie looked him in the eye.

There was plenty of time in Italy for Bill and Janet to get to know each other—both twenty-nine years old, both highly intelligent arts graduates who had had quite different plans for their lives before the war. Although, writing this, I wonder if Bill had any specific plans at all apart from avoiding being a schoolteacher. Janet kept photos of sunny picnics in the Sabine hills, just north of the Rome; of lying by the swimming pool at the golf club outside the city with Masha, a Russian interpreter; of Bill with two of the other Russian interpreters, Andrew Theotakis and 'wicked Michael Tolstoy'. Janet is pictured meeting young Italian women making shoes out of old tyres, and with children who are being monitored by nutrition experts from the United Nations Relief and Rehabilitation Administration (UNRRA). There are photos of a 'first trip to Venice' in August 1945, with Janet buying sandals so as 'not to be outdone by those Italian girls at the swimming pool in Rome'. There are photos from a trip to Siena, and of a parade by a battalion of returning Italian partisans who had fought with Tito.

On VE day (8 May 1945), when the Germans finally surrendered unconditionally, millions of people marked the occasion with fêtes, parties and other expressions of relief and happiness. A 'Victory Dinner' was held at the Eden Hotel in Rome, a very grand establishment in the heart of the city, and the home of British senior officers stationed there. Somehow the menu, with Bill's autograph on it, survived and ended up in a collection of papers that Janet left to me.

Hors d'Oeuvre Alexander

Consommé Mark Clark

Contre Filet Eisenhower,

Salade à la Springbock,

Asperges Montgomery, Sauce Indienne,

Crème McCreery,

Savoury à la Freybourg.

The atmosphere—of pride, satisfaction and celebration—must have been memorable.

In August, once the Allies had finally agreed who would control which parts of Vienna, a flight was organised for the British staff to transfer from Rome to their zone. Bill, in what seems a characteristic gesture of individuality, managed to get hold of a jeep and drove there instead, with another officer, George Sullivan. Their route took them through the spectacular mountains of the Dolomites, an area that Bill would love for the rest of his life. His parachute wings may well have persuaded someone to 'lend' him this jeep. Janet described it as his most prized possession, and it was clearly a powerful weapon in his campaign to win her attention. Until it was stolen by some Russians in Vienna, it allowed them to spend summer and autumn weekends escaping into what must have felt like a magical world of natural beauty, cultural richness and sunshine.

Between 1935 and 1945, Roy from the Rhondda had become a sophisticated and well-read European. It was Hilary Mantel's essay on how she re-defined herself as European rather than English that helped me grasp this part of Bill's identity. She writes:

> As I grew up I came to see that Englishness was White, male, southern, Protestant and middle class. I was a woman, a Catholic, a northerner of Irish descent. I spoke and speak now with a northern accent. And if I tell an Englishman my date of birth and my religion and ancestry, I am telling him, without needing more words, that my family are working people, probably with little education.
>
> All these markers—descent, religion, region, accent—are quickly perceived and decoded by those who possess Englishness, and to this day they are used to exclude. You are forced off centre. You are a provincial. You are a spectator. If you want to belong to Englishness, you must sell off aspects of your identity.
>
> Possibilities of self-redefinition were presented to me. I could become educated, go and live in the south if I liked, abandon my faith and change my accent. I did some of these things.

Although Mantel could not consciously link herself to the ancient idea of Europe, to 'the common culture that is shaped by our inheritance from Greece and Rome', nonetheless, when she began to write in her early twenties, she defined herself 'from the first as a European writer.' When I read this account, it struck me that the Bill we knew was never English but always European. He had none of those essential markers: descent, religion, region or accent.

He was confident about this identity, not threatened by but admiring of the fact Janet had taken the special subject on the Italian Renaissance while at Oxford. Some combination of the jeep, his gift with languages, his wings, his good looks (what Bigeard called his 'gueule d'amour'), and his worldly intelligence did the trick, and on 26 August, six months after they left Liverpool, Janet wrote to her mother in London that she was going to marry her 'parachute major'. In her letter, Janet is confident Lilla will like him 'very much indeed—he's not at all the type of some of my more tiresomely intellectual friends'. Bill 'has prospects with the Foreign Office or the British Council for a job but isn't very keen on either. Anyway I have the utmost confidence in his ability to get what he wants—he is very sensible about the important things, and very firm, you will be glad to hear.'

My mother confessed to me decades later that she knew it would not be an easy marriage, and that Bill had threatened to volunteer again with SOE, still active in Burma, if she refused him.

Janet Russell's background could not have been more different from Bill's. She was educated at home with her younger sister by well-trained governesses (and a local vicar who took care of Latin). Her formidable Australian mother, Lilla Russell, was widowed in 1917 when Janet was just two years old, but felt her English husband would have wanted his daughters to grow up in England. She set up home for them in rural Hampshire near her eldest sister-in-law, Lady Mary Kelly, widow of a Boer War general. Lilla considered Janet 'too excitable' and 'highly strung' to be sent to school, but the unorthodox education that she organised for her daughters served them well. Despite her youth, their last governess, Helena Haughton, prepared

Janet sufficiently thoroughly to win a scholarship in 1935 to Somerville College, Oxford, to read History (just a year after Roy had arrived at King's College London from the Rhondda). Having launched Janet and her sister into their university degrees, Helena then applied, successfully, to be the last in a stream of ill-treated governesses employed by Lord and Lady Redesdale, taking on the youngest of the Mitford sisters, Jessica and Deborah.

Looking back at her time at Oxford, Janet described herself as being a 'parlour pink'—the right's pejorative term for non-communist, left-wing sympathisers in the 1920s and 30s. She admitted to having been an intellectual snob, but never a social snob and I think that is accurate. My mother never talked much about it, but I always felt she loved being at Oxford and was proud of being a scholar at the best women's college. However, the war—into which her year was immediately plunged on graduation—may have made everyone's pre-war life shrink in significance. Janet had a small, close group of friends, about whom we know more than family recollections would allow, simply because one of them went on to become one of England's most respected novelists—Penelope Fitzgerald. In her fine biography of Fitzgerald, Hermione Lee tells us how Penelope Knox, as she then was, 'had her own set' at Oxford. 'They were known as "Les Girls", and they were admired and envied. Lee describes the women who were part of this 'striking bunch': 'But most importantly there was Janet Russell, bursting onto the scene at Somerville at exactly the same time as Penelope. Janet was a forceful, stylish, strong-minded girl.' Lee describes Janet's mother, Lilla, as an Australian heiress to a big banking fortune, though in reality Lilla's father had been the greatly admired manager of the Bank of Australasia in Sydney's Martin Place. Lee goes on to note that Janet's father, 'son of an old English family, had been killed fighting in Palestine in 1917, when she was a baby'.

'Les Girls' had fun. 'They went to dances and balls and parties, travelled to Europe with their families, hired horses from the Longwall stable to go riding on Port Meadow or Headington Hill or to point-to-points, took trips to the theatre in London, went punting and canoeing and picnicking.' 'One young man, Sinclair Hood (Harrow and

Magdelen), thought that "Penelope Knox and Janet Russell were the two most attractive girls at Oxford" of his time. He had friends who felt the same.'*

While Janet was pursued by intense young men, she was not susceptible to them, perhaps because of the way her mother had worked hard to ensure that both her daughters believed they should grow up to be practical and useful to society. This did not, however, prevent Janet enjoying every distraction that was on offer at Oxford. Looking back, she felt that she 'didn't do anything except have a good time—my impression is that latter-day students are in general much more serious-minded, and rarely as frivolous as we were'. She graduated from Oxford rather hoping to get a job at the Victoria and Albert Museum in London.

It was not long before the outbreak of war in September 1939 meant everyone's lives were changed, and almost at once this intense group of Oxford friends began to fragment. Penelope Fitzgerald and Janet went to work for the Ministry of Food, though Penelope then moved to the BBC where she worked for the duration of the war as a producer in the features department. Janet wrote to her cousin Pam early in 1942, describing her hope of getting a job as an announcer with the BBC but confessing that she didn't think the interview went well. By early 1945, it probably did not take much for Michael Wormald to persuade Janet to give up her job with the Ministry of Food, especially as Lord Woolton had recently moved on to become minister for reconstruction in Churchill's War Cabinet.

As they sailed to Naples and settled into their temporary offices in Rome, Janet would have quickly learned something, at least, of Bill's war experiences with intelligence and SOE. She believed he was back with his original regiment, the Royal Warwickshires, and he wore

---

* Harrow is one of England's most prominent public schools, while Magdelen is one of Oxford University's most prestigious colleges in history, wealth and academic achievement. It is not uncommon for the English upper class to use this shorthand of school and college to indicate someone's status.

their insignia along with his parachute wings. She also believed him when he told her he had found this good way to see out the rest of the war, running the interpreters' pool.

Janet's letters from Vienna to her mother in London are often about the weekends away and short holidays that she and Bill manage to take. In February 1946 she describes a skiing holiday above Kitzbühel in the French-controlled section of Austria, saying that Bill is a 'very dangerous skier'. Not that Janet makes any claims for her own abilities, but she had at least learned to ski in Austria before the war. She had also spent the summer of 1935 in Vienna 'trying to learn some German' before going up to Oxford. Bill was dangerous because he would never have put on a ski before, and he probably wasn't letting on. There were several trips to Venice which included shopping, lots of good food and looking at sheets—'one could set up house wonderfully there of course'—and walking in the Dolomites. Janet's mother, Lilla, meanwhile, was preparing to sail to San Francisco as a representative of the Association of Country Women of the World, to participate in the establishment of the United Nations.

Bill was always in uniform, as were their friends in the commission. Janet writes nothing about what he was actually doing, though social photos often include interpreters of different nationalities. Growing up with my mother's photo album, I simply thought of post-war Vienna as a glorious place for romance and weekend trips to some of the most desirable spots in Europe.

It is only once I set out to document as much as possible about Bill's war that I begin to see Vienna in quite another light. The histories of the Intelligence Corps that I collect remind me of the intensely political period when the war ended, and the West was left to confront the military successes of the Soviet Union in Europe. The Red Army had entered Vienna in April 1945, just weeks before the capture of Berlin from the Germans. Once the four Allied powers were all in place, Vienna quickly became a vigorous hive of intrigue, with the occupying intelligence agencies vying with each other. John le Carré's 'perfect spy', Marcus Pym, is sent to Vienna by his commanding officer at the 'Intelligence Depot', to give him 'a chance to get the feel of the place before you're pushed out into the field'. Three months after Pym arrives in Vienna, 'Marlene asked him for his protection. Marlene was a Czech interpreter and celebrated beauty.' Possible defections were a constant source of interest. Vienna was open to freedom of movement and the international zone within the city allowed for less risky communications between the East and West. It was host to several spy agencies, such as the CIA and MI6, along with the forerunner of the KGB. All worked carefully throughout the city to gain intelligence about one another.

My helpful historian at the Military Intelligence Museum confirms that before the war, 'the universities were stamping ground for SIS and MI5 who managed to collect an eclectic bunch of traitors to work for them based on their "vetting", which amounted to how well known and acceptable to society their grandparents had been'. Attendance at Eton and Trinity College, Cambridge, were evidence of a man's bona fides, and language abilities were a particular asset. While this kind of vetting led to the likes of Guy Burgess and Kim Philby being 'picked up' as British agents, it is not clear how Roy would have passed muster given his grandparents spent their lives covered in coal dust. As Germaine Greer learns, 'Intelligence, more perhaps than any other branch of the services, relies on the old school network, upon known backgrounds, family relationships, proven loyalty'. But perhaps in the pressure of war, Bill's linguistic gifts were enough to counterbalance his inappropriate class background which he was, in any case, very good at disguising. His wartime experience certainly gave him plenty of opportunities to study the infinite niceties of class distinction within the British army.

The idea that Bill was simply running the interpreters' pool suddenly begins to look rather implausible. I return to the Intelligence Corps historian and ask him what he thinks Bill was doing there. His reply is straightforward: 'After the war, he was indeed posted to the Allied Control Commission in Vienna where he would almost certainly have continued his intelligence work. He would probably have liaised with Intelligence Corps field security sections, some of whom were running agents across the borders. He would also have continued with his links to MI6/SIS.' It would not do to advertise his intelligence role in Vienna by wearing Intelligence Corps insignia, so reverting to wearing the Royal Warwicks insignia was a diplomatic nicety.

But what perfect cover for a gifted linguist. When Bill's service record finally reaches me, I see that after a year working in Vienna, he was promoted to the rank of Temporary Lt Colonel. Somehow this also seems an unlikely reward for running the interpreters' pool. I make a note to re-watch the *The Third Man*. This 1949 British film, written for the screen by Graham Greene, is a paranoid story of social, economic and moral corruption in a depressed, rotting and crumbling Vienna following World War Two.

Looking back on his life as a spy, le Carré's Marcus Pym is amused by the way this great power rivalry in Austria came to an end.

> A few years later to everyone's amazement the diplomats agreed they wouldn't bother with a sideshow while there was Germany to squabble over, so the occupying powers signed a treaty and went home, thus notching up the British Foreign Office's one positive achievement in my lifetime. But in Pym's day the sideshow was going gangbusters.

Meanwhile, reading the brief notes my mother made for me on the work she did in Vienna, I see that she says her role at the secretariat sometimes required her to sit in on the monthly meetings of the generals who headed each sector. I begin to wonder why it never seemed to have occurred to Janet that Bill might have been doing something more than managing the British interpreters.

*

On 13 November 1945, an announcement on page six of *The Times* (next to the Court Circular) informed readers that 'a marriage has been arranged and will shortly take place between Major William Roy

Probert DSO Royal Warwickshire Regiment and Janet Way Russell, elder daughter of the late Captain Charles Russell, Indian Educational Service, and Mrs Charles Russell, 71 Bedford Court Mansions, London WC1.' Janet's father is given the military rank with which he died in 1917. It is notable that the parents of every other man who is to be married are named, whether alive or dead, as are their hometown and county. The announcement about Major Probert is silent on all fronts.

Their wedding at Christ Church, Woburn Square, London, was one of fourteen marriages published on the front page of *The Times* two weeks later. This is how Bill's family learned of his marriage, according to Denzil. Bill would not have been able to present his parents as deceased in such an announcement because his mother was very much alive, so he must somehow have made it clear that there was to be no mention of them. Janet had only her mother and younger sister in her immediate family. Since Bill and Janet were both in London on leave from their jobs in Vienna, the small nature of the event is not surprising.

It is my growing appreciation of what can be learned from birth, marriage and death certificates that makes me search seriously for their marriage certificate in the family documents box. The first thing I notice is a poignant reminder of the deception that was under way. The certificate required both bride and groom to name their fathers and to fill in a column headed 'Rank or Profession of Father'. William Edward Probert is entered as Bill's father, but he is described as a 'Mine Manager'. In fact, he died as a colliery blacksmith. Janet's mother, Lilla, is one of the two witnesses, but it takes me months to work out the hard-to-decipher name of the second witness. It is Sidney Lamert, a long-standing friend of the Russell family, known to all as 'The Lamb'. I remember visiting his rather grand house in East Sussex as a young child—a memory that survives probably because of his name, which any child would remember. Later I find a letter from Janet to her mother about the wedding plans and discover she had suggested that Sidney Lamert might give her away. My mother had told me that the Lamb used to give handmade walking shoes from Jermyn St to the better-looking women among his family connections, and that she had been in receipt of a pair. Before the war he would present Janet and her sister Ann with £5 'tips' and boxes of Players No 1 cigarettes whenever he saw them.

Sidney was a very wealthy financier who saved the De La Rue company in the 1920s and became its long-standing chairman, setting them up in Regent Street in the West End of London and taking a lease on a beautiful house in Mayfair in 1944 for the purpose of entertaining customers from all over the world. I ordered the company history once I realised that he was present at Bill and Janet's marriage, wondering what Bill might have made of him. He was a serious gourmand, and one of England's most well-known experts on the wines of Burgundy, losing about 1500 bottles of priceless domaine-bottled wine when the cellars below the company offices were damaged during the Blitz. Bill would surely have respected his gourmet reputation, as well as his business success and his ease with women. If he had not already upgraded his father's occupational status on meeting Janet, having Sidney witness his marriage might have been the incentive. And Sidney's involvement probably explains why the wedding was announced in the rarefied columns of *The Times*.

I let myself imagine the scene where both Bill and Janet's fathers are alive and meet at the wedding. Charles Russell with his double first in Greats from Oxford, and Welsh-speaking William Edward Probert, with his admired metal-working skills. I know a great deal more about the character of my Russell grandfather than any Proberts, but I think it is not unrealistic to imagine they might have managed the event with grace.

Meanwhile, Bill and Janet returned to their jobs in Vienna, setting up their first home together in Janet's flat at 16 Neueweltgasse, not far from the Schönbrunn Palace which the British delegation was occupying. The palace was also home to several Field Security sections of the Intelligence Corps, who continued counter-intelligence activities and kept close watch on an internment camp outside the city holding Yugoslavian refugees. A few months later Janet was with the 'political branch' in the political division of the commission, writing to her mother: 'I have moved over belatedly and at last to start my diplomatic career.'

*

As far as I know my mother never asked Bill any questions about his family or his childhood. When I first considered this, it did seem odd. The question I am asked most often about Bill's story is whether Janet knew any of it. People find it hard to believe that she didn't know and, equally, that she didn't ask. When I re-read Germaine Greer's book, I found that she had the same experience. As she searched for her father, everyone kept asking her: 'Doesn't your mother know who she married?' Her response to the question makes perfect sense to me.

> I don't know if she even cared ... Why would anyone doubt the information he gave for the Register? Of course, his parents were overseas if he said they were ... Most people thought he was 'English' and he seems to have wanted them to. The reasons they thought him English were bizarre: 'He always wore gloves when he went out of the office, even on the hottest day', according to the man who worked beside him in 1933, 'so we assumed he was English'.

There is something immediately plausible about this explanation. It was, after all, only after Bill died that we learned the truth about his origins, and nothing before then would have made any of us question his identity. Bill's guard never slipped, even if with the benefit of hindsight, I can see that he was not quite like the other fathers we knew. They generally had occupations that anchored them in the familiar—dentist, bank manager or insurance broker—and in the local. I can see now that Bill seemed detached from ordinariness, in part because his working life constantly took him to places that seemed almost mythical from stockbroker-belt Kent (Beijing, New York, or the Amazon basin). It was also because he had no family who could be used to locate him, ground him somewhere specific and make him like the rest of us. I think his 'aloneness' increased his authority and contributed to the sense of a powerful presence that others noticed. All this may help explain our lack of curiosity about his origins.

What is clear, at least, is that Janet did not care about his origins. By not caring she was signalling that the question of where he came from was irrelevant to her. Bill must have been aware of this, and in this respect, she enabled him to construct a plausible minimal past that was slightly economical with the truth. His relationship with her could develop without any past before the years he spent at King's College.

My mother, when I asked about her ignorance, seemed to blame herself. 'I regret that in my impatient way, I practically put the words into his mouth I think, when very rarely anything about his family or life pre-war came up.' I think she did not need to be so hard on herself. There are very specific elements of Janet's own upbringing that help explain her apparent lack of interest in Bill's origins. Her somewhat intimidating Australian mother, Lilla, had lost her own mother when she was not yet three years old and had been brought up in Tasmania by a spinster aunt and a busy Victorian father. Despite having been deeply in love with her English husband, she was never able to speak with her daughters about their father. Janet told me that Lilla 'never talked about him as a person and we never asked'. The British upper classes are famous for their emotional reserve and insistence on the stiff upper lip, but in Lilla's case it seems to be more a function of her own emotionally thin upbringing. A little later Janet wrote to me saying, 'I have been thinking how little I <u>really</u> minded when mother died, and what a pity it was that Ann [her sister] and I had such a superficial relationship really ... The family inability to talk about personal relationships, very English in a way, which wouldn't have been as bad if my father had lived, I feel.'

The war brought Bill and Janet together across an enormous social divide, and the peace seems to have released in both of them an intense desire for intimacy, together with an acute awareness of their 'luck' in finding each other. They began their life together at a moment when no one of their age wanted to look back. The second half of their twenties had been taken over by the war which was now over. The photos that have survived from their time in Vienna reveal a very good-looking couple; Bill almost always in uniform, looking handsome, confident and fit, almost self-consciously holding himself upright and in an open-chested, broad-shouldered way; Janet looking like a woman confident in love. There are a few photos of them in their bedroom in Vienna, in pyjamas and nightdress, presumably taken on a timer by Bill, that exude a sense of physical intimacy.

The only time Bill seems to have mentioned his family was when he knew that he was going to have a child himself. When I asked about this, my mother wrote back: 'I remember very clearly sitting in the Wienerwald, and talking I suppose about my pregnancy, and him saying clearly that if a boy, he would like him called Colin, after what I thought was his only brother.' It is impossible to know if Bill's brother Colin was somehow particularly important to him, or whether he chose the name because this brother was safely dead and buried, alongside his wife and only child, and could therefore be acknowledged. Bill and Janet named their second son William, and we assume this was after Bill himself and the other Williams in his family. My brother William has the middle name Charles—clearly after his English grandfather—but he also has the middle name Edward. Did Bill want him to be named after his own father, William Edward Probert? It seems unlikely that he could have made this case without revealing more than he wished to, but I have come to think that this might reflect Bill's love for his long-dead father. I hope it does. The family joke is that William was given the extra middle name, in front of Charles, because without it he would have been W. C. Probert—and vulnerable to ribbing about lavatories. My middle name is Mary, which could have been in memory of Bill's mother, but I think it is after my Russell great-aunt, Lady Mary Kelly. (My mother wanted to call me Dido as she loved Purcell's opera, Dido and Aeneas. Fortunately, Bill put his foot down, and I became Dido's faithful handmaid, Belinda.)

*

A year after their marriage, on Tuesday 17 December 1946, Bill was at Buckingham Palace with his wife for the investiture ceremony at which he received his DSO from King George VI. It was this event that made the front page of the Welsh newspapers, where it was spotted by the young Denzil. They were expecting a baby in March and it was, as my mother described it, 'time to look for a civilian job. On demobilisation, like everyone else, Bill was given a suit and a hat—the first time I saw him in "civvies"—I think!'. Bill was in luck because his double-breasted suit, made from high-quality fabric, fitted him well. He had now spent seven years in uniform, all of them overseas. He had never lived in England apart from the years he spent as an undergraduate in London. The transition to civilian life under these circumstances might have been intimidating to some, or at least a cause for some anxiety. But he was now a man deeply in love and full of ambition. When they became engaged Janet told her mother that she believed Bill would have liked to find a job abroad, but this was hard to plan from Vienna.

It did not take long after their return to England before he landed his first job, with Turner and Newall, the world's largest producer of asbestos and asbestos-related products.* Based in Rochdale in Northern England, the company owned asbestos mines in South Africa and Canada and made asbestos cement building products; they also manufactured car parts that relied on asbestos—such as brake linings, gaskets and clutch facings. By 1948 they owned Ferodo, for example, a name prominently displayed at all motor racing circuits. By 1949 they had built a new factory in Montreal and formed Turner and Newall (Overseas) Ltd in Canada.

Why Bill accepted a job with Turner and Newall is hard to know, but it is not difficult to see why they would have been interested in him. Within a year the company sent him on a four-month tour of mines and oilfields in South America. Janet wrote to her mother that he

---

* Their scandalous failure to act on the emerging science warning of the risks of contact with asbestos eventually destroyed the company but not until 2001.

was first to be sent on an advanced Spanish conversation course at Manchester University.

Bill departed in December 1947, while Janet and their nine-month-old son, Colin—or Chuff, as Bill called him—decamped south for the duration, to stay with her much older cousin Pamela Russell, always called Aunt Pam, who was living in Sussex. While he was away, Bill wrote twenty letters to Janet that have survived; one every few days as he moved from country to country, from one mining town to another. Janet, despite not having a sentimental bone in her body, kept all these letters and gave them to me shortly before she died. I did not look at them carefully at the time but added them to the family documents boxes that I keep.

Before the reunion with my brothers in San Francisco, I decided to do a bit of sorting in the family boxes, not wanting to leave all this stuff to my children to deal with when I fall off the perch. I was also probably avoiding a writing project that I had started, and which was turning out to be much more difficult than I imagined. I opened the packet of Bill's letters to Janet and began reading.

I was mesmerised. Bill comes suddenly to life, jumping off the pages with energy, intelligence and emotional openness. When my brothers and I sit around the dining table in Marin County, California, a few months later, discussing our father's possible motives for erasing his Welsh family, these letters are—for me—powerful evidence that he was not 'ashamed' of his origins or hiding any insecurity. On my first reading of these letters I am bowled over by the way Bill describes his feelings of intense good fortune in finding Janet, having a child, and being able to plan their future together. He emerges as a man full of confidence about his own talents and self-worth, planning a new life with a wife he clearly both adores and admires. It is hard to see these letters as the work of someone trying to pass himself off as someone that he wasn't.

On my return from this trip to California I photocopied all the letters for my brothers, wanting them to see this side of Bill's character, and especially the way he expresses his love for us. They are almost impossible to read once photocopied since they are on the flimsiest of airmail paper—almost see-through. They won't last long if I keep looking at them, so I decided to transcribe them for safe keeping. I tackled a few every day, and as I typed I began to take more notice of where Bill was, what he was visiting, who he was meeting, and I could not help but ponder what he was really doing in South America. As I was learning more about his early life and the secrets he kept, I started to wonder if he was still playing some role in the intelligence world. With my more sceptical eye, I was finding it hard to believe he needed an advanced course in Spanish conversation. Surely his Spanish was more than adequate for touring mines? Was he perhaps sent on a rather different kind of course?

*

Bill's letters were usually written at the end of the day, on hotel writing paper, and he was staying in the best hotels that were to be found—in Santiago, La Paz, Lima, Guayaquil, Quito, Trujillo or Oruro. In Bolivia he occupied the vice-president's suite at the Sucre Palace Hotel for a couple of days. Moving to the Anglo American Club in the mining town of Ororu, 'a hell of a country—hard, brutal and tough', he describes how he then travelled to Catavi, the biggest tin mine in the world. With only two trains a week he decided to hire 'an "autocarvil" which is just a motor car fitted with bogie wheels and which is driven along the railway. Very luxurious but neither fast nor comfortable. Hardly any brakes, so that when you see a llama you have to start slowing down immediately. We also had a siren fitted so every time we hooted, we sounded like the New York cops in a gangster film.'

In Peru, staying at the Gran Hotel Bolivar in Lima, he writes about travelling by train to see the Cerro de Pasco silver mines which are at an altitude of 15,000 ft, causing 'an old but very nice American' to pass out next to him as they went up over the highest point. 'I got him fixed with a few shots of oxygen, administered from an oversized hot water bottle with a nozzle.' From there Bill headed to northern Peru for a week of visiting oilfields, and then on to Guayaquil, Ecuador's major port, where he visited more American and British oilfields. Two weeks later he wrote from Trujillo, 600 kms north of Lima—a trip he chose to make by bus rather than plane so he could see something of the country. He was about to go to the world's biggest sugar plantation at Casa Grande, and then on to the oilfields at Talara and Lobitos. Having met up with an American drilling man, they decided to charter a small plane for these visits. He tells Janet that he 'went out in a Stinson and back in an old Piper Club tied together with bits of string. Flew low up the river through a drizzly rain and saw some crocs. Glad when we landed as our old crate gave some disquieting burps now and then ... I always carry your photographs and keep my fingers crossed.' On the itinerary still was Chile, where he was to visit 'the Nitrate fields and one or two other places'.

There are clearly a lot of lengthy reports that get written, even though the altitude in La Paz (where martial law had been declared) hurt his eyes so much that he was unable to type. But why Turner and Newall were interested in all these mines is something of a mystery. Later in the year, they ostensibly sent Bill to Cairo, from where he wrote to Janet that 'the Shell people are putting me on a plane to Ras Haneb—down on the Red Sea somewhere, I believe ... I shall return to Cairo on Tuesday, then quick trip from here to Port Said, Khartoum.' None of this seems to relate to the business of mining asbestos or manufacturing asbestos products.

It is only when my brother William and I visit Denzil's widow in Brecon in 2023 that I hear about Denzil's theory that his Uncle Roy was, in fact, engaged in Nazi hunting in South America on this long trip. This is not a ridiculous suggestion, but then again Denzil wanted to believe that Roy's disappearance was somehow to be explained by his life as a spy. When it became clear that the war was turning against them, Nazi contingency plans were activated. The most prominent of these were Argentina's 'ratlines', a system established by the Perón government and the Vatican. War criminals and collaborators were smuggled out of Europe (Germany–Spain–Argentina) to start new lives with barely disguised identities. German prosecutors now estimate that between 1500-2000 Nazis went to Brazil, 500-1000 went to Chile, while Argentina took in 5000 through the ratlines system. These escape routes also led to Paraguay, Colombia, Uruguay, Mexico, Chile, Peru, Guatemala, Ecuador and Bolivia. While all this is true, Denzil's theory is probably fanciful.

As well as describing his trips to mines and oilfields, Bill also wrote about the people he met, either for work or simply in the cosmopolitan world of the grander hotels. While staying at the Gran Hotel Bolivar, he describes going to a bullfight in Lima's newly built bullring: It 'was like a Roman amphitheatre—a blaze of colour in the brilliant sunshine. Most wonderful of all was the bullfighteress Conchita Cintrón who is on this same floor in the hotel. She's very attractive—face like a Madonna only more refined. Apparently she doesn't like men, although someone who had danced with her told me he'd experienced a very strange sensation.' Bill reports that 'Conchita gave the most incredible performance as '"rejoneador" i.e. she pranced around the bull on a handsome grey stallion and stuck it full of barbed darts, evading its charges with amazing skill. Then she dismounted, did the red cloak act and finally killed the bull with a sword.' He finds it 'attractive and repellent à la fois', leaving after the fourth bull vowing never to go to a corrida again. 'But somehow I feel sure that I'll go again next Sunday!'.

In La Paz, Bill reports that he nearly fainted from altitude sickness when he stepped off the plane, but soldiered on because he'd been invited by the commercial attaché to have dinner with Christopher Isherwood. The writer was on a six-month tour of South America, before publishing *The Condor and the Cows*. Bill told Janet: 'Actually I saw him in the hotel last night tight as an owl, but in an inoffensive way. So typical of what I'd imagined that bunch of writers to be—old sport coat, grey slacks, untrimmed hair hanging over his forehead, but apparently he's quite a nice type—we shall see.' In the same letter Bill describes the flight to La Paz from Lima, looking down onto Lake Titicaca, 'a great plaque of black, sinister water. And then we came in to land at the airport, which is a flat arid tableland about 15000 ft up. It was like a paysage from "Childe Harolde" on the "Waste Lands".' Bill seems to be at home in Byron's 186-verse poem, perhaps identifying with a world-weary young man, disillusioned with a life of pleasure and revelry and looking for distraction in foreign lands?

As I transcribe Bill's letters and make notes about where he is and who he is meeting, I become increasingly aware of how he writes. He is an observant traveller, constantly noting the appearance or idiosyncrasies of local inhabitants and those of the stream of international characters he meets, and he can be very funny. I am even more struck by his familiarity with classical literature (much greater than my own), and the fact that he employs literary allusion with such ease. There is nothing pretentious about his writing. From Guayaquil he describes looking out 'on a waste of corrugated iron roofs, honey—"je suis comme le roi d'un pays pluvieux" and I'm very homesick for you and Chuff'. I have to look this up to learn that he is quoting Baudelaire from *Les Fleurs du Mal*. In another letter he describes a Boxing Day dinner in Viña del Mar with Chilean business people he has met. 'There was a young Spaniard playing the most wonderful accordion music and a Spanish refugee waiter who sang plaintive songs. He was a maquis type, and I was so sentimental by this time that when he sang "Cielo Andaluz",* I almost cried ... Then we had a Trimalchionic dinner, after which I danced with the two chaps' wives.' Trimalchionic? I learn from the internet that Trimalchio is a first-century character in Petronius's Satyricon who throws insanely lavish dinner parties at which slaves serve courses such as live birds sewn up inside a pig.

There is nothing in these letters that suggests he is trying to impress his well-educated wife, or that reveals anxiety about his status. On the contrary. From Lima he writes that he is sure Janet would like the city. 'I can see you loping long-leggedly around the museums and churches, sun glasses in one hand, Baedeker in the other. I wish I could have brought you out, darling, it's not fair that these archaeological pearls should be cast before an unappreciative swine like myself, while you are stuck in the middle of Sussex—(what I'd give to be there right now!).'

---

* A famous Pasadoble composed by Pascual Marquina Narro.

Later in the same year Bill was sent to Portugal and Spain. From Madrid he wrote to Janet about going to the Prado 'all for your sake, because I want to appreciate the things you love. There was a wonderful series of pop-eyed, red nosed curly-lipped Bourbons by Velasquez. Lots of nice Brueghels, luscious Rubens etc, but very few of the French school.' At the same time he felt free to complain to Janet about her spelling of BRITANNIC, joking that he would hate people to think he had an 'illiterate wife'. We also remember his attempts to improve her French pronunciation, which reflected the extraordinary English upper-class habit of deliberately pronouncing French words as though they were English. But what is interesting to me at this point is the evidence this provides of Bill's self-confidence and his ease in multiple different worlds. It was ten years since he graduated with his B.A. from London University, and he had just spent seven of them in the army. What did he read and what did he think about and with whom did he talk in those long periods in any war when nothing was happening?

*

While Bill's letters provide an absorbing commentary on the politics, society and landscapes of the countries he was visiting, they are not primarily about the mines, bullfights or political upheavals he'd seen. They are essentially letters about love and longing, and his hopes for the future. On 7 March he tells Janet from Lima that he has decided to leave Turner and Newall—perhaps fifteen months after he joined them. He despises his boss and wants to work for 'a man—and not a pompous old school-mistress in trousers'. He has ambitions to live in the south of England, as opposed to the industrial north, in a 'nice country spot'. He was thinking about what kind of job he might do next.

At the embassy in Lima, Bill met a man who trained with him at Aldershot in 1939 (presumably also destined for the Intelligence Corps), who was now the commercial second secretary. 'I wouldn't mind a similar job somewhere but I wouldn't accept anything less than a 1st secretaryship. One gets a nice house and a fairly easy time and I don't believe the social side of it is very onerous.' A few days later Bill informs Janet that when he is New York he will 'arrange to put an advertisement in the N.Y. Times asking for a job with an American firm as resident representative somewhere in S[outh] A[merica]. They pay very well and I wouldn't mind a year or two in some pleasant spot ... I wouldn't mind setting up on my own in Brazil with a few good agencies—it's the only way to make real money. We could retire in 10 yrs and buy some place in England. I've all sorts of confused plans for us darling—and Turner and Newall figure in none of them.'

South America seemed a useful place to be. 'People and coincidences keep cropping up.' Bill met with many different officials in embassies, with American businessmen, with Germans from the large immigrant population in Bolivia, and an assortment of sometimes eccentric émigrés from Europe. In Quito towards the end of his trip, at the lovely Hotel Cordillera, he met a lot of British officials and lunched with a British minister who 'apparently used to swim and dine at our hush-hush camp in N. Africa where he was consul-general'. The lunch, he writes, was prepared by 'an Austrian cook—lobster, filet mignon and meringue Chantilly.' He also met the 'Dunlop rep' for the region. The rep lived in Lima, earned a very good salary plus living allowance. Bill thought he had a good chance of getting a suitable job when he got back. After the lobster and filet mignon lunch, he tells Janet that he is thinking about the ad he is planning to put in the *New York Times* and how it will look a 'damn sight more interesting to employers than my last one.' He is a citizen of the world. It is hard to see anything of the Rhondda in this.

All these reports on his experiences and his ideas for the future are embedded in letters that begin and end with declarations of his love for Janet, and how life would have so little meaning without her. Shortly after he arrived in South America, he writes that, 'It's such a wonderful feeling to have a wife who loves you, and a little son! I think that before I met you, I'd been alone too long and something had dried up in me.' To his 'sweet darling' he is constantly sending his 'tenderest thoughts'. Later he writes about how overwhelming it was when he first saw his son—'tiny, asleep. I love you honey, and I need you, too. How empty, useless and unhappy my life would be without you. I often realise that out here. I meet all sorts of people, see fascinating places and have amusing experiences—but darling, I'd swop anything to be with you ... I don't think you can ever realise what it means to me, darling ... Kiss Chuff for me darling. My tenderest thoughts, honey-pie.'

From Guayaquil's sticky heat he writes: 'Think I'll have a double Scotch with ice-cold soda water first—and drink silently to you, honey—<u>the</u> most wonderful person. I love you so much that I'm sometimes afraid—about wars, or accidents and things. Hasta luego, honey—and a nice kiss for Chuff. I love you, darling Janet.'

I am struck by Bill's use of American terms of endearment, as though his feelings cannot be adequately expressed in the English or Welsh he grew up with. But perhaps this is also the language he learned watching American films. I suddenly notice his use of 'sport coat' and 'slacks', which no Englishman would have said. I am not surprised by the intensity of his feelings, but it gives me pleasure to know that he could express them so clearly. What I am more surprised about is his occasional expression of vulnerability—and his insistence that he takes none of this for granted, and that he needs Janet in a profound way. It is possible that this ability to show vulnerability disappeared over time, but I never doubted that he went on needing Janet as well as loving her.

*

Within a year of Bill's return from this tour of South America he had left Turner and Newall for a job with De La Rue, in London, and Janet was expecting me. De La Rue was the world's largest printer of banknotes and passports, with expertise in security printing of all kinds. They also made playing cards, fountain pens and board games. The chairman, Sidney Lamert, had a serious interest in Bill and Janet's future, and Bill could obviously be useful. In the early 1950s De La Rue was licensed to make and sell Formica decorative laminates in

Europe, which kept Bill travelling to Europe, especially Paris. It is perhaps hard to remember how big Formica laminates were in the post-war years, with the boom in kitchen building.

Bill and Janet were once again relying on Pam for a home, this time in Essex, where Pam was living in a large house not far from the Russell family home at Stubbers. The last owner of the estate, Janet's Uncle Champion, had recently died, and both his younger brothers were also dead, including Janet's father, Charles. Champion's eldest son, Max, suffered from a brain injury that meant he was living in a nursing home, while his second son was killed on the Somme in 1916. Champion's youngest son, John, did not wish to take on the family estate, so by this time it was clear that the Russells and Stubbers must part company. No one was looking for fine old country houses, and it was eventually given to the Essex County Council to be used for educational purposes. They too could not afford its upkeep and it was demolished in 1960. This was not uncommon. In 1955 alone, for example, country houses were coming down at the rate of one every two-and-a-half days.

I was born in Brentwood at the end of 1949, and Pam became my godmother. Writing this I am beginning to appreciate just how long Bill and Janet must have lived with Pam. Did this reflect their need to save for their own house and the lack of rental accommodation in those post-war years? I feel that despite Bill's silence about Pam he must have liked her and respected her, for otherwise it simply would not have worked. I want to think he did, as she was talented and admirable as well as generous.

In early 1951, expecting their third child (William), Bill and Janet bought a good-sized house on the Pilgrims Way, near Sevenoaks in Kent, within commuting distance of the city of London. It had an acre of gently sloping garden with a small wood of copper beech trees, backing onto the North Downs. Parked at the garden gate was a 1929 Bentley in which, family legend has it, William was almost born—before they could reach the hospital.

I began to think about how I could reconstruct our father's life, putting the before (Roy) and after (Bill) together, and placing him at the centre of his own story. I thought I might as well start with the question of how he came to own a vintage Bentley in 1951.

William turns out to have by far the best memory when it comes to our childhood and suggested that the Bentley might have something to do with Bill meeting the man Janet's sister married. Peter flew planes for the RAF during the war, before he married Ann. We remember him as a distant, fruity-voiced man who wore neck scarves and smoked a pipe, and liked to race speedboats, fly planes and drive interesting cars. But I also think of Peter as someone whom Bill derided much later in his life, when they were both living in France. So it is something of a surprise to discover that in the early 1950s Peter was taking Bill on joy-flights to France. His oldest son, our cousin Mike, was able to check his father's flight logbooks and reported back to me that Peter and Bill took off from Thruxton, a World War Two airfield in Hampshire, on 15 July 1951 for a five-day European jaunt (this was less than a month after William was born, and not long after the family moved into the house in Kent). Landing for customs and refuelling, they flew to Lyon, Cannes, Milan and on to Bolzano, where they took the train to the Dolomites, before returning via the same route.

Mike is also able to confirm that his father had about six vintage Bentleys over the 1950s. Peter admired the famous victories of these cars in the twenty-four-hour Le Mans races in the 1920s, and after the war these large and expensive-to-run cars were comparatively cheap to buy, and to maintain—if you were able to look after them yourself. Peter had always believed that 'they certainly stood out when visiting his bank manager in Andover for a loan'. They were, Mike tells me, also 'ideal for settling noisy troublesome babies—just pop them in the back and switch the engine on—the slow rumbling and steady vibration soon put the child to sleep!!!'

Bill loved fast cars and would not have minded having a supercharged old Bentley to drive, so I am sure Peter helped him find one. But he may well have considered that it might help him to get a bank loan.

Janet had no money of her own apart from what could only have been meagre personal savings; and Bill had only what he would have saved during the war and earned since joining civvy street. This may or may not have included some extra income for continued intelligence work. But they would, in any case, have needed a substantial loan to buy that first family house.

Before long, beside the Bentley there was a black Ford Popular (Britain's lowest-priced car when it was introduced in 1953)—or it might have been the slightly more upmarket Ford Prefect—for Janet to drive. I have no recollection of Bill ever tinkering under the bonnet of the Bentley, but he formed a strong relationship with Bert Welstead who owned the local village garage and petrol station, and who probably loved the opportunity to maintain such a romantic and famous car. The relationship endured and the reason I remember Bert in his brown overalls so well is that he gave me the only driving lessons I had before taking my driving test aged seventeen.

In 1956 the flight logbooks show that Bill and Peter made a trip to Le Mans for the twenty-four-hour car race held on 28 July 1956, which was won by a Jaguar that year. It took Bill another decade before he had a new one of those. But at least we now know how he was inducted into the world of Bentleys. The Bentley is also the car of choice for Marcus Pym's father, the ultimate literary con-man from *A Perfect Spy*.

Chapter 6
Success: International Business and Life in the Stockbroker Belt

The house on the Kent North Downs that Bill and Janet bought in 1951 was our family home for seventeen years. Called 'The Halt', it sits between the villages of Otford and Kemsing on the Pilgrims Way—an ancient route taken by pilgrims from Winchester in Hampshire to the shrine of Thomas à Becket at Canterbury, made famous in Chaucer's *Canterbury Tales*. For most of those seventeen years Bill was working for the Mitchell Cotts Group, a large global trading company based in the city of London, engaged in everything from growing pyrethrum in Kenya to running international shipping lines, from engineering in Britain to grain cleaning in the Middle East. It was a match that made perfect sense on many levels, and he rose through the group's different companies until he reached the top.

It would be a mistake to think that Britain in these years after the end of the Second World War had become less class conscious and more egalitarian. Bill was right to see that an obviously working-class man from Wales was going to find his career blocked on many fronts. David Kynaston's first volume about post-war British society uses the Mass Observation Archive as well as diaries and letters to capture an 'intimate, multilayered, multivoiced, unsentimental portrait' of *Austerity Britain* between 1945 and 1951. He characterises the country at that time:

> A land of hierarchical social assumptions, of accent and dress as giveaways to class, of Irish jokes and casually derogatory references

to Jews and niggers. Expectations low and limited but anyone in or on the fringes of the middle class hoping for a 'job for life' and comforted by the myth that the working class kept their coal in the bath.

In fact, he suggests that 'fundamental social and cultural continuities remained—indeed, were arguably strengthened rather than lessened by the war', quoting Harold Nicholson who fears that 'class feeling and class resentment are very strong'. You could, with luck, become a 'self-made man', but self-made men were still looked down on and could not belong in any meaningful way to the class above them. In the late 1950s Kynaston still describes the city of London as 'that ultra-hierarchical, status-conscious, age-respecting, largely male preserve'. 'Deference, respectability, conformity, restraint, trust— these were probably all more important than piety in underpinning "the 1950s"'.

I do not think Bill's ambition was ever focused on making a lot of money, and he never talked about the importance of money. Nor was there anything ostentatious about the way he lived once he started to have some. In this he and Janet were totally aligned. In one of his letters to her from Cairo, probably in late 1948, he remarks on this: 'I got your two letters when I returned from Alexandria and you seem to be very happy. It's a miracle to me how you can be happy with so little—but we really have got a _lot_—haven't we honey, but I can't think for the life of me why you love _me_.'

Nonetheless, from his South American letters it is clear that Bill was determined to make a good living, and to make it quickly. Like many people who have experienced real poverty, he hated to feel indebted in any way, and avoided anything that involved lending money. He was also determined to secure his financial position for the long term, which he did by building up a portfolio of bonds and making the most of tax avoidance opportunities. I think he wanted to be able to help his children should they be in need.

Bill was also motivated by his ambition to live a particular kind of cultured, comfortable but also stimulating life. Alongside which, I can now see, there was his fear of boredom and his need to act when it loomed. And this fear never left him, no matter his successes, or how old he got.

*

From the outset, Bill was constantly travelling and was often away for what seemed quite lengthy periods. Janet was supported at home by a series of 'au pairs' until we were all safely at school. We did not know anyone else who had an au pair, but there was probably a good supply available from impoverished post-war Europe.

The first two who came to The Halt were Italian. Carla was the beauty queen of Bolzano, who eventually married an American in military uniform, while Gingi Scolari was an impecunious contessa from Tregozzano in Tuscany. Janet learned to make potato gnocchi, and Italian tomato sauce from the long, slow cooking of tomato paste with a lot of olive oil, onion, and a little rosemary and sugar. The combination of these two elements, gnocchi and tomato sauce, was a childhood favourite for us all and the sauce lived on as we grew up and moved away. The Italian au pairs were followed by Monika, a young German woman, whom we loved dearly and called Monkey. She eventually left us to train as a nurse at the Royal Free Hospital in London.

My brothers and I have no recollection of minding about our father's absences, or of the house feeling in any way disturbed by them. My mother may have been 'excitable' about books, interesting people and ideas, but we remember her as a calm, reliable and loving presence in our childhood, even if my brothers also think she may have been somewhat 'cool', unlikely to be physically affectionate. My mother wrote to me when my first child was a baby, reflecting that 'darling Henrietta is our fourth beloved grand-daughter' and wondering how her friend Nell felt about her fourteenth grandchild—'but perhaps I am more like Mother [Lilla] than I think, I remember resenting her being so "cool" about you all'.

The coolness should not be misunderstood, however. She told me on more than one occasion, when we talked about how important my career was to me, that she had felt the most intense moments of happiness waiting outside our junior schools for us to come cheerfully running out. Janet had a very marked capacity to notice and take pleasure in small things. A year after Bill died, she wrote to me that 'glum-ness comes rarely and I do positively enjoy my life mostly'. She reminded me that she shared with me a capacity for moments of pure happiness, writing that 'We are both very, very lucky'.

*

With the benefit of hindsight, Mitchell Cotts closely resembles Ian Fleming's fictional company Universal Exports, which provides cover for James Bond and the British Secret Service when they are abroad. Ian Fleming was a senior naval intelligence officer during the Second World War and knew a thing or two when he created 007. My belated efforts to understand what Mitchell Cotts actually did were miraculously facilitated by the discovery that just as Bill joined the company, a glossy 'house magazine' was launched, in part to 'help our executives in the different branches in all parts of the world to acquire a better appreciation of the business of the Company' and also 'give to all members of the organization a sense of belonging to a big family, with all the consequential benefits'. An almost complete set of the *The Cottsman* was donated to the British Library by the son of the man who was managing director and then company chairman during Bill's time with the group. I was alerted to this just in time to factor in three visits to the British Library during my research trip. The publication was an invaluable resource in understanding Bill's working life.

The company was established in 1885 by a young but entrepreneurial Scotsman who was drawn to South Africa by the gold mining boom in Witwatersrand. William Dingwall Mitchell Cotts soon realised that gold mining was a crowded space, while there were enormous opportunities in the development of transport and infrastructure to support the Natal coalfields as well as the booming gold mining industry. By

1897 his company had an office in London and branches in all the principal ports of South Africa. In another move that became central to the expansion of the company, Mitchell Cotts became the marketing agency for all Shell oil products in South Africa. Beginning with paraffin, and expanding into petrol, this business alone was worth sales of £2.5m by the 1920s. 'The four gallon petrol tin became one of the commonest sights on the veldt.'

From this base it made sense for the company to move into shipping and trading in other commodities in South and East Africa, which led to the acquisition of a series of major shipping companies in the 1930s. This in turn brought cotton classifying and grain cleaning plants into the business, so that during the Second World War Mitchell Cotts was operating in Ethiopia, Djibouti and Aden, with offices in Egypt and Libya. Offices were also opened in Italy, Lebanon, Syria, Malta and the Far East. It was, in other words, a company operating in countries with which Bill had become very familiar during the war, many of them French as well as Arabic-speaking. His knowledge of South American mines and oilfields would also have added significant intelligence to the Mitchell Cotts Group.

It was only after mapping out Bill's career with Mitchell Cotts in detail that I began to see how extraordinarily well-suited Bill and the company were. He would not have lasted long in any company with a narrow focus, however large—such as a major chemicals manufacturer or a major car production firm—where the work is highly routinised and predictable and also closely monitored. A scholarly monograph on the history of Britain's largest trading companies in the nineteenth and twentieth centuries describes the kind of managerial competencies they needed as the environments in which they operated changed constantly with the decline of the British empire after the Second World War. 'There was a strong ethos in many companies that they were "merchant adventurers" who could turn their skills to anything if it was a good deal ... The difference between "successful" and "unsuccessful" diversification strategies was not in the degree of "opportunism" but whether the firms had the competencies to manage the opportunities that presented themselves.'

151

Since managers needed to be able to shift their focus from one product to another in any region, or from one global region to a different one, it was surprising to read that like all British companies of the time, 'the trading companies stressed "character" and social background in selecting their managers'. In making appointments, there was a preference for a 'respectable, privately educated young man preferably with some sporting achievements at school … This approach fitted the general British preference for "character" and social skills as the main qualification for management.' So potential employees might be expected to be 'extensively questioned on their family backgrounds, their family's position in society, and the occupation of their relatives.' Sporting or athletic qualifications were highly valued because trading companies were 'looking for a particular type of character who would take risks, albeit in a team context'. By now Bill had surely learned to look the part and would have been able to focus attention on his language skills (also highly valued) and his military career. It is also possible that MI6 facilitated his move through personal connections with the top of the company. But it nonetheless confirms that he was right to conceal his origins.

During the 1950s Mitchell Cotts continued to expand into new industries such as sisal, cattle-ranching and seed distribution. They also bought into the pyrethrum trade between Kenya and America. Pyrethrum, as a natural plant-based insecticide, became a hugely successful line of business for the group, and led to the establishment of vast pyrethrum plantations in Ecuador, overseen by Bill, to provide an alternative to Kenyan supplies. Agricultural projects in Africa led to an agreement between Mitchell Cotts and the imperial Ethiopian government to establish a large cotton plantation in the desert area in the Awash valley which was so successful that Queen Elizabeth toured the site with Emperor Haile Selassi in 1965.

At the same time the company was buying into steel and engineering businesses in Britain and Canada, and began to make plastic products, mining machinery, industrial fans, carbon brushes and steel mesh. Mitchell Cotts did not, however, forget the value to be had from acting as agents and sole distributors of vital products such as motor vehicles (like the Land Rover) in Africa, supporting this trade with bus assembly in Sudan and heavy mobile equipment in the Arabian gulf area. By the early 1960s Mitchell Cotts controlled over eighty subsidiaries operating in thirty countries on four different continents. It had world-wide assets totalling £60 million.

*

Bill travelled so often, first for De La Rue in the early 1950s and then for Mitchell Cotts, that at one point he had to have three passports stuck together to hold all the visas and stamps he was accumulating. We loved to look at this and decode the place names where he had entered or left a country. If he went on writing letters to Janet, she stopped keeping them by the mid-1950s. All that can be gleaned from those that survive from this period is that between 1952 and 1953 he was in Rio de Janeiro, Berlin and Geneva. From Berlin he writes that he is 'feeling futile after doing practically nothing since I left London, except two afternoons spent "faisant l'antichambre" for the Chinese in the Eastern sector. Quite fruitless!' He ends: 'Did I ever tell you I love you?—the word is inadequate, darling, for my complex and final attachment to you. Bill.' From the Hotel du Rhone in Geneva the letter is brief. 'My Sweet Darling, Surprise! Just to tell you I love you now at this moment and always. Also Colin, Belinda etcetera—especially the etcetera. Bill.'

In amongst the work trips, I discover that Bill was in Paris in September 1954 to greet his wartime collaborator Marcel Bigeard when he landed at Orly airport on his return after eight years spent fighting in Vietnam. The French had suffered an overwhelming defeat at Dien Bien Phu, and of Bigeard's elite parachute regiment only forty of the original eight-hundred men survived. Bigeard had spent the last six months imprisoned by General Giap. I only know that Bill was there on the tarmac with Bigeard's wife because I found several descriptions of Bigeard's emotional reaction—both in Bigeard's own writing about his life, and in more objective accounts of his military career. An academic discussion of Bigeard's role in the defence of the

French colonial empire captures the meeting. Barnett Singer and John Langdon describe how, after a long flight home with other survivors, Bigeard was reunited with his wife and his 'wartime buddy, Bill Probert. And Bigeard himself wept.' In a magazine interview decades later, but while Bill was still alive, Bigeard returns to this moment. He reminisces about fighting with Bill in the Ariège, and his feelings of emotion as he landed in France from Vietnam on that day, which again brings tears to his eyes.

> After six months in captivity, I land at Orly airport on a beautiful morning, and who do I see beside my wife? Major Probert ... What more beautiful example of 'fraternité'? We fought together ten years previously, and he was there, come to meet me, to comfort me, even though we had not had any contact since that battle.

Reading about this event, almost seventy years after it happened, I discover that my mother was also there (leaving the three of us in England with one of the au pairs, I assume), and that Bill and Janet then spent a few days with Bigeard and his wife and daughter at his little villa in Lorraine. In Bigeard's own account of this reunion he writes about how he and Bill talk again about the Ariège but admits that he has 'a lot of difficulty working out what he is doing ... peut-être agent dans un Deuxième Burcau, peu Importe, vieux Bill!' [Perhaps he is an agent for a counter espionage service, no matter, old Bill!].

It is only once I begin to wonder if Bill stayed connected to MI6 after he was de-mobbed that I see how improbable this reunion was. How could Bill have known that this military plane was bringing Bigeard home to Orly on that day at that time if Bigeard had had no communication with him since they parted company in Paris ten years earlier? It took my brother Colin, generally sceptical about reading too much into anything, to point out the obvious—that MI6 would have sent Bill, perfectly positioned to obtain a first-hand 'de-briefing' from his old comrade in arms. MI6 were most certainly interested in how France's war in Vietnam was lost, with Britain engaged in similar struggles in Malaya until 1960. Bill's questions while they were together clearly alerted Bigeard to what was going on. Deuxième Bureau indeed.

*

In 1957 Bill was investigating the commercial possibilities for pyrethrum in the South African market, which took him to Johannesburg, Durban and Cape Town. A few months later he visited Paris, Milan and Rome for discussions with the selling agents and principal buyers of pyrethrum products. As I read these accounts of Bill's travel in *The Cottsman*, it seems reasonable to conclude that my sense of having an absent father was the result of his literal absence as much as the conventional psychological absence from family life of so many fathers in the 1950s. I do not recall missing my father when he was away, perhaps because even when he was not abroad, his working day was long and he took little part in our day-to-day care. In this, at least, he was probably representative of his generation.

Our childhood memories of Bill's travel are condensed around the excitement of knowing he was about to come home, and the immediate opening of what I remember as a large suitcase to reveal some exotic souvenir or other. This is how we all recall his trip to China in 1958, when he was so tired that he fell asleep on the train home from London and missed our station at Otford. This is perhaps not surprising given *The Cottsman* for that year notes that 'A new Chemicals Division has been created and W. R. Probert will be in charge. Now appointed a Director of the Company, Mr Probert recently returned from a tour of nearly two months' duration entailing visits to Moscow, Peking, Tokyo, Seoul (South Korea), and Hong Kong. Although most arduous, his journey was of extreme interest and value.' My mother made a note for me that he was one of the first Western businessmen to visit the People's Republic of China. Some of this travel looks like it would have been of interest to MI6.

When he finally did arrive home, in the suitcase there were the most beautiful traditional embroidered silk jackets, including a small, exquisitely made red silk child's gown for me. I associate this trip with learning about Mao Zedong's mobilisation of the Chinese people to eliminate the Four Pests (flies, mosquitos, rats and sparrows). Bill's description of Chinese children banging pots and pans so that the sparrows could not rest until they fell, exhausted, out of the sky, was sufficiently dramatic for it to stick in my mind.

Perhaps even more memorable were the shrunken heads he pulled out of his suitcase on his return from a trip to Ecuador in 1962. Bill described to us how, in the area of the Amazon basin where Mitchell Cotts was clearing forest for a tea plantation, local tribes practised head-shrinking of their enemies. I have no idea how the ones he brought back for us had been made, but they were extremely convincing, including the sewn-together lips. I know the year we got them because I took one to school for some kind of 'show and tell' and my otherwise worldly form teacher decided that it was not 'appropriate' for girls in the Lower IVth to see such a thing.

Among the other travel trophies my brothers and I remember, there was also the much-loved camel saddle which I assume came from Egypt—a wooden frame with red leather padded cushion on top. It may well have come home from the one trip Bill took that left an indelible mark on me, only because he took Janet with him. In Janet's photo album there are five photos on one page headed 'With Bill in Egypt and Lebanon'. Janet had a habit of trimming her photos to remove anything that was not integral to the scene, thus allowing her more photos on one page than would otherwise be possible. Here there is a photograph of Janet holding what I am sure is her Egyptian *Baedeker*, walking in the Valley of the Kings, and another of her standing—with the book open—in the Karnak temple complex near Luxor. From Lebanon there are two photos from the ruined city of Baalbek, the temple of Jupiter and the temple of Bacchus. The last photograph is a roadside shot under which Janet has written: 'It seems unlikely but I think this was on the frontier between Lebanon and Syria—we went on to Damascus.'

There is no date for these photographs, but I think it must have been 1956, when Bill, still new to Mitchell Cotts, was area manager in Cairo, a position 'brought to an end by the Suez crisis'. 1956 makes me now think about the crisis over the Suez Canal and what Bill might really have been doing in the Middle East that year; but at the time the only crisis that mattered was entirely provoked by Mrs Wood, who moved into our house to take care of us while our parents were away. Mrs Wood had occasionally cleaned house for Janet and lived—with her husband and a budgerigar—not far away, on the local council housing estate.

The social gulf between anyone living in a council house and any other kind of house was particularly wide, but even small variations in housing type could be used to express superiority. David Kynaston describes VE day celebrations where there had to be two street parties, divided by about two hundred yards, to ensure that children in semi-detached houses and detached bungalows would not interact with poorer children living in terraced houses.

I must have visited Mrs Wood on the council estate at least once as I remember the budgerigar being let out of its cage to fly round the 'parlour'. Budgerigars had become popular pets in English working-class homes during the twentieth century. During the Blitz, Churchill was being driven through a London slum and sent his detective to see why people were standing in a very long queue. The answer was birdseed. My trauma had nothing to do with the budgerigar, but only Mrs Wood's unmotherly ways, and expectations of behaviour that were not at all like our mother's. Looking back, William and I both feel that she behaved as though she was in her own house, bringing her niece with her, together with her expectation that we should always be neat and tidy and not answer back. Failure to conform led her to use the flat of my hairbrush on us. The day when our parents were expected home, I remember running away and hiding in our little copper beech wood as their car drove up, unable to manage my emotions. I probably wanted my mother to understand how much I had missed her, but I would have found it impossible to put this into words at the age of six.

Bill's role in Cairo was short-lived after Britain's ill-fated reaction to President Nasser's nationalisation of the Suez Canal, which saw British and French paratroopers dropped along the canal before they were forced to withdraw in the face of intense pressure from the United

States and the Soviet Union. Mitchell Cotts' assets were sequestrated by the Egyptian government. The company was also running into difficulties in Saudi Arabia, primarily because the Saudi government was unwilling and unable to pay for the vast building projects that had been commissioned by the Royal family, including a huge new palace and harem.

While searching for information about the nature of Mitchell Cotts' business interests in Egypt, Lebanon and Syria, I discover something that sends me off down a new secret service rabbit hole. In 1946 Mitchell Cotts bought a successful Saudi Arabian company called Sharqieh Ltd, based in Jeddah. It was involved in an attractively wide range of business activities ranging from oil to armaments, transport, banking, construction and utilities. Nothing surprising here, apart from the armaments perhaps. But the man who was selling this company to Mitchell Cotts was called Harry St John Bridger Philby, an eccentric Englishman who, through years spent exploring the Arabian Peninsula between the wars, became an expert on the history and geography of Arabia, as well as its birdlife. After the sale, St John Philby agreed to stay on as a local director, not least to help the new owners get around local rules that caused commercial difficulties—such as restrictions on non-Muslims visiting Saudi Arabia.

St John Philby had converted to Islam in the early 1930s and lived for much of his life in Jeddah. In the 1920s he was judged to be admirably qualified as a secret intelligence service—or MI6—agent for the area. In 1920 he had been minister of internal security in British-controlled Iraq, and a year later he was named head of the secret service in Mandatory Palestine, working with T. E. Lawrence—better known as Lawrence of Arabia. By the late 1920s, however, he was seen as politically unreliable. A security review describes him as 'a very intelligent, potentially hostile person'. Philby was 'the one individual in Jeddah, who, if he were otherwise than he is, could solve our difficulties,' being 'second to few Englishmen ... in his knowledge of modern Arabia.'

St John Philby's sympathies in the Middle East were indeed not always with the British, and there has been much speculation about which side he was backing at certain key moments. Even when he began his career in the Indian civil service in 1908, he described himself as a socialist, and a supporter of Indian independence.* But for me, all this pales into insignificance beside the fact that he is the father of Kim Philby, Britain's most notorious double agent.

In the early 1950s, St John Philby was obliged to leave Saudi Arabia temporarily (having offended the new king with some frank criticism) and he moved to Beirut, where his son was then living. Kim Philby had once again been allowed to work for MI6, despite the growing evidence that he was a double agent working for the Russians. By 1956, the time of Bill and Janet's trip, St John Philby was back in favour with the Saudi royal family and had returned to Jeddah, where Mitchell Cotts hoped he could help them extract hundreds of thousands of US dollars owed by the Saudis for the palace and harem built for the king's uncle, Emir Abdullah.

It seems most unlikely that Bill would have been travelling to the Middle East in his first years with Mitchell Cotts and not been in contact with St John Philby. When I share my discovery of this—admittedly tenuous—link between Bill and Kim Philby with my brother William, he points out that Kim went to Westminster School. William knows this because both he and Colin went to the same school.

My brothers and I had talked about why they were sent to Westminster at our reunion in San Francisco, along with the curious question of the Bentley. Looking back, Westminster was not an obvious choice. While being one of the great British public schools for boys, it was quite unlike the places usually chosen by the ruling class and the aspiring ruling class, such as Eton, Winchester or Harrow. In the

---

* Philby's career trajectory was in some ways identical to that of Janet's father, who joined the Indian Educational Service after his Oxford degree and fell in love with India. Philby says that 'I was earmarked at a very tender age for the Indian Civil Service, which was regarded in our perhaps excessively military family circle of those days as a glittering prize open only to the best "Brains" in the country!'. The training of this class of British administrators in India was long and deep, and it is entirely possible that St. John Philby and Charles Russell might have met at some point before the First World War.

1960s it did not take sport seriously and did not even have a rugby team. There was no school blazer or uniform as such, and boys simply had to wear a pale-grey suit. It was, above all, a seriously intellectual and cosmopolitan school, with a number of European Jewish refugees teaching there. There were many day boys as well as boarders, and my brothers commuted there by train, taking the same daily route as Bill.

As we now realise, Bill would not have been familiar with the British public school system, nor could he have boned up on it with the internet. Despite their visibility, only about eight percent of English students attended private schools in the 1960s. The choice of school generally depended on family connections, or family ambitions, together with word of mouth in the right circles. Bill had no relevant networks or personal knowledge to rely on. Nor would he have wanted to discuss the options with his colleagues since that would inevitably lead to questions about his own schooling.

On Janet's side, her father was sent to Loretto in the 1880s, a very small public school in Scotland with a distinctive and revolutionary character. 'The outward and visible sign was the dress of the boys. No caps, flannel shirts open at the neck, shorts or knickerbockers and no waistcoats. Coats off when the temperature reached 60 F, open windows and a cold bath every morning.' The headmaster insisted on the value of organised games, reflecting his intense belief that education should be one great whole, 'including every part of one's being, and that character could be trained only if body, soul and spirit were all being educated together'. Meanwhile our cousins were down to be boarders at the same public school in Berkshire that their father had attended (having already been sent as boarders to his old prep school). I imagine that Bill would not have cared for that kind of place, which was more focused on 'character' and sport than intellectual development or academic achievement. Janet, at least in retrospect, used to say that the boys should have gone to the local more modest public school in Sevenoaks.

We all began our education at local fee-paying preparatory schools.* The only children we knew who attended the local authority primary school were the daughters of Mrs Dalgarno, who came to clean our house several mornings a week, and who lived a little further down the road from Mrs Wood. Unlike Mrs Wood we liked Mrs Dal. In the late 1950s, most English schoolchildren faced the eleven-plus exam which determined if you could move to a grammar school (if, that is, there was one near enough and your parents could afford the uniform and extras). The majority of those who sat this exam would default to a secondary modern school where the emphasis was on vocational training to age fifteen. Until the fiercely fought decision was made to introduce comprehensive secondary schools, this moment was often life-defining. A similar moment had been life-defining for Roy. It was still life-defining when Fiona Hill was at school in County Durham in the 1970s. As the daughter of a coal miner in County Durham, she came to fame in 2019 when she testified before a committee of the United States Congress as part of the impeachment inquiry against President Donald Trump. An expert on Soviet and European foreign affairs, she had been appointed to his national security staff. In her subsequent autobiography she gives an extraordinarily powerful account of how people from her working-class background are defined and constrained by the English educational system.

When I asked my brothers if they know anyone who went to our local secondary modern school in Sevenoaks, Colin reminded me of Andrew Ross who lived close by and was thought of as slightly dangerous because his mother was divorced (something not to be discussed), he had greased hair swept back into a quiff, and a 500 cc Norton motorcycle. They couldn't think of anyone else. I know no one who went to a state secondary school. Yet secondary modern schools were educating seven out of ten children in the state system. My own school, established for the daughters of Christian missionaries in 1838, was a fairly modest establishment in Sevenoaks, but we played

---

* Boys' fee-paying primary schools were called 'prep' schools, but private primary schools for girls were usually called 'junior schools'. So, I went to a junior school while my brothers went to a prep school.

lacrosse instead of hockey in winter (better for our deportment), and this connected us to the poshest of girls' boarding schools. Visiting the stately homes and grounds of Benenden or Roedean for Saturday matches, we gave ourselves away by shouting 'Hip hip hooray!' at the end of a match, while our hosts shouted 'Hip hip hoorah!' There was no escaping the niceties of class distinctions in England in the 1960s.

It is hard to overstate the significance of class and accent in shaping English schooling, even today. As recently as 2019, a large poll revealed that over half of those surveyed thought that a regional accent was a barrier to graduate corporate jobs, and twenty percent said that they needed to change their accent to be successful. Listening to the hugely popular podcast, *The Rest is Politics*, I have given up counting how often the school backgrounds of the two presenters are mentioned, or the schooling of any English political players they might be discussing, as though this in itself can tell you what they think about any particular topic. The assumption that you can tell a person's political position from the school they went to is so entrenched that any deviation from the norm requires some explanation. When someone who went to a comprehensive school becomes an extreme ideologue on the right (like Liz Truss) it is as surprising as when someone who went to Eton resigns from a corrupt and vicious Conservative government (like Rory Stewart). In this world it is not surprising that Bill chose to close down any possible enquiries about what school he went to.

As we mulled over our parents' choice of Westminster, Colin's initial view was that Bill would have cared a lot about the quality of the education that his children were to receive, but that he would have had no truck with status as such. I don't think boarding schools would have been considered, so it is possible that Westminster, which could be reached by commuter train, emerged logically as the best choice in Bill's eyes. But it is still a very large leap from Porth County Boys, and a very big decision. What, after all, was wrong with Sevenoaks school? As we spoke about Westminster, I discovered that the boys' fees were in fact paid by Janet's cousin, Marjorie, who had married Ellery Sedgwick—the editor of the *Atlantic Monthly*—and gone to live in Massachusetts after the war. This was a revelation to me, as Bill hated the idea of being indebted to anyone, literally or figuratively. But it also makes sense, as it is hard to see how he could have afforded the fees otherwise in 1960. This was a man who started from scratch after the war, with nothing but his own education and ambition.

The other possibility is that the idea of sending his sons to Westminster came from St John Philby, and even his son Kim. While reading up about this remarkable father and son, it became clear that they both cared deeply for Westminster School and what it represented. In his autobiography, *Arabian Days*, St John writes at length about the school as he knew it, and its traditions:

> The six years I spent there, in the shadow of the Abbey and Houses of Parliament with the chimes of Big Ben spelling out the fleeting hours, were years of real happiness ... I liked the work and the games, the social and intellectual activities of the school ... Yes, those were good days indeed at Westminster; and the greatest thrill of my life, which has not been devoid of exciting moments, was probably provided by the announcement of my selection as Captain Elect of the school for the ensuing year.

Perhaps more surprising is his son Kim's devotion to the school. Ben Macintyre, in his book about Kim Philby's personality and character, suggests that Kim's most treasured possession, even on the eve of his defection to Russia from Beirut, was his old Westminster scarf. (He also provides ample evidence about the role class snobbery played in protecting Kim, allowing him to survive so long in MI6 despite the growing evidence of his disloyalty.)

Bill would, I think, have admired St John's deep knowledge of Arabia and his love of languages. He might also have been sympathetic to his support for Nasser's nationalisation of the Suez Canal in 1956, as well as St John and Kim's work in exposing British and French invasion plans. I was, I admit, excited to discover that all St John Philby's papers are now held by the Middle East Centre at St Antony's College, Oxford—eighty-nine boxes of them. I let myself imagine opening the ones that have been catalogued as involving Philby's relationship with Mitchell Cotts and finding evidence that St John and Bill met.

Between the Rhondda and the British Library I squeezed in two days at St Antony's (gnashing my teeth again that the archives closed for a long lunch even if you had come from Australia to see them). St John Philby's papers provide many insights into the challenges of doing business in Saudi Arabia, covering not just the drama of trying to extract payment for the royal palace and harem, but also the business opportunities in areas such as the sale of tents for the hajj (which came to be known as Philby tents), distribution of Land Rovers (especially after American Jeeps were temporarily banned), and negotiations over the purchase of fighter aircraft and arms orders (and the 'importance of not talking to any Jewish person about them'). Among the letters are two from Rolls Royce about the Saudi king's desire to purchase a RR Phantom IV with a custom left-hand-drive (sadly not possible), and the possibility that Mitchell Cotts in Jeddah might obtain the Rolls Royce and Bentley franchise in Saudi Arabia. There is also a lot of correspondence about St John's decision to buy a RR Silver Wraith for himself.

In long letters to Mitchell Cotts head office in London, St John worries about finding competent British managers for the Saudi-based company, who need to 'have experience of working with eastern peoples (not in the British Empire)' and who speak Arabic. Incredibly, he suggests that 'the only one I know who happens to have the requisite quality of adaptability is my own son! Why not try him?'

> [Kim] did extremely well during the war in charge of a branch of the Secret Service, in which he continued with the best of prospects until that Burgess-McLean affair, which involved his own department, and left him with little option but to resign ... He had several years of experience in Turkey while in the Secret Service, and soon had a grasp of the language, while he is also fluent in French, German and Spanish ... I therefore suggest quite seriously that you should discuss the idea with him.

The potential value of employees with intelligence experience is also the focus of earlier correspondence between Mitchell Cotts head office and the manager of Sharquieh in Jedda which describes the appointment of a Mr Wybrow. 'I believe he has a good military record and was in the Middle East in Intelligence and secret work during the last war, also in the First War.' It would seem that Bill was likely to fit right in.

From the correspondence in the Philby archive, I can see that by the mid-1950s St John had developed a close and frank relationship with G. McIntosh White (Mac) in the London office. Apart from dealing with the decision of the Saudi government not to renew Mitchell Cotts' trading licence at the end of the decade, St John seems genuinely interested in Mac's school-aged son David, and his academic and sporting progress. He responds to the news that David is to start at Lancing (a boarding public school in Sussex with what some think is the largest and grandest school chapel in the world) and points out that the school is supposed to be 'good at squash'. St John obviously loves cricket, writing at other times about seeing a test match at The Oval and wanting to know about David's cricketing prowess and scoring history. I do not find a record of any meeting between Bill and St John in 1956, but it would be surprising if it did not occur. It is not too fanciful to imagine St John telling Bill that he should put his two young sons down for Westminster, and Bill subsequently taking the advice.

Back in the city, it seems that there was frequent communication between Mitchell Cotts executives, senior civil servants and their government departments, particularly the foreign office. The managing director of the group did not work for MI6, but his son informs me that he had frequent contact with them. There would have been no difficulty in arranging for Bill to do some work on the side when travelling for Mitchell Cotts.

In London, Bill had another bolt-hole that he used from time to time: the Special Forces Club. This club was created in the immediate aftermath of the Second World War, just as the special forces that had evolved during the war were disbanded. Those who had served in these often-clandestine units were mostly returning to civilian life. They were warned never to speak of covert operations, and some, especially those who had worked with foreign agents, were made to sign the Official Secrets Act. They were aware that to divulge any of their wartime activities could, in theory, result in imprisonment.'

General Gubbins, who signed the recommendation that Bill be awarded his DSO, was the last director of SOE, and wanted to create a club where former members could meet for lunch or dinner and talk about their wartime experiences. He also hoped to preserve the 'bonds of comradeship and mutual trust which had been formed between a special group of men and women in the war years'. Such is the secrecy that still surrounds the club, they refuse to confirm anyone's membership, let alone provide any information from their records, so it is impossible to know how often Bill went or who he met there. It remained a place he would stay, avoiding any social commitments, even after he had retired and left London.

*

When Bill was not away on these international business trips, he took the daily commuter train from Otford to London. The train was divided into first- and third-class carriages since second-class travel had become uncompetitive with third-class travel, and second-class carriages were largely dropped before the war. In 1956, third class was renamed second class, and this is how I remember train travel as a child. The early morning train to Victoria Station was full of men in city suits, and in first class there were certainly still men in bowler hats, though not on Bill's head. From Victoria he travelled by London Underground to Liverpool St Station and then walked to Cotts House in Camomile St, E.C.3. This was a new, nine-storey purpose-built office building in the heart of the city, with entrances in Camomile and Outwich streets. I think Bill left early in the morning, probably before we left for the school day, and returned late, often arriving back at Otford Station around seven in the evening. For some reason we remember knowing that Bill's suits were now being made by Moss Bros. (pronounced familiarly as Moss Bross)—the company that supplies most of the morning suits to be seen each year at Royal Ascot, or Eton and Harrow cricket matches. 'The biggest single operation in Moss Bros. history was Queen Elizabeth's coronation in 1953, when morning suits, striped trousers and top hats left the shop in battalions.'

Working for Mitchell Cotts was certainly setting us up financially. Before long the Bentley was disposed of, and we had the first of a series of more conventional large family cars, a Vauxhall Velox. This was followed by a blue Ford Zephyr which took us to Spain on our first overseas holiday as a family in 1957, and cost £608. While this car may not have impressed a bank manager as much as a Bentley, it was not just a family sedan. 'The motoring press greeted the Zephyr Six with wild enthusiasm for its spacious interior, handling and ride. In Europe, Dagenham's sporting reputation was set in stone when Maurice Gatsonidès's Zephyr Six defeated Ian Appleyard's Jaguar Mk VII and won the 1953 Monte Carlo Rally.'* 'A Zephyr Six seemed as much a harbinger of a Britain slowly emerging into colour as films starring Diana Dors' platinum mane and Laurence Harvey's pompadour.' When we were in our senior schools Bill had progressed to a Jaguar in British racing green. By the time we were finishing school and Bill and Janet were living in London, he had moved up to the imposing Jaguar XJ6 with dual fuel tanks, one on each side of the boot, requiring a very large wallet to fill. While this progression of cars clearly reflected his success as a businessman, they were also cars that he liked to drive. He never lost his interest in cars, from his beloved wartime jeep to his last Honda.

These cars were central to our family summer holidays which generally involved a very early morning drive to Dover for the channel ferry, a quick stop for moules et frites washed down with Stella Artois in Calais or Boulogne, and then long drives south to the Côte d'Azur or northern Italy or the Costa Brava. Bill would drive relentlessly on these holiday trips, with the three children taking it in turns to

---

* Dagenham in East London was where Ford cars were manufactured in England.

sit in the passenger front seat, reading the custom map provided by the Automobile Association, and telling him—from our vantage point, sitting on the left—when it was safe to overtake. Janet always sat in the back, wishing we could stop more often and earlier.

When we were young, we generally camped on the way, and Janet and Bill cooked up fried eggs to be eaten with a baguette on the side of the rural lane into which we had turned, looking for somewhere to spend the night. How we fitted an old canvas tent with wooden poles, cooking stove, utensils, clothes and beach equipment into the car I have no idea. These kinds of holidays, which we took for granted, were in fact unusual in the 1950s, with less than two percent of English families going abroad at the start of the decade. Looking back, I can see how much France had influenced Bill in what we ate and how we cooked (and how lucky we were in this). He was very particular about some things. We bought freshly roasted coffee beans in Sevenoaks, ground them in our wooden grinder with a drawer, and made espresso, using an Italian stove-top moka pot; our green salads were dressed with olive oil and vinegar; garlic was ever present; and Bill would make steak and chips, insisting the beef be rare ('saignant' even) and the chips be fried twice as in France, to achieve the right crispiness. He even went so far as to buy what was probably one of the first electric deep-fat fryers when they came onto the market so he could have perfect frites.

Sunday lunches were either a sirloin of beef, a leg of lamb or roast chicken. The lamb would be distinctly pink, and Bill carved it horizontally so that each slice got more rare, unlike the English practice of over-cooking it and then carving down onto the bone like slicing bread. In all this he and Janet were in complete sympathy, and I still remember Janet's pleasure in discovering Elizabeth David's *French Provincial Cooking* which was published in 1960. Elizabeth David had spent most of the 1940s in Athens, Alexandria, and Cairo. After the war, back in England and staying in a hotel in Ross-on-Wye, she writes about the terrible food:

> And still there was no excuse none, for such unspeakably dismal meals as in that dining room were put in front of me. To my agonized

homesickness for the sun and southern food was added an embattled rage that we should be asked—and should accept—the endurance of such cooking.

To comfort herself she began to write down descriptions of Mediterranean and Middle Eastern cooking. 'Even to write words like apricot, olives and butter, rice and lemons, oil and almonds, produced assuagement.'

Sunday lunches and later, as we got older, Sunday dinners were a consistent feature of Probert family life, and even after we had all moved out, they continued in London, including any girlfriends, boyfriends and friends from our childhood. Several of these friends remember that Bill was very generous with the drinks. They were one of the few moments when Bill was genuinely present. He enjoyed the role of pater familias in this context, dispensing generous hospitality, and I think it pleased us that our friends could experience it.

Throughout our childhood Bill was definitely not present, however, before Sunday lunch, as this was when he played golf. While he was on the links, Janet took the three of us—for as long as she had power over us—to holy communion in the Norman church in Kemsing, conducted by a very high Anglican vicar. Bill had no truck with any religion and Colin remembers him as a committed atheist. But these differences did not seem to be a source of any marital tension. Golf was not, of course, a game played by the working class and certainly not in the Rhondda. Nor was it played by anyone in Janet's family. But it was entirely appropriate for business executives, and the English like to joke about all the deals that get done on the golf course. It is also a game that you can play by yourself or with just one other person, which suited Bill's preferences. While it was a signifier of middle-class status, there was still room for status hierarchies in the game. In Sevenoaks there were two private golf clubs: Knole Park and the Wilderness. As my brother William puts it when I ask him about his memories of them: 'The Wilderness golf club was definitely the gin and Jaguar nob golf course'. We both think that this is why Bill played at Knole Park, where he always played with the same man, whom we knew only as a plumber. My mother found it hard to believe that a plumber was allowed to join Knole Park golf club when I asked her what she knew about him. But William and I think that Knole was less exclusive than the Wilderness. Bill was not trying to impress anyone by playing golf, it would seem, and he continued to play with serious enthusiasm even after moving to live in France—settling by chance near a town with the oldest golf course in France, a country far less enthusiastic about the game than England.

Despite no longer having a Bentley, Bill was able to arrange a substantial extension to our house on the North Downs by 1960, creating a new kitchen, a larger drawing room with parquet flooring, and a fourth bedroom and second bathroom. The one moment of consumer excitement that I clearly recall was his purchase of a rather beautiful hi-fi player in dark wood, standing on elegantly tapered legs in the new drawing room. Domestic hi-fi (high fidelity) became available from the mid-1950s, when recording quality began to improve with a fuller frequency range, and consumers realised that they would get much better sound from separate components put together in various kinds of consoles. The term 'hi-fi' became synonymous with componentry designed to deliver accurate sound reproduction. On our new player we listened to everything from Mozart's horn concertos played by Dennis Brain and recorded in 1953, to Burl Ives and Harry Belafonte. All his life Bill was interested in good equipment for playing records and tapes and finally CDs, sometimes asking my advice.

Bill was obviously musical, and could sing and whistle when he chose, unlike Janet who loved music but admitted to being totally tone deaf. When we found out about Bill's childhood home in Ynyshir, we also learned that there was—in this tiny house—what Denzil's widow described as a music room, with an organ and piano. Or rather, what might have been the front parlour was devoted to music. In our home we used to sing along to Belafonte's 'Banana Boat' song with Bill and laugh out loud listening to Victor Borge performing his phonetic punctuation. There were, however, no Welsh songs, and no evidence of Bill knowing what to do with a keyboard.

*

Reading the glossy magazine put out a couple of times a year by Mitchell Cotts in the 1950s and 60s provides not only insights into the nature and scale of the group's activities around the world in those decades, but also the social world inhabited by its executives. It was most definitely a man's world. In the photos that include Bill, whether in London or in Ecuador or Japan, there are no women except executive wives and geishas.

In issue number four (1957) there is a photograph taken at a luncheon at the Savoy, a luxury hotel on the Strand, to farewell a retiring director. In this picture Bill is seated with a number of identical-looking middle-aged men, and they are all focused on whoever is giving the farewell speech. The average age of the directors of Britain's large companies at this time was fifty-five, and most had never changed their job. Bill is noticeably younger than the others, only forty-two, and still new to the company, but he is smoking a very large cigar, dressed in an immaculate double-breasted suit, revealing a light-coloured pair of socks, and exuding confidence.

It is tempting to interpret the photograph in terms of Corelli Barnett's withering description of British industry in the 1950s.

> At the summit of the industrial system stood an elite predominantly blessed with the accent of the officers' mess: men bowler-hatted or homburged, wearing suits of military cut either bespoke or at least bought from such approved outfitters as Aquascutum or Simpsons of Piccadilly; gentlemen indeed, confident of manner, instantly recognizable by stance and gesture. They lived in large, detached houses on a couple of acres of garden in the suburbanized countryside that surrounded the great cities all within 'exclusive' private estates adjacent to the golf course. They drank gin and tonic; had lunch in a directors' dining room resembling as near as possible a club in St James's; dined in the evenings; drove a Humber, Rover, Alvis,

Lagonda or perhaps a Rolls Royce; and were married to ladies who played bridge.

Bill's colleague, who became chairman in the late 1960s, lived in exactly such a house in just such a location, beside the Wilderness golf club, where I remember him wielding the first electric carving knife I had ever seen. And the chairman did indeed have a Rolls Royce, though a driver drove it.

A few pages further on in *The Cottsman* there is a new two-page section headed FEMININE GENDER, which leads with a long piece about the year's Paris fashions. It includes a paragraph exhorting readers to TRY THIS SUMMER SALAD. Reading this recipe made me acutely aware of just how much Bill had protected us from English cooking.

> Heat two cups crushed pineapple. Add sugar and salt, stirring until dissolved. Melt two tablespoons of gelatine in hot pineapple mixture. Cool, and when mixture begins to thicken add four tablespoons lemon juice, one cup grated cheese, two tablespoons chopped green peppers, two tablespoons pimento, and finally fold in one cup whipped cream. Place in jelly-mould and garnish with slices of tomato and cucumber. Serve with mayonnaise.

The casual sexism of the times is evident, just as it was portrayed in the brilliant television series *Mad Men*. There are execrable sexist jokes sprinkled throughout *The Cottsman*.

> 'Women are not much, but they are the best other sex we have.'

> 'Why waste time trying to change your wife's character? Today, it's much easier to change your wife instead.'

Or from Gary Cooper:

> 'I don't always have horses in my pictures. Women are good to look at, too.'

Confronted with this evidence about Bill's workplace and his colleagues, I don't think he subscribed to this way of thinking about women. While he appears in black tie at company dinners, where everyone else is accompanied by their wives, Janet is never there. Perhaps because he was younger than most, and she had three children on her hands, but she would not have wished to go, and I do not believe he would have thought she needed to. As we know from the love letters he wrote her, he took her intellect seriously, and this did not change during his life. The only photograph in which she appears is from 1969 or 1970 (by which time they are living in London). It is taken at Grosvenor House, Park Lane, where the Road Hauliers Association is having its annual dinner. By this time Bill was in charge of the enormous transport and distribution businesses that Mitchell Cotts had bought into. In his black tie, cigarette in hand, Bill is looking bored. Janet, looking very elegant, is listening politely to the evening's entertainer, John Slater—a well-known character actor who usually played lugubrious, amiable cockney types. It is hard to imagine anywhere more incongruous for Janet to be, but she had a great capacity to be gracious in the most unlikely circumstances.

I imagine Bill's attendance at such events was mostly grudging. As our childhood friends have remembered him to me, he had little patience when anyone said something stupid. While he could be very charming indeed if he wished to, it was not often that he wished to. Indeed, Bill showed little interest in any kind of social life, despite Janet's ability to make friends and find common interests in the most varied of settings. The only friends of his that we ever met were Dicky Flynn and Michael Beswick, or Beeswax as we all affectionately called him.

Bill met Beeswax when they were both working for De La Rue in the early 1950s, before Bill joined Mitchell Cotts. Beeswax spent his whole working life managing the company's grand London facilities (and perhaps the wine cellar), a career almost the exact opposite of Bill's ambition and need for new experiences. Beeswax always wore brown corduroy trousers, brown brogues, and tweed jackets with leather patches on the elbows when he visited, but had a surprising sense of dry humour, could tell excellent shaggy dog stories, and took notice of children. The family visitor's book tells me that he came to stay quite often, bringing his second wife to stay in Wales as late as 1981.

It is hard to work out the basis of their friendship at this distance, but it was sufficiently strong for Michael to ask Bill to be godfather to his son, Nicholas. While Bill was competing his way through Porth County Boys, Beeswax was being educated at Bryanston School in Dorset, in an educational philosophy diametrically opposed to that of E.T., Porth's headmaster. Bryanston was a distinctive progressive public school that was established around the principles of the Dalton Plan in the 1920s. In this pedagogy, pupils work at their own pace and receive individual help from teachers when needed. There is no formal class instruction, but students draw up their own timetables and are responsible for completing their work. They are also encouraged to help each other with their work. Despite their backgrounds, Bill and Beeswax were probably drawn to each other by their shared enthusiasm for vintage motor cars and claret, with Beeswax being as devoted to his Bullnose Morris from the 1920s as Bill was to his Bentley. It also seems likely that it was Beeswax, a longstanding club golfer, who introduced Bill to the game and to its club structure—neither of which Bill had probably encountered before.

There was no reason to think that Bill was anything other than what he seemed, as he commuted to the city and played golf. But looking back I can see some interests and enthusiasms that were incongruous for a middle-class Englishman. While his sporting interests were varied, they included some which were distinctly working class or Welsh. He 'did the pools' with Littlewoods, for example, a huge betting concern after the war. From a printed list of football matches each week the challenge was to predict eight draws from fifty-five fixtures. Bill would mark his coupon and post it off, like literally millions of others. At 5 pm on Saturday, once we had a television, we would watch the reading out of the football results, game by game, division by division. David Kynaston says that it 'was an absolutely normal part of the urban working-class routine… All over the country, the ritual checking of scores was sacrosanct.' Winners received the money in that week's pool, minus Littlewoods profits. Many working-class men saw it as a safe form of investment, guaranteed by the integrity of the pool companies, unlike some seedy gambling operations. It felt as though 'the individual skill of the punter could lead to the winning of some life-changing jackpot cheque which was presented by a sporting personality or celebrity'.

We did not get our first television set until the late 1950s, from which point we children watched the usual popular programs such as *Popeye the Sailor* and the long-running *Adventures of Robin Hood* with Richard Greene, as well as the earnest BBC *Children's Hour*. In the early 1960s I think we all watched *That Was The Week That Was*. None of this was exceptional, but I think Bill's fondness for Benny Hill's TV show, with its slapstick and relentless sexual inuendo (not to be confused with Monty Python's 'nudge nudge, a nod is as good as a wink') came from his working-class origins.

We also grew up watching professional boxing on television, and Bill would occasionally go to watch a boxing match in person. Now I think about it, I don't think any of my school friends knew the difference between a south paw and an orthodox boxer, or between a technical knockout and the real thing. Henry Cooper and Joe Bugner, both British heavyweight champions, were admired by us. Writing to Janet from Spain in 1948 Bill complained: 'I'm quite furious that with the fourth test on and all the Olympic games, I get so little news. Only learnt by chance that we've got a new world boxing champ—old Freddy Mills.'* Janet would have had zero interest in this news (or any other sporting news), but as children we learned to share his enthusiasm, and never thought it unusual.

Boxing, I learn, was historically particularly popular in Wales, integral to regional culture and extremely popular with the working classes. Since the early twentieth century Wales has produced a notable number of professional boxers, including several world champions. It was adopted as a sport for the underprivileged in industrial South

---

* Freddie Mills became a friend of the notorious London gangsters, Ronnie and Reggie Kray, and died from a gunshot wound in 1965.

Wales, and Gareth Williams compares it to life in towns like Merthyr, with its terrible health and living conditions. The high rate of industrial injury and death in these places reminded the working class that life was short and brutal, just like boxing. A boxing-booth showman reported that Ferndale, just a little further up the valley from Ynyshir, 'was the roughest place in the valleys'. The mountain fighters 'used to come to the fairgrounds from the collieries with their gangs with them, most of them half drunk, and the very sight of them was enough to freeze the heart out of a bull terrier. Broken noses, black eyes, cauliflower ears, lumps knocked off 'em.' There is an extraordinarily violent description of a bare-fisted mountain fight behind Merthyr in Jack Jones' novel, *Black Parade*.

Kenneth O. Morgan, in his history of modern Wales, informs me that 'Freddy Welsh' from Pontypridd, just down the valley from Ynyshir, became lightweight champion of the world in 1914; and Jimmy Wilde from Tylorstown, a couple of miles further up the Rhondda Fach, became fly-weight champion of the world in 1916, 'probably the most skilful and successful British boxer there has ever been'. It is not surprising then that Bill should have been interested in the sport. It was, however, shocking to find a news report as recently as 2021 which featured a fight between the two best Welsh bare-knuckle boxers, in front of a sold-out crowd in London, during which both fighters received 'brutal injuries'.

Bill's enthusiasm for rugby union, which was also surely a product of his Welsh childhood, could pass for a regular upper middle-class interest in Kent, being played only in private schools in England. Like me, Colin remembers being taken to watch an international rugby game at Twickenham—or 'Twickers'. Colin also remembers Bill taking him to see his first Manchester United football game. This had a profound impact on Colin's life as he became a Man U 'tragic'. Less easy to place is Bill's love of motor-racing. As children we would always be taken to the Boxing Day Formula 1 race at nearby Brands Hatch (which from 1964 hosted the British Grand Prix). We saw the great Argentinian driver Juan Manuel Fangio as well as Stirling Moss race there, and later Jack Brabham and Jackie Stewart, and loved the sight of tyres being warmed up and the smell of high-octane fuel. Talking about sport with Bill or watching it on the television with him remain happy memories for each of us.

*

While Bill's interests do, in retrospect, seem a little out of the ordinary for stockbroker-belt Kent in the 1950s, they seemed quite ordinary to us. As did our strangely lop-sided extended family. The only grandparent we knew was Australian, and the only family connection that came with Lilla when she moved to live in England was her Australian niece, Joan, who became my godmother. Joan also moved to England after her first marriage in Australia ended in divorce. She then married an Englishman, and her three Australian children—our second cousins—were sent to boarding schools, in the stately homes of Charterhouse and Westonbirt. They did come to stay with us occasionally, but the youngest tells me that she found Bill very intimidating, remembering vividly her fear of being spoken to in French at the dinner table. Janet's mother showed as little interest in her own Australian family as she did in ours, being far too preoccupied with the United Nations and the Association of Country Women of the World. I do not recall her ever mentioning her twin brothers. It is not surprising that we did not think of ourselves as being part of an Australian family, or indeed as having any connection to Australia. It is all the more surprising that I have spent my entire adult life in Australia, and now feel distinctly Australian.

Even though Janet's father, Charles Russell, died in 1917, and Lilla never talked about him with his daughters, it is nonetheless his family to which we three Probert children feel we belong. I now find it curious that we showed so little interest in how we come to have a relatively uncommon, yet obviously Welsh, surname. I remember feeling slightly relieved when Rumpole of the Bailey took on a pupil called Liz Probert in the popular TV series.

When I ask my brothers if they think they are Proberts or Russells, without hesitation they say Russells. There are several possible reasons for this. The first is that the Russells are the only side of the family whose history we know—and it is a long history, embedded in the Essex countryside not a huge distance away from where we grew up. Janet experienced happy days before and during the Second World War staying at Stubbers, when it was home to her Uncle Champion and her much older cousins, Marjorie and Pam.

In our Probert family we played Edwardian games like 'Racing Demon', 'Charades' and 'Up Jenkins' because Janet had played them at Stubbers. We visited large country gardens when they were open to the public because gardening ran in the Russell genes. We read Edwardian children's books and children's poems from *The Golden Staircase*. Aunt Pam encouraged us to learn a poem off by heart for her visits. The ballad of Sir Patrick Spens was worth two shillings and sixpence.

The second reason we are Russells might be that Janet's cousins were very obviously interested in being our aunts—perhaps because neither had children of her own. Even when Marjorie moved to Massachusetts, she would send the best Christmas presents we ever received, while Pam would draw or make woodcuts of beautiful birds for us, creating a memorable Alphabet Bird Book for William. They were affectionate and engaged, and we had no other relatives like that. Or that we knew of at least. The third factor was that the Russells seemed to be admirable as well as likeable. They were well educated, enlightened, cultured, interested in the natural world as well as the social world, without snobbery. It is not surprising that we liked the idea of being Russells. I even gave my daughter the middle name Russell, despite knowing she might only ever meet one of them, namely her grandmother Janet. It is as though the Russell story simply expanded into the very large gap left by the absence of other relatives.

Janet took Bill to see the family home in Essex when they were married. The Russells had lived at Stubbers for over three-hundred years, getting Humphrey Repton to redesign the large gardens in 1796. Janet wanted Colin to have the middle name Champion, after her father's oldest brother who was still living there then. It was a name going back more than two centuries in the family.

It is impossible to know what Bill made of the Russell family and their privileged lives. When Janet found out about his working-class Welsh origins, she berated herself for never having wondered what he might have made of such a family home, and for not having considered whether he might have been intimidated by it. She asked her daughter-in-law, Jane, whether it might have been her fault that Bill kept his origins secret. Janet was herself singularly uninterested in questions of social status which explains, in part, her imaginative failure here. I think she was intrigued by the relatively exotic nature of Bill's family origins, and only distressed by the possibility that she had been insensitive with him. My brothers and I have no recollection of her feeling angry or blaming Bill for this late discovery of his Welsh family.

In thinking about this, both Colin and I find it hard to imagine Bill being intimidated by anything at that stage in his life. He had jettisoned Roy from the Rhondda and fully realised Bill-with-parachute-wings by the time he began to meet Janet's family. Nonetheless, I notice that in many of his letters from South America, Bill ends with sending love to Janet's mother and to her sister Ann but fails to send any to Pam—even though Janet was living with Pam while he was overseas. Bill and Janet were also living with Pam when I was born and Bill was looking for work in London, before they bought their own house. He did eventually write that he didn't know why he kept forgetting her. Was it because he was repressing anything that made him feel indebted to a Russell? Learning now that Bill accepted money from Marjorie to send the boys to Westminster School and knowing that he was able to take significant advantage of Pam's hospitality on two occasions, suggests to me that he appreciated them both and did not feel in any way threatened by them, or the Russell family's status. He was always far too prickly about owing favours or feeling indebted for him to have accepted these things otherwise.

*

It is difficult to write wisely about your own mother or father, at any time. It is certainly not easy to fully realise the social context in which they were formed, especially when such revolutionary changes have occurred in attitudes to family life in general and relationships between men and women and their children. It is particularly problematic when a parent turns out to have been keeping so many big secrets. Trying to dig them up is both risky—who knows what may emerge?—and somehow improper, although I am perhaps a throwback in this era of over-sharing. I am as curious about my parents as the next person, but I don't think I have a 'right' to know everything. And as I have been learning, the uncovered secrets require interpretation. I am writing this story about my parents, and I am aware they are not here to challenge it.

*

After I read his letters from South America, before we started on the project, I concluded that Bill loved and needed Janet from the moment they got to know each other in Vienna, and that despite their conventional division of family labour, he saw her as his intellectual equal. I think that at a profound level, he never stopped feeling that he was extraordinarily lucky. This is in no way to ignore the way their life was shaped by his priorities, nor the way the black moods he experienced as he grew older were unreasonably directed at her—or any one of us who happened to be present. I don't know when I first started to think of my father as 'difficult', but when friends who never met him ask me to tell them what I mean by the term, I find it hard to say. It certainly involved his capacity for getting angry and the difficulty of knowing what might trigger this. Colin thinks that, in middle age, this behaviour was linked to his growing frustration at work, the experience of 'disappointment and disillusionment' when he could go no further at Mitchell Cotts. He enjoyed reading the satirical *Private Eye* and *Le Canard Enchaîné* as he became increasingly disenchanted and cynical about business life. For a man who did not know how to stand still, it was perhaps unbearable. Drinking was a pressure-release valve, but it meant that the discharge was not directed at the problem. Colin tells me that knowing more about Bill's life fills him 'with poignant feelings'. Talking about him as we have learned more has given Colin 'a fresh perspective on him and the arc of his life'.

Bill's difficult side cannot, however, be reduced to the frustrations of a clever, brave and ambitious man thwarted by his time and place. There was also, I now think, some kind of deep-seated insecurity that might provoke an attack. I am suddenly reminded of one occasion when William and I arrived together to stay in the newly built house in Wales, driving down from Lancaster where we were living. I think we were larking about, being close in our own particular way, and Bill did not like it. I do not remember how this expressed itself, but I knew he felt left out or rather threatened by our intimacy. This in turn reminds me that he did not like it when the big boxer dog he inherited in the Béarn showed a preference for one of us instead of him. This is perhaps somehow connected to Bill's childhood and the severing of his relationship with his mother. But he is not here to lie on the psychoanalyst's couch for me.

Janet wrote to me after they were settled in the Pyrenees with uncharacteristic clarity about Bill being difficult.

> I am very pleased with my new laid-back 1985 self—it's working a treat. We've had a very peaceful happy month. What have I got to get into a tiz about? Why argue about domestic trivia or be critical? As a result we don't get into the situation when OGP [Old Grumpy Patch] feels threatened and attacks and then feels worse and must justify it and the black dog appears and it's all tears and sprained ankles. And in case you feel I am giving way all along the line, I don't have to speak for him to know how I am feeling!

*

As I began digging up as much as I could about Bill's life, I felt reasonably confident that I would not come across a mistress or even an extra-marital affair, despite Bigeard's descriptions of him during the war. His good fortune was to have married someone who must have understood him in some profound way. Not only that, but Janet had a remarkable ability to adapt to the upheavals he caused in order to ward off whatever demons or sheer boredom he was experiencing. When this involved uprooting her (and she was very good at putting down roots in all types of soils) and moving her from Kent to London, from London to Pembrokeshire and from Pembrokeshire to the French Pyrenees, she might have been forgiven for feeling aggrieved. There is no doubt she set off without enthusiasm on each occasion, but she also insisted that she always ended up being eternally grateful for the experiences that these moves made possible. In the meantime, as children we were not uprooted, living on the Pilgrims Way until we were ready and eager to leave.

My brother William reminds me of warm family moments with our father, like when he would ripple his biceps under his jumper, saying there was a mouse loose in there; or play with our hamster on the cleared dinner table on Saturday evenings. William suggests that the hamster, who was called Gubbins, was probably named after General Gubbins of SOE. Sunday morning breakfasts were another family affair, with coffee, bacon and eggs and the *Sunday Times* and the *Sunday Observer* providing each of us with a piece of the paper to read once the colour supplements were introduced. We all remember at least a few long summer evenings when Bill might take us to the outdoor swimming pool at Hildenborough after he got home from work, or play French cricket with us on the lawn.

Very occasionally Bill would read out loud to us (usually sitting round the coal fire in the drawing room), and the works we clearly remember are *Tales by Saki*, the pen-name of H. H. Munro, a British writer of witty and sometimes macabre stories satirising Edwardian society and culture; and Jim Corbett's *Man-Eating Tigers of Kumaon*. Saki's story 'Shredni Vasta' involves an unloved child, Conradin, and his polecat ferret, kept in a shed in the garden. Conradin prays that Shredni Vasta, the ferret, will organise retribution against his unkind guardian aunt, and when the ferret kills her, Conradin calmly butters another slice of toast. While these tales were disturbing but fascinating, the stories about man-eating tigers were truly terrifying and on one occasion William and I were about to climb out of our upper-storey bedroom window to get help from the missionary down the road who had spent time in Africa, since we were convinced that a tiger was killing our parents down the hallway. As we were about to lower ourselves out of the window, the lights came on in the hall and Janet appeared to turn on the hot taps to release the boiling water which was rumbling in the tank in the roof. Bill also encouraged us all to read C. S. Forester's Hornblower series, and later Simenon's Maigret detective stories, followed by Nicholas Freeling's Van der Valk books. In the first series of these, the Dutch detective has a French wife, Arlette, whose gourmet cooking is regularly contrasted with that of stodgy Dutch wives, allowing Freeling to write about his experience of being a chef and his love of food. Arlette undoubtedly appealed to Bill, and to me. All this reminds me of the cosmopolitan and outward-looking way our household operated.

Perhaps I am enjoying these discoveries and memories because I have been quick to think critically about my father ever since I was a teenager, finding his unpredictability difficult to handle, and being quick to fight back. Keeping him at an emotional distance was always my protective mechanism, my way of not minding too much when he went on the attack. I have been reminded of my eight- or nine-year old self who found that a school friend had the father that I really wanted. We would occasionally spend the day at each other's houses or even spend the night, so he was not just a figment of my imagination. I would dawdle on my morning walk to the bus-stop for school, hoping that Mr Medd would drive past me on his way to the railway station and we could wave at each other.

In my teens I started to spend all my weekends on a sheep farm owned by an eccentric gentleman farmer, who gave me total freedom to learn by doing. When I was about thirteen, we were driving up through the fields in his old Bedford van, when he stopped at a closed gate and told me to take over. He did the same with his tractor when ploughing a field, never protesting when I hit a gate post as he must have known I would. I think my enthusiasm for these weekends was, in part, a desire to avoid risky family situations. When my own teenage children were not getting on, my mother wrote to me saying, 'I remember how trying it was when you and Colin couldn't bear each other and became both v. disagreeable. Luckily you disappeared to Death Hill [the location of the farm] whenever possible!'

At the same time, those weekends gave me the kind of confidence in my practical abilities that any teenager might enjoy. Perhaps they offset the growing sense that I was, in some respects, a disappointment to my father—an argumentative tomboy rather than an elegant young woman with a subtle and feminine intellect. When I was a bit older, I remember two men—family friends whom I liked and respected—managed separately to let me know that they understood Bill was not an easy father to have, and this created an unexpected and much appreciated sense of validation.

*

I realise I am prickling defensively when I read an account of how Bill dealt with Janet's Oxford friends. Hermione Lee, in her biography of the most famous of them, Penelope Fitzgerald, writes that Mops, as she was known, saw less of Janet after her marriage, as Bill was 'jealous of her old Oxford friends', and actively distanced Janet from them. Indeed, Janet wrote to me that while Bill liked Mops' husband, he 'took instantly against Mops ... when I took him to some Knox party, thinking he'd be sure to like her'. After Bill's death, Hugh Lee—who was part of the tight Oxford circle that included Penelope and Janet—wrote to her to express his sadness, noting that he had been lucky not to 'get bitten' by Bill. Ham, as he was known, thought that he probably escaped this fate because he understood Bill's attachment to his Bentley. 'I think it was that I shared his love for that old Bentley, all too soon given up for the Ford of a family man. He even invited me down for manual labour in Wales, do you remember?' In the photo album I find pictures of Ham and his wife visiting Bill and Janet around the time I was born, and then again years later, at The Halt. My mother told me that Bill accepted both Ham and Margaret, another member of their Oxford group. But it is true that none of her other friends stayed close.

This is a difficult topic. Janet was never putty in Bill's hands, but it was also the case for all of us that you did not attempt to reason your way out of any major disagreement when Bill had become angry. He did indeed bite. But did he particularly dislike Janet's friends for some reason? He would not have been intellectually intimidated by them, but might he have been jealous of the kind of friendship they shared? Or did he know that despite his erudition he might always be an outsider in that tight, intensely connected group of friends? He would occasionally accuse Janet of being 'frivolous' (just as she accused herself about her Oxford days). This seems a ridiculous criticism of any of her friends as individuals, but perhaps there was also a collective frivolity that grated with Bill. As a group, did they represent a kind of taken-for-granted intellectual privilege about which he was scornful, precisely because of the precarious nature of his own education and their blissful ignorance about working-class deprivation?

Aware that defensiveness might be clouding my judgment, I was particularly happy to find convincing support for my speculation in David Kynaston's account of how the public received Kingsley Amis' novel *Lucky Jim*, published in 1954. Reviewers recognised in the central character, Jim Dixon, an anti-hero who 'after getting a scholarship and Oxford or Cambridge degree, finds his social position both precarious and at odds with his training'. As Amis himself explained later:

> [Dixon] is a plausible figure in his world: there are certainly many like him in that they are the first generation in their families to have received a university education, they have won their way up by scholarships all through, they are not the conventional Oxford-Cambridge academic type, they don't embrace the manners, customs and pastimes of that type ... but stick to their own, to the ones their non-academic contemporaries share (beer, arguments in pubs, amorous behaviour at—and outside—dances, jazz). Dixon has seen, throughout his life, power and position going to people who (he suspects) are less notable for their ability than their smooth manners,

their accents, the influence they or their fathers can wield. The money thing is less important; Dixon is hard-up himself, and is a bit suspicious of the rich, but is far more so of Oxford-accented 'culture'.

Whatever the reason, there is no doubt that Bill had few friends of any kind. He did, however, take a real interest in several of our teenage friends, some of whom sent me their recollections as I tried to reconstruct these years. A friend of Colin's who came regularly to the house wrote:

> Throughout my teenage years and indeed my life, Bill was a benign presence, and always very welcoming. I remember the gallic shrugs and the expressive pouts (if that is the word), how he would sometimes speak in French to express his thoughts and ideas ... I was often in attendance for Saturday night suppers ... I remember his presence and moods seemed to dominate the table usually in a positive way. He had a good sense of humour and although often critical he also liked a lot of people.

I am not sure how many people Bill really liked, but he seemed most at ease with young people who were not intimidated by him, especially if he could show them how to make proper frites and a vinaigrette, or an Old-fashioned cocktail. The only person of his own age that he saw regularly and willingly outside his work was the plumber with whom he chose to play golf every week, and whom none of us ever met. Later in his life he found it easier to be friendly with a canny Welsh farmer who was probably slightly crooked than with any well-educated Englishman. As for Marcel Bigeard, it seems that once the evidence of his involvement in the torture of Algerians who supported the Algerian national liberation struggle in the late 1950s and early 1960s started to surface in France, Bill rejected the prospect of having anything more to do with him.* In an almost plaintive voice, Bigeard writes in one of his later memoirs, 'Where is Bill and his beautiful wife?'

---

* It would seem that the British instructor at the SOE camp in Algiers, who noted that Bigeard's attitude to interrogations 'was far too aggressive', was prescient.

There is a pattern here which somehow seems less odd once Bill's origins in the Rhondda become visible. But I hesitate to say I understand it. In researching his life I have found only two real friends, both of whom were close to him in North Africa. What do Dicky Flynn and Michael Wormald have in common? I think he respected both of them, intellectually, and in the way they conducted themselves during the North Africa campaigns. The intensity and proximity of army life, the possibility of adventure, and a shared appreciation of the desert and the island of Madagascar created strong bonds for a young man who was increasingly detached from his past. Bill was quite capable of forming golf-course friendships and I do not doubt his fondness for Beeswax, but he came to rely completely on Janet for intimate company. He did not mind leaving her on his relentless travels, but he did not like her to leave him. She wrote to me about the difficulty he had 'in making close relationships and in showing affection' and the resulting 'crucial importance' of his wife. Indeed, she was taken aback when he encouraged her to come and stay with me in Melbourne when my first baby was born.

Knowing nothing about the emotional patterns in the Probert household in Gynor Place it is unwise to speculate about the basis of Bill's social isolation. But that is surely where the answers lie.

*

It is not surprising that Janet was the practical centre of our lives, with Bill on the periphery. He was not away from home any more than his work (and golf) required him to be, and there are several photos of him re-organising the garden. He cared about our academic success, and Colin says Bill was all over his homework. I have no such memories, but we all agree that Bill knew very little about our school lives, and we do not believe he ever set foot in any school we attended. He would, however, occasionally take me to some distant lacrosse pitch on a Saturday, or collect me from a tennis tournament somewhere in Kent. I have one clear memory of him coming to collect me from Sevenoaks railway station, perhaps after a game for the East of Kent.

Several other team members who were school boarders, together with our distinctly attractive sports mistress, were also waiting at the station and I remember the sense of pride as he drove up in his Jaguar and offered to pile everyone in and drop them back at the school. This surely reflects the rarity of such an event.

The first time I remember Bill giving me a 'clip round the head' was when, aged about seven or eight, I took some scissors to my unruly hair and cut off my curly fringe. I think he arrived home from work, came upstairs to my bedroom, saw what I had done and was very angry. It is hard to understand why. David Kynaston writes that it is 'undeniable that many 1950s parents—especially fathers—could be harsh or authoritarian or remote figures to their children'. But somehow this does not capture our experience. Apart from Mr Medd, the fathers of our friends were mostly very distant and much stricter than Bill. William reminded me how we were allowed to smoke cigarettes, even at the dining table, when we were quite young. He vividly remembers being a small boy and Bill suddenly putting him on his lap while driving into Sevenoaks, suggesting that he could steer.

Bill was, however, unpredictable. My brothers and I remember sitting at Sunday lunch, knowing that somebody was about to be on the receiving end of one of his outbursts. This did not happen very often, but our wariness stemmed from never knowing what had provoked any particular outburst, and the fact that there was nothing that could be done to prevent it. I can see now that my anxiety was caused by his unpredictability. But because of this unpredictability it was also particularly rewarding when he decided to be utterly charming to a friend or visitor, who would find it irresistible. Colin thinks that Bill knew how to use his charm in what could be manipulative ways. The problem was that you never knew when he would turn on one of us. William describes it more charitably as Bill being 'inconsistent', but the effect is the same: you never could be certain about what might make him angry, so you needed to be on your guard. Even being on your guard did not help, though, as there was nothing you could do to deflect it.

Asking my brothers to describe their relationship with Bill as children, I realise again how differently we experienced him. Colin reveals, to my surprise, that he 'idolized him', fearing his anger and disapproval but feeling 'it was always for my own good and my benefit'. Colin thinks that part of the reason he has 'been plagued by insecurity, fear and anxiety ... may have been my boyhood feelings of inferiority, of not measuring up. Perhaps he was the standard I would never measure up to.' I think Bill felt protective of his youngest son, William, perhaps from a very early age, but William tells me as he grew older he did not feel able 'to be myself with him and had never been able to feel at ease with him'. They have both found moments in our re-thinking of our father's life to be quite overwhelming. I, in turn, am deeply touched by their reactions, but I can see that I was never as vulnerable as them. This must surely be because it is natural for sons to want to admire their fathers, be loved by them, and to live up to their father's expectations. As the only girl, I was perhaps freer to defy him when I needed to, knowing that my mother had my back.

*

Bill's unpredictable outbursts were never aimed at anyone outside the family—to their face, at least—as far as I remember. But he was a man that nobody took for granted. Our cousin Mike remembers him as always very positive, but capable of being 'shouty' and 'grumpy', 'possibly overbearing'. 'He was not easy to disagree with!' Mike says that 'we were all a little careful around him'. He could get angry. He remembers Bill shouting 'Basta!' very aggressively to someone beating their dog in the Spanish seaside town of L'Estartit (while we were all on holiday together). Others remember his capacity to be crushingly dismissive about anyone he despised. In a letter Bill wrote to me I have a perfect example of this, in a description of one of Janet's eccentric cousins in which his contempt for the way she squandered her unearned wealth leaps off the page.

As we got older, more potentially dangerous points of tension emerged. We became teenagers just as the sixties began to swing, and some elements of a wider cultural revolution reached down even into the Kent countryside. Bill was in no sense a conservative and did not care for the emerging racist politics being promoted by Enoch Powell, with his 'rivers of blood speech' opposing mass Commonwealth immigration. I don't know how he voted, or if he voted, but I am fairly certain he would have baulked at voting Labour, mainly because he doubted the capacity of any government to fix a serious problem. When I made the mistake of sticking a Vote Labour poster to our front window after we moved to London in 1968, this provoked a major rage. A few years later, after inviting me to join him on a short fly-fishing holiday in the Republic of Ireland, we fell out dramatically over some political argument. I have no recollection of the subject, but a friend still remembers me talking about it, so intense were the exchanges.

I don't know what provoked this particular response, but not long before he moved to France, Bill wrote to me:

> Your notions about politics astonish and dismay. One of the few honest politicians in this country pointed out that to administer a country, there had to be continuity and that politicians who stay in power must therefore and of necessity be venal and corrupt. This is patently true.

He was not really capable of a calm discussion about opposing views, perhaps partly because he was unable to admit to or explain the origins of some of his most strongly held beliefs. If you have so painstakingly erased your own past, you must keep the lid firmly screwed down on many things. I was not good at calm discussion either.

While Bill was alive, the risk of an explosion between us was always there. When I moved to Australia in 1976, we could exchange affectionate letters, which he often signed off as O.G.P. or Old Grumpy Patch—the sobriquet I gave him at some point and which he happily adopted. Over time, our reunions—in France or Australia—involved my own family, and somehow this reduced the chance of conflict. But when I visited the Béarn on my own, I would be wary.

Even before I fully appreciated the dangers of political disagreements, I began to feel that I was a disappointment to him in some ways. He was, for some curious reason, very opinionated about how women should look. Even in his love letters to Janet when they are first married, he wants to stop her wearing what seems to have been her favourite red dress, and he does not at all like a shorter haircut she adopts at that time. His reaction to my fringe cutting is of the same kind, I suspect. What he wanted, quite explicitly, was a wife and daughter who were elegantly dressed and traditionally coiffed, though we did not have to bite our tongues. I never felt he wanted me to be quieter. Now that I have seen those rare photos of Roy as a dandy, I think he both enjoyed clothes and used them to signal his attitude to life from an early age. He might have changed his style over time, but style mattered to him.

After they went to live in France (and probably while in Wales), Bill would regularly insist that Janet go and buy some new, smarter clothes. Shortly after they settled in the Pyrenees he wrote to me:

> Your Mum looks very well and seems to be settling down to a pleasantly active exile. It is my sneaky intention to change her habit of dressing like a dishevelled bumble bee à la Oxfam and gently to persuade her to 'faire valoir' her natural charm and elegance. She doesn't have to look like Ivy Leonard, does she? Write soon and small, darling, so that your letter will be longer altho' the same size. Profound and deferential affection from your old Dad.

Ivy was one of my mother's closest friends from the Pilgrims Way and also my piano teacher (with a back-scratcher for administering admonishing taps when I hit a wrong note); she was unconventional and dowdily dressed. Janet wrote to me not long after this letter from Bill arrived. 'As soon as the weather changes, I shall go shopping for clothes—Bill is constantly harrying me to buy some expensive clothes. Shopping, or trying to, is a bane when you don't know where to go.'

From the 1950s Janet always wore her hair up (grey from a young age), in a French roll which suited her perfectly, and she only suffered rebukes from Bill about stray hairs that had to be tidied before dinner.

She was also naturally tall and elegant, wearing the sheath dresses of the sixties with style. I, on the other hand, had impossibly inelegant curly hair (inherited from Bill) and was happiest in jeans on a farm. I was also inclined to argue and was incapable of turning the other cheek. As for Bill himself, he is remembered by our childhood friends as always well-dressed, even casually. He always had a comb to hand to settle his wavy hair into place if needed.

*

While I felt that I failed to live up to Bill's expectations about how women should look, I have no recollection of feeling that I failed to live up to any other expectations he may have had. Rather, I felt that he was not interested in the life I had chosen—or fallen into. Janet, at least, sat down with me when I told her I was thinking of taking a job in Australia (and reluctantly agreed it was a good idea). I do not recall Bill expressing a view (but this may be my faulty memory). I am more certain that he never congratulated me on finishing my PhD, or getting a book published, nor my university career. Bill had always liked that I was good at languages, but he had no time for the social sciences. He would be much more interested in my driving an old panel van across the Nullarbor, or doing up an old house. From time to time, he would come up with an idea which resembled his sheep farming plan for William—like buying a place in the country for me which he could use as a base for fishing or bush-walking in Australia. I quite liked the ideas, but they made no sense in the context of my actual life. When planning his move to France he wrote to say, 'Why not take a sabbatical and prepare some kind of thesis or book on a French subject—live among real intellectuals for a while. I would subsidize you generously and we'd love so much to have you with us for a while.' Nothing that I have learned about his secrets really helps to explain this parental approach. Living on the other side of the world probably meant I minded less about this lack of attention to the realities of my life, and it was compensated for by what I saw as my mother's approbation—which was far from undiscerning.

*

The years of family life on the North Downs were stimulating enough for Bill to keep boredom and frustration at bay. Work for Mitchell Cotts was neither routine nor predictable and took him almost every year on lengthy trips to North Africa, South Africa, the Middle East and Europe and then North and South America. I can now see how perfectly Bill was matched to his job and appreciate how it allowed him to enjoy travelling to so many interesting countries, using his gift for languages, and making keen observations about unfamiliar places. He was also lucky (or was it his genius?) to have married someone who had her own interests, who studied textile art as soon as we were all at school and became a talented artist herself. I had no sense that she resented his absences. We, his children, had never known anything different, and it was more exciting to have a father returning from Cairo or Quito with mysterious souvenirs than a man in a bowler hat returning from the city with his briefcase.

Chapter 7
Boredom and Frustration: From the City to the River Teifi

In 1967 Bill decided his family should leave the Pilgrims Way and move to London. Then in my last year of school, I remember going with Janet to inspect some three- or four-storey townhouses in Kensington and Notting Hill Gate and being surprised and impressed that we could afford to look at such desirable places. There were several possible reasons for such a move, but it was an unusual thing to do at that stage in a man's life. I suspect that it happened because Bill was increasingly bored with Kent. He may also have tired of the long daily drive into the city in his Jaguar, smoking cigars and listening to Jack de Manio's morning news program for the BBC. His job was also evolving.

The Cottsman tells me that in 1965 his work took him to Gibraltar, the USA, the Bahamas, Ecuador, Italy and Iran. In 1966 he was again in the USA, but also Romania, Bulgaria, Egypt and Lebanon. Later that year he made two more trips to the USA, one of which extended south to Ecuador, probably for his last visit. The magazine announces that with effect from 1 July, 'W. R. Probert has been transferred to Mitchell Cotts Group Ltd in which company he will hold executive responsibility ... for the activities of all operating companies in Cotts House and for Group pyrethrum sales. He will also be concerned with the development of commercial activities of an international character throughout the Group.' The group comprised about 130 companies in twenty-one countries, with 27,000 employees—mostly in Africa. This represented a very wide spectrum of businesses, creating what some might have seen as challenging responsibilities.

Until this time, the group had derived most of its profits from activities carried on outside the United Kingdom. But Mitchell Cotts, like many of the biggest British trading companies was now refocusing its businesses within Britain (and Australia); opportunities overseas were shrinking as vigorous anti-colonial regimes emerged. In the words of the newly appointed chairman, Ken Dick, 'the tempo of political change overseas had steered the group's efforts towards the type of equilibrium that could only be ensured by greater participation in commerce and industry at home'. In 1967 Mitchell Cotts began investing strongly in UK transport, haulage and warehousing, creating Mitchell Cotts Transport Ltd as a 'vehicle for expansion', with an initial fleet of 1200 vehicles and a vast twenty-six-acre warehousing project in Staffordshire. This was followed by the purchase of the West Kent Cold Storage Company, the largest cold store business in the south of England, only eighteen miles from London's docklands. *The Cottsman* reveals that following this re-organisation, 'W. R. Probert becomes additionally responsible for all the transport and warehousing activities of the Group in the UK.' In 1968, as another element in this refocusing strategy, the company expanded its engineering interests and industrial manufacturing in England, and these were also added to Bill's responsibilities.

As I read all this, I can better understand how he was able to afford a nice house in London. But, for the first time, I can also appreciate his talents as a businessman. Bill was in his early fifties by then, and had a great deal to show for his time at Mitchell Cotts. I feel something like regret that I was too busy joining in the noisy anti-imperial and anti-capitalist protests of the late 1960s to notice what he was doing and how much he had on his plate. As well as the twinge of regret, however, there is enjoyment to be found in reading these accounts of his achievements and seeing the photographs of him—from his early forties to his late fifties—staring confidently out of the pages of *The Cottsman*. It occurs to me that he had not just done well, but that the work he found with Mitchell Cotts gave him great satisfaction.

The move to London made sense for us all only if you ignore the fact that we three children were unlikely to stay much longer in the family home, whether it was on the Pilgrims Way or in Notting Hill Gate. But it certainly made short-term sense. Colin had left Westminster with two A levels (because it seems Westminster did not deem it necessary for their boys to do three like everyone else), and Bill discouraged him from bothering with university unless it was Oxford or Cambridge. His view was that Colin would learn more from three years' experience working for a good company, so he got him to apply to the top fifty companies in England. In those days that meant sending off fifty type-written letters and waiting to see what came back. Colin tells me that Bill had an idea advertising would suit him. 'I thought he thought advertising was insubstantial and superficial and that I was too—probably because I was so into rock and roll and popular fads like longer hair and Chelsea boots.' First though, Bill suggested a sort of 'gap' year, and took Colin with him on a trip to New York (which Colin remembers as an extraordinarily exciting city) and then on to Ecuador, where he left him to spend time in the Amazon basin on the new Mitchell Cotts tea plantation, trying to avoid being bitten by piranha fish.

On his return from the Amazon, Colin got his first toe-hold at the bottom of the advertising industry without difficulty and began as a proof runner in the traffic department of a top London agency called Pritchard Wood. He ran round the agency with proofs of ads that had to be signed off by the writer, art director and account executive before release to publication. Within a year he had been promoted to assistant account executive. This should have alerted us all to the possibility that he was going to have his own stellar career. But for now, he was twenty, living at home and still commuting with Bill to London every day, patiently waiting downstairs at Cotts House until Bill left the bar on the top floor and drove him home in the Jaguar.

William was still at school at Westminster, also commuting every day on the train, and I had opted for an economics degree at University College, London (UCL). Janet had no desire to move but would have stood little chance in the discussion. This should not, however, be taken to mean that her views counted for nothing with Bill. I think it is rather that she would have found it difficult to mount a persuasive counterargument in the face of our collective enthusiasm for leaving the Kent commuter-belt.

Bill and Janet agreed on a handsome four-storey, four-bedroom terrace house just south of Kensington High Street, with a garage in the basement. Shortly after moving in, Bill came home with the enormous Jaguar XJ6. And then insisted on getting a yellow Mini-Moke for Janet who, while being a great enthusiast for convertible cars and having the roof down in all weathers, would have preferred to stick with her convertible Triumph Herald. Perhaps the Mini-Moke came his way from his work with the Transport Group, but it was certainly a standout in Kensington. Janet and I ended up enjoying ourselves with it, since it was still possible to drive around London with relative ease at that time. I remember cruising through Knightsbridge on my way to see university friends in Hampstead, feeling extremely cool. (It was also cold and draughty in most seasons, with flapping, zipped-up sides.)

Despite the obvious career success, the purchase of a very desirable house in London, the powerful car in the garage, it is easy to see in retrospect that Bill was no longer really enjoying life. As he began to travel to Birmingham as opposed to Cairo or Quito, he became more difficult to live with, more irascible, more likely to drink hard and late. There was no more Sunday morning golf with the plumber and nothing to take its place. We were all tiptoeing around him at home, and if he returned late my brothers and I sometimes lurked in the TV room in the basement, hoping he would not bother to check us out. The danger was the familiar one of an unpredictable explosion, only the risk was now greatly increased by his habit of ending the day in the rather nice bar at the top of Mitchell Cotts House. We held our breath as he swung his large expensive car into the very narrow driveway and down under the house. He was a good driver, but it was a miracle that he managed to get it in sometimes. I think there were a few tell-tale pockmarks around the front door keyhole. When he drank he seemed to start looking for trouble, and usually ended up making it. We were not frightened in any sense, but certainly apprehensive. I think we always knew that we were not really the target of his outbursts, and that they were about his own inability to deal with things that we simply did not understand. And at that age, like most young adults, we were focused on our own lives, not that of our parents. This was undoubtedly a bad time for Janet, but she never shared any of her own difficulties with us. She would have considered that completely inappropriate.

At the same time as his work was becoming more humdrum, Bill was being given plenty of reasons to find his children increasingly irritating. It is hard to remember from here just how pervasive the generational clashes were in the late 1960s—over drugs, haircuts, clothes and music as well as the meaning of life and politics. In France the student movement almost toppled the government, while anti-war sentiment spread from the US across Europe. My brothers went in for the drugs and rock and roll, while I went in for the increasingly oppositional politics. Re-reading Bill's letters I found one, written from France in 1983, that really surprises me. He had found himself unexpectedly listening to that 1966 hit song 'Winchester Cathedral', through his satellite dish.

> This made me feel intensely nostalgic for that long-ago when my three children, whose names momentarily escape me, were growing up in the enjoyment of that happy, intoxicating ferment of the time. I wonder if your recollection of the period is as vivid as my own? You were fortunate to be young <u>then</u> and not now.

As a student at London University, I was spending a lot of time protesting against the Vietnam war outside the US embassy in Mayfair or marching between University College and the London School of Economics opposing or demanding something or other. Bill was lucky that Germaine Greer's *The Female Eunuch* wasn't published until I was too busy doing finals exams to read it.

I don't recall the substance of any particular blow-up with Bill over politics, and it was in any case usually impossible to know the cause of any particular falling-out. It was as though he wanted to provoke—or was it that he couldn't bear to see his children adopt stands he thought profoundly stupid? He must at least have been aware of my tendency to take the hook. Looking back, I can see one moment that could easily have been a flashpoint, with my naïveté crashing into his substantial life experience, but where he held back.

Seeking some way to get involved in student politics I volunteered at the University of London student newspaper, which was then being edited by an older American draft dodger. My one and only assignment was to go and interview the then principal of King's College about the Vietnam War. General Sir John Hackett was a man whom the draft dodger may well have assumed was an unmitigated militarist. I was a green undergraduate, probably full of moral zeal but ill-informed about most things. I remember being received graciously by Sir John in his office, and trying to scribble down what he said in answer to my questions—which I assume were largely about his attitude to the Vietnam War, and the student protests.

Until I set to work researching Bill's war experiences, I had completely forgotten this embarrassing event, or perhaps I repressed it, for I must have known I was way out of my depth. I was certainly given no more journalistic assignments. It came back to me when reading background material about the North Africa campaigns, where I learned about John Hackett's highly respected military record with the most elite and eccentric of units, such as the Long Range Desert Group, Popski's Army and the Special Air Services. He was another gifted linguist. In 1943 Hackett went on to command the 4th Parachute Brigade, set up in the Middle East. Bill would certainly have known about him and possibly met him during the war, as he was also a key figure in the training of operatives like Bill for political warfare and SOE. Reading about these military units, it suddenly dawned on me that this was the man I interviewed in 1969, about whom I had known absolutely nothing except that he had been a career army officer. And this realisation brought back a clear memory of Bill's agitation when I told him I was going to be doing the interview, which I now see as evidence of his legitimate concern about how I might comport myself. Sadly, Bill said nothing about his knowledge of Sir John, and what I assume would have been respect for his military activities during the war. And if he had, would I have been able, at that time of generational conflict, to hear what he was saying? Now that I know a great deal more about Bill's own wartime experiences in North Africa, I think it is quite remarkable that he did not explode at the very idea of my challenging Hackett. But then again, his explosions never seemed to be about anything obvious.

The worst blow-up between me and my father occurred in a black cab when we were both, for some reason, travelling from the Mitchell Cotts offices in the city back to our house in Kensington. Bill had, I think, been on the top floor having a drink or three which is possibly why he was coming home in a taxi. At some point on the way home he started to get stuck into me (who knows what about, and it is in any case irrelevant). As we inched around the traffic at Hyde Park Corner, I couldn't stand it any longer, opened the cab door and got out into the traffic (and surely slammed the door shut). I stayed away from home for several days; I was not going to back down. Bill was not going to back down. Janet signalled to me that she could see he was sorry and wanted me to come home, but we knew that he could never bring himself to say this.

We all reacted differently to these explosions, though I was the only door-slammer. Later Janet would say that she felt bad that she was unable to protect us, but she knew that if she joined in it would only make things much worse. Sometime around then she told me that the way she coped with it was to tell herself that he was sometimes ill. I found this very useful as it prevented futile attempts to apply reason to the problem. But looking back, I also think it led to a kind of wary distance between me and my father. It helped me not mind as much, but it made me care less. It ended up being a kind of wall between us that made me less vulnerable to his outbursts, but which also made me love him less.

My solution was to get away. I found out that I could get a bigger maintenance grant on the grounds of family problems, and I moved out to a lonely flat at the bottom of Hampstead Hill, where I could not afford to put coins in the electric heater. I have one memory of discussing the grant application with Janet in the kitchen in Kensington. As I recall, Janet said something like, 'If things don't improve, I may move out too.' Her words were more elliptical, as she would never have said anything so crude, but the meaning seemed clear to me. This was the only time I ever remember her letting me see how she felt about the way that Bill was behaving. Decades later she could write to me about the challenges of living with Bill.

But whatever my fights with him, in the end I would unbend and return home, or signal the end of hostilities, knowing that Bill probably regretted what had happened. There were good things to return home to, quite apart from Janet and the house and its location. There were still Sunday dinners, with our friends welcome. There would be gin and tonics all round, a perfectly cooked roast of some kind, always a pudding, wine, and a lot of conversation. And Bill could be calm and supportive about just the thing you might imagine was going to cause trouble.

I have mixed feelings about the idea of analysing the relationship between one's parents, perhaps because at some more fundamental level I think children should be able to take their parents for granted. At the same time, I know that each person's expectations of intimate relationships must be coloured by their perceptions of the way their parents related to each other. In thinking about how extraordinarily lucky Bill was to have found Janet, I am struck by the occasions where Janet insisted that she was equally lucky to have found him. My brothers and I agree that this was a relationship of equals at some vital level. Reading the letters Bill wrote her in the late 1940s and early 1950s, it is abundantly clear that he was in no doubt about his good fortune and was profoundly grateful for it. I think his feelings did not change in this respect. He did not mellow as he aged, but he was able to find new enthusiasms to engage his intelligence which somehow helped disperse the black clouds.

I was the only one in the family who spat the dummy, walking out, unable to sit and take it as much as unwilling. I am the one most like him. Looking back, I can see that my reactions were probably influenced by the women's liberation movement in the 1970s. My mother kept a letter I wrote to her from Belfast in January 1972, in which I describe how I had just finished reading Germaine Greer's *The Female Eunuch*.

It gave me tremendous comfort in a way. A coherent explanation of many of the very real personal frustrations and miseries I sometimes have. There's an element of 'grasping at straws' in my enthusiasm, and yet it's powerful and compelling. I'm not sure if I'd recommend it to you, though I think you'd see in it a lot of familiar experiences. It's polemical, full of bile and anger—but also for me a book of hope. I can't really get down, at present, the way it relieves me to find a <u>book</u> which articulates so many of my own doubts and worries and inhibitions.

*

A few years after he died, Janet wrote to me:

> I've been wondering what you've inherited from Bill, now that you've controlled a tendency to get in a rage! An ear for music and a gift for languages certainly. A courageous and enterprising attitude towards life and in your career—? Me, left to myself, I'd probably be still living in Kemsing, like Ivy, Rhoma, Nelly—oh horror! ... Goodnight dearest girl, xxoo Mum.

These women were her long-time friends, but she did not regret having had to move away from them.

After graduating from University College in the summer of 1971, I remember sitting in the dining room and telling Bill that I was planning to move to Belfast to study the conflict that was now rapidly escalating between Unionists and Republicans. I had been profoundly influenced by the professor who taught international relations at UCL, and who was working on how to negotiate peace in intractable conflicts such as Cyprus or Northern Ireland. He had invited me to lunch with Bernadette Devlin*, together with John Bayley, a young lecturer in his program—and it was as though I had been noticed by an important adult for the first time.

---

* A radical civil rights activist from Co. Tyrone, elected at age twenty-one to the House of Commons in 1969.

Bill expressed scepticism about this Belfast idea—which I had to discuss with him, even though I was twenty-one since I was going to need an ongoing parental subsidy of some kind. More questions from Bill revealed that in truth I was going because I wanted to be with John Bayley, who had decided to throw in his stellar academic early career to test out conflict resolution theories in Belfast. I was definitely in love. Bill had met John and I think John had charmed him. They were both capable of being very charming indeed. In a typically unpredictable (to me) response, Bill found this rationale perfectly acceptable, unlike my intellectual enthusiasms. He was still probably hoping I would come to my senses and join the Foreign Office. But this was 1971 and I would no more have worked for the government than for a colonial multi-national company.

Looking back, I think my brothers and I are all surprised at the things he did not get mad about. He never said anything when his military medals (not to mention Janet's silver candlesticks) were stolen and pawned by his youngest son to pay for his heroin addiction. Bill never said anything critical when William ended up in Brixton prison briefly. When I told him many years later that I had given up on finding Mr Right and was going to have a baby on my own, he seemed quite unperturbed and intent on making sure I was going to manage financially. In fact, I think he was pleased, or as Janet wrote 'surprisingly chuffed'. He had never (wisely) made any comment on my romantic attachments or failure to marry or have children.

Janet wrote back from the Béarn after they received my letter about this development:

> Bill is muntering away about you and yr plans, and quite putting me off—we are sitting out on the terrace in the autumn sunshine, our faithful boxer at our feet. He (not the boxer) feels you should get back into yr house for the great event, and says that if this is too difficult financially, we would help you ... He also suggested you might like me to come out in the spring (ours) and he might follow or not as seemed best. Actually this idea had not occurred to me!!

*

My brothers and I had each moved out of home within three years of what might have been a sensible family move to London, mostly not on good terms with Bill. William and I both think we remember Bill coming home one evening and telling Colin, in no uncertain terms, that it was time for him to move out. Colin has no memory of this, however. Which is a salutary reminder about the way siblings can 'see' and remember things quite differently from each other. Before long, William had pretty well disappeared into the London drug scene with his then girlfriend, and I was in my Hampstead bedsit.

Meanwhile, the transport portfolio in Mitchell Cotts was booming, making big profits for the group. They were now acquiring various transport companies in Australia, including Corrigans Express, and by 1968 had seven Australian group companies all offering different kinds of specialist knowledge to the rapidly growing mining industry, including air transport for mining executives. In 1971, as we left home, Bill was made a member of the group board (as opposed to being on the boards of many subsidiary companies). He now appears in annual general meeting board photographs, always a cigarette in hand, but looking jaded or even bored. He had risen as far as he could in the company, responsible for all the major profit-making operations within the group. The group managing director was not going to be giving up that position any time soon (and Bill was right about that as I discover that he was still in charge ten years later). It is likely that Bill could see nothing else to reach for in Mitchell Cotts and began to plan his exit, carefully calculating how long he needed to keep working in order to have enough in the bank for the next stage of his life. He had never been able to tolerate things standing still or becoming predictable. This sense of frustration at work probably increased his drinking and irritability until he could make his exit.

I have no doubt that Janet was, this time at least, keen for a change. There were certainly elements of life in London that gave her pleasure, but she was always someone who preferred to live in the country, and their marriage was at its most strained. I do not know whose idea it was, but suddenly Bill was off in Wales on a fly-fishing course. Is it possible he had fished in the Rhondda like so many hungry boys did in the Depression? The sport gripped him like golf had done twenty years earlier.

Fly-fishing is not for the half-hearted. There is too much to learn about flies and casting, too much equipment (flies, rods and waders) and too many hours out on the beat for it to appeal to most people. As Robert Hughes put it, 'fishing largely consists of not catching fish'. The appeal for Bill is not difficult to see. It is, Hughes writes, essentially a solitary sport, but never lonely. It has also been claimed that fly-fishing can be used to reduce psychological distress of various kinds. When Hughes died, Ben Macintyre—who had fished with him in Long Island Sound—wrote that 'in his reviewing and writing Hughes was loud, impatient, and sometimes cranky. But with rod in hand, you have to be quiet and focused, a shadow, a mimic'. Macintyre knew that Hughes 'was a naturally combative character, a pike on the page' and exactly the same could be said about Bill. The pike is a voracious fish with a large mouth, filled with sharp teeth. But Bill was at his best when showing me how and where to cast my fly.

There are plenty of excellent places to learn to fly-fish in the south of England—in Hampshire or Somerset, or further west in Devon, for example. Bill could have been on the River Test in less than two hours from Kensington. But for some reason he learned to fish in Wales, on a river that is about four and a half hours' drive from London. He started some time in 1973, in Llandyssul, where there was a fly-fishing club on the Afon Teifi. Within a couple of years Bill had designed and organised the building of a house near Newcastle-Emlyn in Welsh-speaking Carmarthenshire. The terrace had a spectacular view, looking away to the south where the Teifi runs through, a river known for its excellent salmon, sea trout and wild brown trout.

At the end of March 1975, at fifty-nine years of age, Bill retired from Mitchell Cotts and from his life in London. They did not want him to leave, persuading him to stay on the board, but even that he gave up almost immediately. The house in Kensington was sold and two months later Bill and Janet moved into their new one, Trem-y-Gorwel in Cwm-cou.

Believing that his recently acquired red Mercedes Benz was encouraging Welsh tradesmen to double their prices for him, he rapidly replaced it with an old second-hand Rover—a 3½ litre mustard-coloured sedan with remarkable acceleration that did not look at all flash. In fact, when I borrowed it, I noticed there was no tread on the tyres. Janet could have another Triumph Herald convertible.

*

It is only after Bill's death that we realise that his route to and from the River Teifi, and the site of their new house, passes only fourteen miles south of the place where he was born and went to school. Not far away is the cemetery where his brother Colin is buried with his wife and young son; and also his father and mother who were buried with the baby sister he may never have known about. Ada's grave was re-opened twice, to 9 ft, to receive her parents. A short walk from the cemetery he could have found his brother Ron, living next to his wife's family. After his working life as a car paint-sprayer and factory fireman in Coventry, Ron had retired back to the Rhondda, living with his wife in Trealaw where she was born, in a house next to his mother-in-law and sister-in-law. Ron lived in Trealaw until he died, aged seventy-nine, in 1987. There is no reason to assume Bill knew how close Ron was, but he certainly knew where he himself had lived for the first eighteen years of his life.

When Bill and Janet went walking in the Brecon Beacons, they were a few miles from where his sister Lily was still living, near her son Denzil—the admiring nephew who eventually found us. The same year Bill made this move to Wales, his oldest sister Rene died, aged seventy-three, in Aberystwyth, just an hour's drive north from Cwm-cou.

I have no doubt a psychoanalyst would have plenty to say about how someone can compartmentalise their life to this degree. Or why someone might consciously or unconsciously wish to return to the place they came from. Then again, Bill may simply have known that there are beautiful parts of south and west Wales, where the fishing is as good as anywhere in Britain, and where land is relatively cheap. He may also have been determined to avoid the snobbery often associated with fly-fishing in Britain. Whatever the case, his ability to never let on that he came from Wales is remarkable.

*

As Bill and Janet settled into life in Cwm-cou, the rest of us were dispersing. I finished a PhD on the Troubles in Northern Ireland (about which I do not recall Bill ever expressing any interest) and, unable to work out how to fit into anything or anywhere, accepted a university lectureship in Perth, Australia. I think I rationalised it as a temporary visit, allowing me to get to know something about my Australian roots. Colin was married with a young baby, and on a visit to Wales was inspired by Bill's radical move to make one himself. Having risen rapidly with his second big advertising company, he fell in love with the idea of California, and thought it would be fun to work there for a while. He headed off despite having no visa, moving his family to New York from where it would be easier to get one than in Los Angeles. Almost fifty years later he is still living in America, long settled in California, with no regrets.

When we eventually discovered the truth about Bill's Welsh origins, my limited sociological imagination began to see our family as an example of the failure of social reproduction. None of us seems to be doing what one might expect from a privileged stockbroker-belt upbringing. Apart from me, there is downward educational mobility with neither of my brothers going to university. We have scattered to all corners of the world. Our careers range from sheep and dairy farming to advertising to higher education. My mother wondered about this too, writing to me when Colin moved his family to San

Francisco: 'It really is rather amazing how different your 3 lives have turned out to be, more than in most families surely?'

I think I have always somehow felt that I didn't quite fit into the world I grew up in. William says he never felt that our family was quite like the families of our friends, and in that sense we did not 'fit' where we lived. Colin, on the other hand, never felt that he did not belong there. What he learned from Bill, he says, was that he was free to make his life as he wished—and, in a way, that is exactly what I learned too. But was there some centrifugal force at work in our family?

Meanwhile, for Bill, fly-fishing more than filled the hole left by golf—for a time, at least. With a permit to fish on the Teifi, he met a Welsh farmer whose land ran along some of the best fishing in the area. Oswyn was an unlikely friend, involved in a number of dodgy sidelines, but always keen to talk new projects. Oswyn worked his farm with his son, and this seems to have given Bill the idea of setting his own son up on a farm.

William, having got away from heroin, was living in Nottinghamshire with an eminently sensible and practical girlfriend, driving heavy goods vehicles and running deliveries. The irony is that I was the only one in the family who had ever shown any interest in farming, spending my teenage years working on a sheep farm at weekends. But out of the blue Bill suggested that he buy a small hill farm (with plenty of sheep subsidies to go with it), which William and Jane could manage. At first blush this was a hair-brained idea. Jane, at least, was a trained nurse whose expertise could plausibly be transferred from humans to animals, but William had only had the benefit of a Westminster education and A levels in French, English and History—which were unlikely to be useful. But he had also done factory work and has a gift for fixing all things mechanical.

That Bill might have liked the idea of setting his son up in a worthwhile business does not seem out of character. I think he always felt protective of his youngest son—the 'etcetera' to whom he sends special love in his letters to Janet. A very long-standing friend from our childhood wrote to me after I asked for his memories of Bill, divulging that Janet told him one of the last things Bill said to her when he was dying was 'to look after William'. But buying a farm seems a trifle left field. This is, nonetheless, what happened. Perhaps Bill was taken with the idea of farming himself, and this was a way he could give it a go. He had been looking for a small property, with Oswyn's help, for an eccentric cousin of Janet's. He proceeded to find a farm for William, insisting that he marry Jane. Then they all set about learning how to care for sheep and produce fat lambs. This implausible plan worked, but I can see now that it was more luck than prescience on Bill's part. He could not have known that William and Jane would turn into dedicated farmers.

Within two years William and Jane had a baby, and Bill found a new farm for them, between Llandysul and Carmarthen, on part of which he proposed to build a new house for himself and Janet. He'd discovered that there were many aspects of farming life that he enjoyed enormously, from going to buy rams at the market in Builth Wells to eradicating thistles from the fields. He wrote to me at length about their mission to buy rams.

> What a thoroughly pleasant time we had. Altogether I bought 4 rams instead of the 1 I intended—they were irresistible and I had to be dragged away before I bankrupted the partnership. As soon as William and I hefted these magnificent beasts into the back of the pick-up, they started rogering away (a good sign!)—with the B.F.L. [Bluefaced Leicester] mainly on the receiving end. I don't think he's a poofter—he just had no choice—outnumbered and outgunned by the Suffolks.

In one of the happiest photographs I have of him, he is standing in a field in gumboots, wearing one of Janet's old hats, holding a manual grass-seeder which looks like a strange Chinese stringed-instrument. He just looks very pleased with himself and is smiling unself-consciously at the camera. Janet, meanwhile, was making new friends who introduced her to wool-dying and wool-spinning, among other things. There were guilds of weavers, spinners and dyers all over

Wales, and this was a rewarding extension of her long-standing involvement in textile art and embroidery, and perfectly suited to life on a sheep farm.

Once I had moved to Australia family communication had to change. Telephone calls were prohibitively expensive—even 'trunk calls' within Britain, let alone international calls. Blue folded airmail letters took over. I think I kept almost all the letters Bill or Janet wrote to me over the next thirty years (which morphed into weekly faxes in the last decade of Janet's life, after the residents of her French village gave her a fax machine for her eightieth birthday). These letters give me something more solid to rely on than my memory alone as I attempt to reconstruct Bill in this period. His descriptions of farming life are among the most vivid things he ever wrote for me.

> The spring has come and after 16 inches of rain in March, most of April has been dry and clear. Before and over this Easter the sky was consistently cloudless with a sharp sunshine and cool north-easterly breezes. Golden days with that delightful feeling of freshness and renewal one gets at this season of the year. I bought a 1978 Ford 6600 tractor which is a blue and white delight to behold or rather *is* when it is not bespattered with dried cow-dung from muck-spreading.
>
> We have rotavated, harrowed, rolled, seeded, harrowed rolled and fertilised the top field ... Yesterday in the brilliant sunshine the Welsh hills all around us were dazzlingly clear and it was indeed a happy and exhilarating moment when we roared down from the top fields in our respective vehicles. Reminded me of the last stage of Wavell's westward push in the Desert War back in early 1941, when tanks, armoured cars and trucks headed across the flat salt pans and then the stony outcrops with pennants flying in the wind. Should we put pennants on the tractors?

Re-reading this letter now, I am struck by his reference to Wavell's campaign in North Africa, since I cannot recall him ever talking about or even mentioning it before. But even more noticeable in all this celebration of Welsh country life is the fact that there is no suggestion, even accidental, that he comes from this country. By this time William and Jane's young daughters were attending a Welsh-speaking nursery school, but at no point did Bill let on that he had more than a sprinkling of Welsh words, or let any Welsh accent creep in. This seems particularly remarkable as even I want to start speaking with that beautiful musical lilt when I hear it. To all intents and purposes, he was as new to Wales as the rest of us.

And then, as I am proof-reading the text for this book, Colin suddenly remembers that Dad used say 'boyo' a lot. That is indeed a give-away.

*

It was probably inevitable that this father-and-son venture would end in tears and sprained ankles, as Janet used to say. But as usual it is hard to know exactly why. Bill the businessman with very clear views on how to manage assets versus William and Jane who simply came to love being animal farmers? The difficulty of making a living out of a small Welsh hill farm reliant on government subsidies? Bill's short fuse? I got an inkling of the problems emerging in a letter from Bill in March 1982. He begins with lambing, writing 'Priez pour nous! Or as the Latin dogs have it—Ora pro nobis'. (A typical funny, literate aside, mocking scholarly seriousness.) Then he tells me how much he is loving reading Anais Nin's journals, 'an extraordinary woman at whose own intimate life one can only tantalisingly guess'. He is 'entranced' by the diaries: 'a subtle, feminine intellect, and a warm, beautiful and gracile woman too'. He ends by telling me that he is 'beginning to question whether I can go on living indefinitely only at Blaengwen, satisfying tho' it is for your Mum and Brother.

> Maybe I can find some compromise to rid me of this stultified feeling I get with increasing frequency. I find it increasingly difficult to go on 'cultivating my garden' when on the one hand the nights are drawing in (it may soon be curtains) and on the other so many new experiences and places are still attainable—if only one reaches out for them. The problem is to do this without causing real anguish and

anxiety to your near—and sometimes dear ones. An idea is slowly formulating in the recesses of my shrivelled brain—perhaps I'll write to you about this when it becomes clearer. Love Dad.

It has been tempting to look for complex psychological reasons behind Bill's decisions to make radical changes in his life (and therefore Janet's). But there is also the relatively simple theme that keeps re-occurring: when Bill found his life becoming boring or when he could see nothing new ahead of him, he was going to find something quite different to do, or somewhere different to live. He had an extraordinary appetite for new projects. And as far as possible, he was going to avoid doing things that he found uninteresting (like attending our school speech nights). As I am wrestling with this period of Bill's life, Colin writes to me: 'I wonder if Dad always found family life boring. I feel that his efforts at it may have been duty-driven and performative.' 'He loved us all but found family life at home very dull.'

Was this low boredom threshold the result, in part at least, of Bill's war experiences? I have no way of knowing, but as I think about its possible origins, I realise that I have a not dissimilar need to avoid boredom. When I entered my sixties and began to imagine radical changes in my own life, I would think happily of how Bill and Janet had successfully started a new life in France as they approached their seventies—one that gave them both enormous satisfactions.*

Fishing and farming might be considered surprising new interests for a businessman of his age, but Bill's decision to try life in France, aged sixty-seven, fits into a very long and deep attachment to that country. Janet wrote to me about this moment:

> It's amazing what the past 4 years have done for him, his interests in building & farming are very genuine—he would love to farm in France now, tho' that is hardly on. He is at his happiest when making plans & bringing projects to fruition—unlike me who am inclined to be rather negative!

---

* For the story of my own attempt to avoid boredom see *Imaginative Possession*, Chapter 1.

Janet had, as usual, made good friends in Wales, developed new skills around her long-standing interest in textile art, found a group of talented art and craft makers (including a silversmith) and walked all over the hills and along the beaches of Carmarthenshire, absorbing the region's natural history. But she could also see that father and son were going to become even more estranged if they attempted to go on with the shared farming project. The fact that Bill owned the farm and needed some of its value for his new plans meant that the separation was inevitably very painful. William and Jane had to give up their home and their animals.

How the French plan was hatched I do not know, and there was much grief on William's side, even though Bill and Janet both wrote often to me about their intention to 'see them right' financially. In the spring of 1983, Bill and Janet crossed the channel, planning to return to pack up their belongings once they found the right spot in France. In the space of a few years Bill had built two new houses in the Welsh countryside (each with an admired garden, designed and maintained by Janet); he had learned enough about hill sheep farming to help William start out in a serious way; and he had become a dedicated fly-fisher, skilled at making his own flies. But this was not enough to keep at bay the development of that 'stultified feeling'.

*

Bill was able with apparent ease to compartmentalise his life in such a way that his first eighteen years as a Welsh boy in the Rhondda could be kept totally separate from his seven years of 'retirement', forty years later, as an Englishman in Carmarthenshire. It is difficult to understand this. What seems clear to me, nonetheless, is that this would not have been possible if he regretted his decisions; he could not have done it with a bad conscience.

Chapter 8
France: Death and Discovery

Bill and Janet's plan for their French move involved getting in the car, crossing the channel, and driving south down the west coast towards Bordeaux, before turning east along France's southern border, looking for a place they might like to live—for now. Janet wrote to me a week after they left England, saying they had stopped in the Dordogne for a few days, staying with her brother-in-law, Peter, who was now remarried and had retired to live in France.

> We decided not to look round yet in the Dordogne, which is obviously crafty and stiff with permanent English. We'll be back, we said and shot off to the Pyrénées Atlantiques. Arrived thro' heavenly country, to see the Pyrénées shining 40–50 miles (?) off and decided on the spot that this was where we wanted to be, between Bayonne and Pau.

They immediately started looking for a house to rent, and Janet posted this letter to me as they were about to talk to real estate agents in Orthez. Having agreed to this French plan reluctantly, she ends the letter by telling me she had 'lived more intensely and variedly in the past 2 weeks than in a year in Wales'. She might not have liked being uprooted so often, but she was even better than Bill at responding openly to new experiences.

Neither of them had any desire to join an English community. The tiny village in which they settled without much delay lies on the ridge of one of the many foothills running up into the Pyrenees, just south of the city of Pau—historic capital of the Béarn region, and seat of the Kings of Navarre. We all came to agree that the road that runs westward from Pau along these foothills towards Biarritz is the loveliest road in the world. From the wide terrace of their modest house in St Faust de Haut they looked south to the mountains and the dramatic Pic du Midi d'Ossau. What was to have been an experiment—with the bonus of the substantial tax benefit from living outside the UK for at least six months of the year—turned into a way of living that neither of them wanted to give up. Even after Bill died, Janet chose to remain in the same house—refusing suggestions from her children that she relocate to Brittany, Melbourne or San Francisco—for another fifteen years, until her death early in 2010.

Bill's first letters to me from St Faust suggest he is happy already:

> It's Sunday morning here and Janet is busy attaching butterflies to the front of your pullover while I am semi-paralysed after a shindig at the village hall with the locals. About 500 of them eating a gargantuan meal and making one hell of a noise, supported by a P.A. system blasting out about 5000 watts per channel of excruciating music. Grilled sheep meat and haricots blancs extruded from my earholes and my tonsils were aflame and afloat in plonk. But no ill effects except that if you offered to cut my throat I wouldn't really object.

Three months later he writes describing how much he likes the village of St Faust and adds:

> I am however, reading quite a lot of French literature, listening to France Culture and France Musique on my trusty hi-fi, and keeping in touch with events via a recently acquired Grundig Satellite.

Despite Bill's ability to write with humour about the rural social life going on around them, he did not suddenly become sociable. He was lucky to be able to play golf again. Luck was needed as golf courses are relatively rare in France. Pau is home to one of the oldest golf courses in the world outside Britain, and by the time Bill moved into the area there was an excellent new course on his side of the Gave du

Pau. He found a French golf partner who again remains a shadowy figure to the rest of us. It was Janet who made friends in the area and got to know an excellent local potter and a skilled teacher of landscape water-colour painting.

What they shared in this new life was a love of walking in the mountains. Their best days involved setting off, perhaps in the old four-wheel drive belonging to Xavier and Thérèse—a local couple with a deep knowledge of the Pyrenees—to explore some part of that great mountain range. In Bill's rucksack was baguette, cheese and wine; in Janet's it was paint, brushes and sketch pad, while Xavier could be counted on for more wine, a hard saucisson and a very sharp knife. However, it was his wife Thérèse whom Bill really liked, partly because she was an excellent driver, always at the wheel on their trips (something Bill rarely liked to cede), and partly because she was not in any way intimidated by him. She was also a good French cook. The natural history of the Pyrenees became Bill and Janet's collective enthusiasm, though Janet was more diligent and before long she could identify every kind of vulture and bird of prey that circled above them.

*

While Bill was alive, the fact that he had chosen to settle not far from the town of Foix in the Ariège did not seem significant. But as we discuss what we are discovering about his life, my brother William suddenly sees this proximity in a new light. Growing tired of the damp hard slog of farming sheep in Wales, he and his wife decided to look for a farm in France, a country that makes serious efforts to help young people move on to the land. They arrived in St Faust in late 1988 and began looking for possible farms in the south-west of France. Bill, William now remembers, was keen to show him potential properties near Foix, the town he had helped liberate in August 1944 and where he earned his DSO. None of us had ever heard Bill talk about his mission to the Ariège, and we remained completely ignorant of his role, even as we played with his medals from the bottom of his chest of drawers. Yet, as we now know, it is the one element of his life that has been well documented, and which is still celebrated in the region.

As he drove around with his son, Bill failed to mention any connection to the area. Looking back now, William is puzzled about why he was so keen to take him there to look at what were never going to be suitable farming properties. What might Bill have been thinking about as they drove through Foix? How could he not be remembering the fighting, the adrenalin, the intensity of those days? Would he not have been tempted to show William the farmhouse where they hid at least?

On balance, I think Bill's ability to separate his past experiences in Foix from his return to the area is of a different nature from his ability to compartmentalise his two lives in Wales. It would not have been difficult to present a glamourised account of the Allied mission in the Ariège, or one that would have made his children proud, but this would have been totally out of character. Bill never told stories about his war, but he was not hiding it. His identity seemed to reside in his being and his doing, the present and the future—never the past.

Bill's silence was not total, however, and on rare occasions he felt moved to tell someone—usually a younger man—something about his war, but it is hard to know what the trigger was. On one such occasion the trigger was obvious, though it takes my ex-husband to remind me of it. We were driving with Bill and our toddler towards the Spanish frontier, not far from Lourdes, and stopped to fill the car with petrol. It seemed that Bill knew the garage attendant as he paused for some time to talk to him. We learned, in a casual mention later, that the man was someone Bill had known as a fighter in the resistance.

Being reminded of this brings back my own memory of a much earlier but very similar experience. When I was about seven years old, we were returning from a family holiday on the Costa Brava, driving north through Spain before crossing the Pyrenees into France near Andorra. On this trip we paused briefly when we reached the French side to fill up with petrol, before hurtling north to the channel ferry. Bill was the only one to get out of the car, but we noticed him shaking hands with the petrol station owner and talking for a few minutes—which seemed unusual. I think it was only much later I discovered that Bill had been briefly reunited—thirteen years after the event—with the man who supplied petrol for his motorbike when he was caught on the wrong side of the German lines in August 1944.

When I ask all my friends who met Bill to tell me anything at all they remember about him, I get another surprising war story. An Australian friend on holiday in the area with his family was invited to lunch with Bill and Janet in St Faust de Haut. David tells me that he remembers that, at some point, Bill left the table to retrieve something to show him. He returned with a letter on grand notepaper, signed by King George VI, expressing the country's gratitude for the things Bill had done during the war which could never be acknowledged publicly. David cannot recall this being part of any conversation about the war. Rather, it seemed that suddenly Bill felt like letting him know something significant about himself.

*

It was perhaps inevitable, living in France, that Bill's war would catch up with him in some way or other—though it was not, as it turns out, the result of his relative proximity to the town of Foix. Janet believed it was Bill's golfing partner, Claude, who, without telling Bill what he was doing, forwarded Bill's address and phone number to General Bigeard. This means that Bill had at least mentioned his connection to this very well-known Frenchman while playing golf. Marcel Bigeard was now seventy-three years old but continued from time to time to write about his deep affection for 'his' English major, Bill, and to wonder where he was. Tipped off in this unlikely way, Bigeard telephoned out of the blue and Bill, having answered, could not escape the conversation. Bigeard followed up the call with a personal note in his large dramatic handwriting.

Cher Bill,

Quelle surprise ... ta voix, ton humour ... en quelques secondes nous étions dans l'Ariège 1944 ... en fait c'était hier.

Je t'embrasse

Bigeard.

This note fills the page, but on the other side he had photocopied or had photocopied—in a sort of random pattern—at least thirty newspaper headlines about himself, such as 'Bigeard: le franc-parler patriot' and 'Le General Bigeard: Une guerre tres speciale et riche'. It seems that he often used this pre-loaded paper in his correspondence.

Bigeard served in the French army until 1974, retiring as a four-star general before being appointed deputy defence minister under President Valéry Giscard d'Estaing, and later taking a seat as a member of France's lower house of parliament. In his retirement (eventual) he wrote many books, mostly memoirs. He had a remarkable gift for self-publicity and self-promotion, and over the next couple of years would send Bill photocopies of press clippings or small extracts from books about himself with headings like 'Bigeard, le magnétique m'a convaincu envoûté'. Later he wrote again, saying, 'you will always be "my" Bill, with that calm and that class', in the same breath announcing that he now despaired of French values. After Bill's death he sent a note to Janet, again expressing his love for Bill, adding that he had never understood why Bill had wanted 'this isolation'. The note was accompanied by more photocopied headlines about himself.

Assuming that Bill had absolutely no desire to be found by anyone from his past, he was lucky to die just weeks before those who were organising a major celebration for the fiftieth anniversary of the liberation of Foix caught up with him. It was Janet who received the communication, presumably because Bigeard had passed on Bill's phone number to the organisers. And every year thereafter, on the same date, Janet was rung by the 'boy' who had shown Bill the way into the school at Foix so he could surprise the German troops.

Bill's resistance to any memorialising of the war, and especially his own role in it, is clear. Whatever the reasons, he went to great lengths to insulate himself from his past, and not just the war. As we know, after his return from Foix, despite having been in North and East Africa for nearly five years, he did not go to see his mother and sisters in Wales; nor did he seem to have made contact with his brother and their cousin in Coventry, Alfred Knight. The Proberts, on their side, seemed surprisingly ready to let him go.

*

The only Probert who was too young to be implicated directly in this family breach was Bill's nephew Denzil—the son of his sister Lily who had married a baker in Brecon in 1928. As a university student before the war, Roy obviously made a strong impression on his young nephew, so that when Denzil saw Bill's photograph in the newspapers in December 1946, meeting King George to receive his DSO, the eleven-year-old longed to be reunited with his glamorous uncle. However, he had to wait over thirty years to be finally free of his mother's injunction not to go looking for Roy while she was alive. Denzil explained to Janet that:

> I was aware that the family believed Uncle Roy wished to lead his own life away from the family and that he never saw his mother after the early years of the war. I was very doubtful of this view and after my mother's death I determined if possible to find out as much as I could. My search now really began.

His initial efforts bore no fruit. It is hard to imagine how he would have gone about his search without the internet to help him, and with all the secrecy that I ran into. He decided to pursue the ministry of defence for an address, knowing that they would have had contact with Bill over the awarding of his DSO. From the ministry he eventually extracted our address on the Pilgrims Way—the last address on Bill's record of service, accompanying the final stamp that marked his commission as 'Relinquished'. Sadly for Denzil, Bill had moved us all to London almost a decade earlier. In fact, by the time Denzil wrote to that address, Bill had retired from the city and moved on to Wales. In 1979, when Lily died, he and Janet were just moving out of their first Welsh home onto the second farm that he bought for William, near Pencader. It is deeply ironic that when Denzil began his hunt, Bill was living less than fifty miles from where his nephew was living. Indeed, Bill and Janet certainly went walking on the Brecon Beacons on at least one occasion during this period.

Denzil's next move was to contact the department of social security (DSS) since everyone working in the United Kingdom must have a national insurance number. DSS initially refused to disclose any information about Bill, as a matter of policy. They did, however, agree that they could forward a letter to him if they received one. Denzil's wife, Audrey, wrote the letter, probably in 1984, together with contributions from Denzil's three children. As Denzil explained it to us, 'Audrey felt that if a letter was to be written for forwarding it might be better coming from her. Audrey thought that she might be able to explain my sincerity in wishing to meet up with an uncle I had always been very proud of.'

By this time, however, Bill was no longer just over the other side of the Brecon Beacons and had moved to south-west France. It is as though he was always one move ahead of his nephew, though there is no evidence to confirm he knew he was being looked for. The DSS letter may never have reached Bill, but if it did, he prevented anyone else from seeing it. Receiving no reply, Denzil told us that he 'gave up all hope of ever seeing Uncle Roy again'. He had been warned by a high-ranking army figure that 'Roy possibly had a D notice or something similar above his name and that no information would ever be given'. He had run into the secrecy that would frustrate my own searches nearly thirty years later.

Ten years after his unsuccessful attempt to use the department of social security, Denzil finally, 'by complete chance', found his uncle, simply because friends of his took a holiday in the Pau area and somehow heard of Bill Probert and found his address. This suggests that everyone who knew Denzil was aware of his intense desire to find his uncle. When they heard about this, Denzil's children planned a surprise sixtieth birthday summer holiday for him in Pau. Luckily for Bill, just as this proposed celebration was revealed to Denzil, he was informed by his doctor that he needed to 'have something removed' and must postpone any travel until this was done. Disappointed to be temporarily grounded, he decided to write to Uncle Roy, and this time he finally had the right address, in St Faust de Haut.

> [I]f I get through my hospital visit successfully I might just take my children up on their offer at a later date this year ... If there is no reply to this letter don't be too surprised if I arrive unannounced on your door-step from my hotel in Pau ... I realise how determined my family are that I should meet with you once again. I have no wish to disappoint them.

Four months before this letter was safely delivered to his house, Bill died from heart failure. He was already safely buried in the village cemetery in St Faust de Haut. When Laurent the postman handed the letter over the gate, the surprise was going to be all Janet's and then ours.

*

Janet wrote back to Denzil to explain that his favourite uncle had recently died, and to tell him we knew nothing about any family in Wales, and that news of Denzil's existence was a bolt from the blue. There was a lot of information about our respective families to be exchanged. In April of the following year, Janet and William travelled to Wales to meet Denzil and his wife, Audrey. In the event, Denzil was hospitalised again, but they went anyway, and met around his bed in the Nevill Hall hospital in Abergavenny. They also went to Ynyshir and stood outside the small terrace house at 44 Gynor Place where Bill lived until he went to university, and where his mother was still living when he married Janet and when all three of us were born. There was affectionate correspondence between everyone for a while. But no one could make sense of Bill's decision to leave Roy and his family behind after the war.

In 2005, I was finally able to make my own first trip to the Rhondda. I found the graves of Roy's father William, his mother Minna, and his brother Colin in the Trealaw cemetery. But as I write these words, I feel like the British art critic and writer Laura Cumming whose book about searching for her biological grandmother is another remarkable story of painstaking research. She eventually finds a photograph of her grandmother as a child:

> [T]he little girl in the hat is Hilda, my grandmother. Except this pronoun is like a stile I cannot get over. The connection between us was diverted, as if a dyke had been thrown in the way. She is my grandmother, and I am her granddaughter, but I can only reunite us with words, the joining of people through writing.

I too have written and then deleted the word 'my', resorting to 'Roy's' father and mother rather than my grandfather and my grandmother.

I had read a little about life in the Rhondda in the 1920s, and I stood in front of 44 Gynor Place, Ynyshir, trying, without much success, to imagine my father's early life. I drove over the Brecon Beacons to meet Denzil and Audrey one afternoon, and we spent an hour or two puzzling yet again about the mysterious Roy but understanding no more than before. It was somehow a disheartening visit.

But eighteen years later, when I return to Brecon with William on this last attempt to make sense of Bill's life, Audrey and her daughter Mitch greet us with great warmth and explain that Denzil had been suffering from extreme depression when I announced my first visit. Rather than begging off, he had insisted on dragging himself out of bed to meet me, almost unable to stand the strain.

Only now do I fully appreciate that without Denzil and his dogged dedication to the hunt for his uncle, we would never have known that Bill was once Roy, a boy from the Rhondda.

Chapter 9
A Family Reconsidered

Almost thirty years after the letter that Denzil wrote to his Uncle Roy arrived in St Faust de Haut, I have now done everything I can to understand how Roy became Bill. I wanted to uncover how he had escaped the poverty-stricken Rhondda of the 1920s and become the debonair man in the city, wearing his Moss Bros. double-breasted suits and driving a Jaguar. The idea of thinking about him not so much as my father, but on his own terms, had seemed a curiously grown-up thing to do. I was not motivated to uncover his secrets because I felt a belated need to examine his relationship with me, but because his life seemed so intriguing—a good story that ought to be told. Nonetheless, this process of discovery became, at least in part, an interrogation of his relationship with me, leading inevitably to unplanned introspection and reflection.

Thinking sociologically, on the other hand, comes naturally to me, and much of my working life has been spent researching class and inequality. I felt I should start at the beginning and try to account for Roy's early life in the Rhondda and his escape to London University. I was an amateur in the ancestry research field, but I had friends who could teach me about archives, and there was the intrinsically interesting (to me, at least) history of coal mining in South Wales waiting to be explored. Roy's early years are the Welsh version of the wider British experience of economic crisis and Depression, and perhaps a more intense and memorable version for that, with the fate of the Rhondda— which came to be known as 'Heartbreak Valley'—representing one of the most extreme examples of industrial collapse. Gwyn A. Williams compares the Depression in Wales with the Famine in Ireland, arguing it 'unhinged this Welsh polity, devastated its communities' and 'dispersed a quarter of its people.'

The Second World War provided another area for research with its own intrinsic interest. It reminded me that I am of the last generation who will feel any personal connection to that war, through the memories of our parents. I had not previously thought of the war as something that gave Roy more opportunities than most, playing to his intellectual and physical strengths, and possibly his temperament. It also gave Roy a way to stop being Welsh and working class. The requirement for conformity in the armed forces allowed him to decode the niceties of English class signals in a highly controlled environment. But when he returned to civilian life, to become a successful businessman, he had to choose how to present Bill to the world so that he could merge seamlessly into a quite different domain. He managed this perfectly; his accent, his clothing, his house and car all conveyed his acquired class status in ways that completely occluded his origins. He also knew how not to overdo it, not to be in any way ostentatious as he became financially secure.

I felt my task was to focus relentlessly on the events of Roy's life for which I could find evidence, minimising speculation or imaginative leaps until the facts took their own shape. Luckily for me, the facts gave me plenty to work with because Roy seems to have caught every major wave of social and economic change that occurred in twentieth-century Britain. The trajectory of his life depended on the specific times in which it was lived. I can see now that his gift was his ability or willingness to take advantage of every conceivable opportunity that social change put in his way—such as the creation of Welsh County schools, the outbreak of war and the long post-war boom. Roy's genius seems to have been his ability to remodel himself many times over as his external environment changed and new possibilities presented themselves.

However, even if I could research Bill's whole life as though it were an interesting historical exercise, I could not escape the personal nature of my investment in the findings. I recognised moments when I reacted proudly to finding something that illustrated his intelligence or his courage, and moments when I knew I wanted to defend him from possible criticism. There were also times when I braced myself, fearing that I might be about to uncover what I would see as moral failure. And alongside the excavation of the facts, there was the matter of the secrets.

While Bill's desire and capacity to keep secrets were revealed shortly after he died in 1994, it is only now, thirty years later, that I appreciate the extent to which he had purposefully constructed a new identity by the end of the war. He was, and probably had to be, a man with a large ego.

When I turned to Bill's life as a successful businessman after the war, it was no longer possible to keep him at arm's length. I was no longer relying only on archives and war records, but describing a world in which my brothers and I were present. Here the material is, of course, richer; and it is not possible to reconstruct Bill's life in the 1950s and 1960s without remembering how we experienced it personally. I began to see how his propensity to lose his temper, the unpredictability of his outbursts, and his ability to lash out at his nearest and dearest—especially after a drink or two—were somehow connected to the strain of becoming Bill.

Most people seem to believe that if you live your life keeping important secrets from everyone, including your own family, there will be some undesirable side effects. In a notebook that Germaine Greer kept during her search for her father Reg she writes:

> A good man cannot live with secrets. A good man cannot watch over himself even in sleep to be sure that he does not give away the secret locked around his heart which dares not murmur its systole and diastole. The only hope is to neutralise the secret by forgetting it, but

227

you can't do that either ... You can never tell, you can never explain, you must let everybody down, you can never justify yourself.

My everyday understanding of psychology suggests that there must be some truth to this. But while Bill had secrets, his lies were few and far between. Unlike Reg Greer, he did not change his name or cover his traces after the war. He seems to have decided to be silent. If he told few lies, being 'found out' would not necessarily cause an existential crisis. He was, in almost every respect, what he seemed to be. But is it damaging in some way to be unable to access your childhood, to be obliged always to appear fully-formed—with no past? And was he ever afraid that at some point that past would be exposed?

I suspect the psychological impact of his secrets probably revealed itself when things over which he had no control got in the way of his desires and ambition. Bill may have been exercising a remarkable degree of existential freedom, but this did not give him power over everything. His career rested on a very large complex global organisation, and his family was not infinitely malleable, so when he was inevitably frustrated, he had few emotional means for dealing with this frustration.

For Greer, her father's lies about his real identity are indefensible. When I re-read her book, at the start of my own research, I was struck by her harsh reaction to the discovery that Reg had hidden his impoverished early life as Eric Greeney—an illegitimate child fostered with many others by the admirable Emma Greeney and her illiterate husband. Eric left Tasmania as a very young man, and changed 'from a semi-literate book-binder to Reg Greer the toff.' She cannot absolve him from the crime of cutting all ties with his adoptive family, especially his admirable mother. 'Try as I might', she writes, 'I cannot forgive my father this cruelty, banal and commonplace as it is, compounded of indifference and lack of imagination.' Her brother Barry, however, reacts to these discoveries quite differently, suggesting that their father 'did what he had to do ... He knew what he could handle, and what he couldn't'. His judgment is much kinder: 'After all that he made a stable family; he brought us all up well. Three out of three's not bad going.' But this assessment does not assuage Greer's disillusionment. Her last line is poignant. 'In finding him I lost him. Sleepless nights are long.'

I wondered how I and my brothers would judge our father's life as we learned more about him and shared our childhood memories. It also occurred to me that the more I learned about Bill, the more distant he might become—less like the Bill I knew. As Greer discovered, and any family researcher knows, there are risks involved in digging up your parents. The biggest hole in our understanding of Bill is the total absence of any reliable evidence about his father and mother. For Greer, Emma Greeney is the real heroine of her story, but Minna is as likely to have been unlovable as lovable, or as likely to have been rigid and unforgiving as motherly and loving.

*

Alongside the risks involved in digging up a parent there have been unexpected rewards. For me the focus on Probert family life in the 1950s and 60s has led to a powerful sense of reconnection with my own childhood and adolescence. In exchanging memories not just with my brothers, but with other people from that time, I feel like I have been reunited with my younger self. The rewards are perhaps greater if, like me, you emigrate at a relatively young age and start your adult life alone on the other side of the world. Here in Melbourne, there are very few people who ever met my father, and few who really know much about my early family life. And indeed, I should say that one of the things that I love about Australia is this lack of interest in one's past. When Laura Cumming is searching for her grandmother, she is puzzled to learn that her recently uncovered Australian aunts never wondered about the identity of the very young girl in a photo frame beside their mother's bed—who was, in fact, their half-sister. Cumming writes that an 'Australian friend once told me that his compatriots can appear incurious about the past, putting it behind them because they are always "just starting".' Germaine Greer makes a similar point about Australia when explaining the lack of curiosity about her father's background. 'Australians detest snobbery and insist that a man is to be valued for what he is in himself, and not the stock he may have come from on whatever side of the blanket.'

It is ironic that I have a faint recollection of Bill and Janet discussing a possible emigration to Canada when I was probably of primary school age. I don't think I was being consulted, and my brothers have no such memory, but perhaps I overheard them talking. Knowing what I now know, I think Bill might well have been less on his guard had he moved us all to Canada or Australia. All English accents seem to flatten out in Australia, and while there are minorities in Melbourne who still ask you where you went to school, there is no assumption that this tells you who is running the place.

*

It turns out that William has the best and clearest memories of our childhood, leading to much emailing and WhatsApping as I collected them up. He wrote to me, as the manuscript took shape, that he found it particularly interesting that 'we all have such different relationships and views of our parents, and talking about our childhoods has thrown up all sorts of interesting facts about how each of us reacted and our different recollections of certain events. So, all in all, what is great about the whole affair is I for one feel reconnected to both you and Colin.'

Individual family members can experience the same family life quite differently, and that certainly turns out to be true for us. We each found our own way, mostly unconsciously, to manage these often-intense relationships. Whatever was conscious or unconscious, it remains the case that by living so far away for almost all my adult life there were relatively few opportunities for serious conflict with Bill, and many for affectionate letter-writing—though I still managed a door-slamming episode on one visit to St Faust when, I think, he started to attack my mother for something or other. After leaving the house in anger, ('digne fille de ton père' as my mother used to say), I went for a long walk out of the village, along the 'crête', before I had no option but to return to the house, by which time I think Bill regretted what had happened, or at least regretted the result. We all think his outbursts were in some sense uncontrollable, and that he felt sorry afterwards, but I now wonder if he knew I was capable of cutting my ties to him if he went too far. This unforgiving temperament of mine was made clear to me when I witnessed a vice-chancellor criticise and demean a dean in front of me, when I was a mere head of school. I clearly remember thinking that, if this vice-chancellor ever spoke to me like that, I would immediately send him my letter of resignation. This would not be a rational thought-out response, but something I simply felt I had to do and would enjoy doing—even if I lived to regret the gesture. Many years later a different vice-chancellor did almost exactly this to me, so I acted as predicted, taking myself into rather early 'retirement'.

I have been surprised to find myself liking my father more as I began to see his life as a whole, since I think that out of all of us (Janet and my brothers), I was the quickest to find him unbearable, or at least was the quickest to judge and slowest to forgive. I love the photos that have surfaced of Roy with Dicky Flynn before the war changed them, suggesting two handsome, confident, possibly cheeky young men living it up as far as it was possible without any money. It made me similarly happy to see how much Bill appears to have enjoyed his career at Mitchell Cotts. And he never took his good fortune for granted. It had been easier to remember his black moods than his love of life.

Towards the end of this project, I asked both my brothers to write to me, independently, and tell me whether finding out so much about Dad's life had changed their appreciation/ understanding/feelings about him, if at all. I also asked them to respond to some specific statements about him, and about the relationship between our parents.

Colin responded without delay, writing: 'I feel a greater sense of the arc of his life and his feelings about it. It has made me more admiring of him, very empathetic to his experience, and very loving towards him.' He disagreed with my statement that 'We did not have a close relationship with Dad.' And he disagreed with my statement that 'We were always a bit on our guard, ready for trouble', writing back, that it was 'only later in life for me—related to alcohol. When there was trouble, I did not hold it against him because I think I understood where it came from.'

In contrast to Colin, I did hold it against him, and had no inkling where it came from at the time. William, like me, has earlier memories of being wary of Bill's unpredictability especially at mealtimes, as do some of our friends. But we agree that we knew, even if only subconsciously, that these explosions were, as William put it, 'not coldblooded attacks against us but more him venting his own frustrations'.

Of the three of us it is William who finds it hardest to reconcile what we have learned about Bill with the father we experienced. Unlike Colin, who can now see a father whom he always thought was there, William now thinks he had no idea who his father was. 'I didn't know him at all'. As this book was being typeset William confessed to me that he had not yet read it as a whole. When I called him to talk about this, he told me that he fears being overwhelmed with regret about not knowing Bill and not having thought about him very much. 'I didn't know who he was and therefore Dad didn't know me.' William thinks it will also be painful to confront his own youthful mistakes, and that he may feel 'ashamed'. The fact that 'Dad never had a go at me about them', if anything, makes it harder. Even thinking about this prospect brings tears to his eyes as we talk, and I curse being ten thousand miles away. William says, and he is right, that we three need to be together again to talk about it all.

It was while checking some facts with William about Bill's farming project in Wales that I was brought up sharp by his descriptions of Bill's difficult and damaging side. It reminded me of just how little time I really spent with Bill after I left home. It also alerted me to the fact that I had been about to write an ending to Bill's story that reflected the emotional distance that I had managed to put between us.

William and his wife Jane both saw a lot of Bill during their years in Wales and had plenty of opportunity to see him when he was at his worst. This generally seemed to involve unprovoked critical and undermining rants against one or other of his family. They did not feel dangerous or threatening—but they were upsetting to experience or witness.

After this conversation with William, I suddenly remembered Janet's five-year diaries which I took home with me after she died. There were four of them I think, with the five lines allowed for each day nearly always filled in. Janet had enough space to comment on the weather, the garden, the main activities of the day and visitors, and she also recorded the days when Bill was really difficult. I could not bring myself to destroy them when she died, mainly out of a sense of archival responsibility rather than any fascination with their content. They lurked around with the other family documents I kept, until the moment I decided to start sorting through the boxes so that my children did not have to inherit their contents. The diaries would have been a valuable resource right now, but in my sorting enthusiasm I had decided not to read them, simply because I did not want to be reminded how often Janet might have suffered from Bill's 'illness'. I did not want this knowledge in my head. So, the diaries were shredded.

*

My brothers and I agree that we never in any way felt physically threatened (despite the odd 'thick ear'), and that our parents loved each other deeply. However, a family therapist might suggest that I moved to the other side of the world in order to avoid, however subconsciously, what I knew would be damaging confrontations. I think this would not be a ridiculous suggestion. Colin, on the other hand, thinks it is a ridiculous suggestion. Meanwhile, William tells me he now 'can't understand how we all ended up living all over the world'. In other words, while we now agree on many more facts about Bill's life, we experienced that life differently and responded differently to it. We do, however, agree that we never doubted Bill's love for us, even before we read the letters that he wrote to Janet from South America in 1948. And we have all turned out alright. As Barry Greer said, three out of three isn't bad.

Barry Greer's suggestion that three out of three isn't bad suddenly reminded me of a moment where I felt a similar sense of family success. Bill did not leave a will, knowing full well what the French legal system would insist on if it got hold of one. He simply made it clear that he wished his estate to be divided between us in a way that reflected our financial needs, and Janet had the power to enact this. Colin had little financial need so would receive one sixth of the total; William had the most financial need so would receive half of the total; and I would get a third. I could afford to think about this in a dispassionate way, but I remember being very proud of Colin's willing acceptance of this arrangement. I also felt proud of us as a family. We all (Janet and the three of us) went to the oak-panelled room provided by Credit Suisse in Guernsey to arrange this distribution, and I can still see the surprise on the face of the banker as we divided up the bonds with little concern for anything except the broad parameters set by Bill. When I asked Colin for his memories of how Dad organised this, he wrote back: 'I was very proud of him. Each according to their need. I had no need of money. But I might have been hurt if he'd left me nothing or a token.'

When Janet died fifteen years later, she too felt no need to leave a will. I had already been given authority to manage her finances, and my brothers allowed me to distribute the remaining estate according to her wishes without ever asking to see the books. This also makes me proud.

I feel I have discovered just what an achievement Bill's life was. I didn't 'lose' him in the process, but I didn't 'find' him either. It just turned out to be a great story.

Chapter 10
Coda

Coda: The recapitulation often ends with a passage that sounds like a termination, paralleling the music that ended the exposition; thus, any music coming after this termination will be perceived as extra material, i.e., as a coda. In works in variation form, the coda occurs following the last variation and will be very noticeable as the first music not based on the theme.

While searching for information about Bill's wartime experiences on my return from San Francisco in August 2022, I came across the website called Forces War Records (FWR). It holds almost ten million entries about the British army from the middle of the eighteenth century onwards. It aspires to help anyone trying to do military family history research, claiming that the official published lists 'are often one of the best ways to trace an officer's career in the British Services'. I found the barest details for Bill initially, with two entries for W. R. Probert from 1944 and 1945, giving his rank as Second Lieutenant since November 1941, attached to the Royal Warwickshire Regiment. Only later did I realise that this was totally misleading since he never served with this regiment. By trying variations of his name including misspellings, I found the record of the award of his DSO in the *London Gazette* of 21 June 1945, as William Ray Probert. From this I went back to the FWR site where he materialised, this time as William Ray Probert, Temporary Major in the Intelligence Corps. I bookmarked this FWR page about him when I found it, just as I bookmarked any relevant ancestry site that would allow me. Thus far, FWR had not

235

told me anything I did not already know, and I cancelled my subscription once I realised that Bill had in fact been working for a variety of secretive branches of the Intelligence Corps, which would not be appearing in these kinds of publicly available war records.

Late one evening in February 2023 I receive an email from the FWR algorithm telling me that 'Another subscriber to Forces War Records has bookmarked and left a comment regarding a record—William Ray PROBERT, which you have also bookmarked', and inviting me to click through to see what this new comment says. I have to resubscribe in order to do this, but I have learned that good leads can be found in the most unlikely places, especially if they involve military history buffs. Within a few minutes I can see the comment, from user ID 3665363, which reads:

> Please get in touch if you have any information about Maj Bill Probert and his life after he returned from Foix in 1945.

Intrigued about this, I immediately type into the Reply box:

> Could you identify who you are? I do indeed have a great deal of information about Major Bill Probert's life after Foix.

ID 3665363 replies twenty-five minutes later:

> It is long story, and somewhat delicate, as I have reasons to believe that Bill Probert is my maternal grandfather. I am happy to explain in more detail. Can I ask with whom I am talking?

Without pausing to let this really sink in, I reply:

> I am Belinda Probert, his daughter. I live in Australia and am writing a book about him because I know he had many secrets. Though I had no idea this might be a possibility.

Then it does sink in. I suggest that perhaps we should continue this exchange by email rather than through the public comment boxes on the FWR website. I add another 'comment', that it is late in the evening in Melbourne and that I assume the person leaving the comments is in the northern hemisphere. I get an instant reply from ID 3665363 who materialises as a woman, called Barbara Iten.

> Dear Belinda Probert, thank you for your reply. Yes I am near Foix at this very moment. I am standing in a field in front of a memorial plaque that would fill your heart with pride and love.

I have to get up and walk around the house, patting my chest in the way people do to manage powerful emotion, and saying, 'oh my goodness, oh my goodness'. I need to tell someone what has happened.

I text my daughter asking if she is still up, and when she says she is, I tell her about Barbara. She warns me not to assume anything until I hear more. I realise that I have no desire to find yet another mystery in my father's life. I eventually go to bed knowing that at least we have begun our extraordinary change on good terms, even if this doesn't make it easier to get to sleep.

The next morning (my time) we start to exchange emails. Barbara explains that thirty years earlier her grandmother, Anne-Marie Vigneau, revealed to her that her real grandfather was 'an Englishman she had met towards the end of the war, Major William Probert from the intelligence service who had been parachuted with General Bigeard to fight with the resistance'. Anne-Marie had never spoken about this to her daughter, Barbara's mother, bringing her up to believe that the man she lived with was her father.

Anne-Marie's sudden desire to share this information, decades after the event, seems to have been triggered by the fact Barbara had just given birth to her first child. She learned that her grandmother had been moved from Paris to the relative safety of Foix early in the war, where she continued to work for La Poste. Foix was then in Vichy-controlled France, outside the German-occupied zone. By the end of 1942, however, the Germans and Italians occupied the rest of France between them, and from then on German troops and the Gestapo were stationed in Foix. Anne-Marie met Bill when he dropped out of the sky to organise the resistance fighters in the area to secure the liberation of the Ariège in August 1944. After he left, she discovered she was pregnant.

Barbara and her English partner, William, are driving back to England from southern Spain, crossing the Pyrenees into France near Andorra (probably on the same route we had taken returning from our family holiday sixty years earlier). Knowing of Bill's role in the liberation of Foix, which is well documented, they decide to visit the town, and learn everything they can about Bill's time there. It is from Foix that Barbara posts her question on the FWR record for William Ray Probert, and the algorithm alerts me immediately when she does so. She tells me later: 'That night William woke me up in the middle of the night saying we had received a reply, your first ever message.' The story Anne-Marie told her granddaughter fits so exactly with what I know of Bill's mission that not for one minute do I doubt that it is true. I wonder how often anyone who posts on such an uninteresting military site hits the jackpot within a few hours.

Barbara spends the next day at the local Museum of the Resistance reading descriptions of her grandfather, seeing him appear as 'a kind man, an intelligent man, a gentle and efficient leader'. They go to find the sign that has been erected at the edge of the forest where Bill and the team landed, and the farm where they were sheltered until the necessary arms drops were organised. It is while Barbara and William are standing in front of this sign that they get my second message saying that I am Bill's daughter. I am an aunt she did not know she had.

As Barbara continues her drive across France, from Foix to Bordeaux and then up to St Malo we continue to email each other with questions and information. Her first long email includes a photograph taken only two years earlier of Anne-Marie on her one-hundredth birthday, with her daughter Margaret who is almost certainly my half-sister, and both of her children, Barbara and Robert, together with four of their children. It dawns on me that if we had made this connection just a couple of years earlier, I could have asked Anne-Marie herself for the story of her meeting with Bill in 1944.

I feel I should reciprocate this sharing of information, but I have no idea where to start. Since they have been in the vicinity, I find myself telling her that Bill is buried in the cemetery in St Faust de Haut in the Pyrenees where he lived for the last ten years of his life; and that he was born in the Rhondda in Wales in 1915. I tell her that I know a lot about his life because I have been researching it for the last six months and will be coming to Britain in May to find out more.

I think about whether I am going to have to deal with the discovery that my father refused to acknowledge the existence of this baby. The idea that this might have happened is painful. Not least because I realise this baby was born just as Bill was falling in love with Janet in Rome. I feel an urgent need to know how Anne-Marie lived with this baby, whether she was supported when it was born, how she managed financially, whether the baby was loved.

During this long and astonishing day Barbara decides to call her mother to tell her how she has found me, and I learn that Margaret lives in Ibiza. It seems that they have never talked to each other about the fact that Bill is Margaret's father. It is as though a small explosive device has detonated in both our families, shaking everything loose. Barbara and I both want to pause our email exchanges so that we can begin to absorb what we are discovering, but we also want to know so much more without delay. I am anxious about how Anne-Marie would have coped, and about the baby's early life. I am equally anxious that I may learn something about my father that will reduce him in my estimation.

I confess to a feeling of relief when Barbara emails me again, after talking to her mother, with new information: when Anne-Marie was sent to Foix during the war she was already the lover of a married man in Paris. His family lived in Foix, and he arranged for her to stay with his brother while she lived there. While very possessive and devoted to Anne-Marie, Auguste was unwilling or unable to divorce his wife. I learn that Anne-Marie remained with this man, living as though they were man and wife, until his death in the 1960s.

Over the day some elements of the story become clearer, and I feel increasingly that perhaps this is not going to be a story of guilt, regret and remorse, but that we will be able to work together, as it were, to bring our sides of the story together. Barbara tells me that she had already formed a view of Bill's character that made her unable to accept the idea that he would abandon a baby. She had managed to find Marcel Bigeard's wartime description of Bill, and his 'gueule d'amour' and seen the photograph of Bill, Bigeard and Royo.

My emotions are swinging wildly between disbelief and alarm, and amazement and excitement. I need something stable to hang on to, so I forward some of these email exchanges between Barbara and me to my brother William in France, telling him I need to talk to him when he wakes up. Not surprisingly, he is quick to call, gobsmacked by this development. As I am talking to him on WhatsApp, my email pings and I see that it is a message from Margaret, the baby in question, who must now be seventy-seven years old. In the subject line she has written 'Deeply moved'.

> Is the least I can say
> Belinda, I wish, if you agree of course, to meet you when you come to Europe in May.
> I'm too emotional at the moment, but maybe we could Skype sometime and pull pieces of information together. I do feel so grateful to you for unveiling the past and revealing a reality full of hope.
> Just now I'm trying to realise...
> It's pure joy
> Margaret

I read it to William, and I think I may have sounded a little hysterical, so relieved, so excited, happy, full of questions. It is extraordinary the real-time speed with which we are all communicating. But I also realise that I am going to be able to answer so many of the questions Margaret and Barbara will have, and this easily offsets the feeling of being weighed down by another story about Bill that I cannot digest. In just twenty-four hours I have gone from shock, to fear about what this story might mean, to exhilaration at the prospect of being able to solve a great mystery for Margaret and her family.

*

I later learn that my half-sister Margaret was nineteen years old and about to marry when she was told about her biological father. She had grown up believing that Auguste, the man her mother lived with, was her father. It was not her mother, Anne-Marie, who told her about Bill, but a family friend of Anne-Marie's parents. It is as though, when Margaret and Barbara were about to start their own families, some sense of duty—that children should know where they come from—led to these disclosures. Margaret's informant was close to her grandparents and told her that her real father was Bill Probert, from British intelligence. Margaret also told me how the man she had thought was her father had taken steps to ensure that Anne-Marie and Bill would not see each other again. Being from Foix himself and having family there, he made it clear to everyone that Anne-Marie and Bill should be kept apart.

Within a few days I learn that Anne-Marie and Margaret never talked about Bill even after Margaret knew the truth.

Margaret tried to explain her upbringing:

> I was her [Anne-Marie's] only child, lived with them in Paris. I always felt paralysed when it came to ask about my real father and saw myself as we say in French 'un cheveu sur la soupe', unwanted. But that of course was my interpretation. I don't feel like a war casualty anymore, that was a child and teenager's impression.
> Be sure I enjoy life so very much though.
> That's it for today.
> I'm happy and excited to meet you.
> Margaret.

*

I find myself poring over every document I have that might tell me how or when Bill met Anne-Marie, and when exactly Bill left Foix with Bigeard and Deller. I know I am hoping to discover that he could not have known about the pregnancy when he left. Margaret sends me a photograph of her mother as a beautiful young woman with glorious platinum-blonde hair. As I check the original mission reports from this time, it appears most likely that Bill and Anne-Marie met on 14 September at the gala event organised by the Allied mission to liberate Foix, for the purpose of raising money for a nearby town that had been devastated by German troops. As I know from my research into Bill's war, everyone was at this gala, celebrating the liberation of the Ariège and dancing late into the night.

I already know that Bill left Foix nine days later, on 23 September, reporting to the Special Project Operations centre in Avignon, en route to Paris. Later, after my research trip to Wales, I read more of Bigeard's accounts of his war in another book, and find his description of that gala evening, where Bill noticed a small blonde woman, very pretty, among those who thronged around the three heroes of the hour. Later in this book, Bigeard describes watching Bill, 'accompanied by his blonde', write up and sign a recommendation that Bigeard be awarded the Military Cross. I find this recommendation in Bill's official reports, and it is dated 23 September, the date they left Foix for Avignon.* As far as it is possible to know anything, it seems that Bill and Anne-Marie had an intense week together, and that he was then obliged to leave—before she knew she was pregnant.

Margaret and I conclude that they exchanged addresses, though these turned out not to be very useful. Anne-Marie gave Bill the address of her parents' hotel in Paris, and Bill gave her his cousin's address in Coventry—which he was already relinquishing as part of his plan

---

* Bigeard describes this as Bill signing his recommendation for the award of a DSO, in Paris—but it is clear from the text that it is the Military Cross recommendation which was signed in Foix or just possibly Avignon. Anne-Marie did not accompany them to Paris.

to make a new life for himself. We think Bill and Bigeard went to the hotel run by Anne-Marie's parents once they arrived in Paris, perhaps simply to pass on information about their daughter's safety and well-being after the fighting in the Ariège. Since Bill never went back to Coventry and severed all connections with his cousin and brother living there, it is impossible to know if any letters from Anne Marie ever reached him. I think it is reasonable to conclude that he never knew about the baby.

Margaret asks if we might meet via Skype and we start to get to know each other. I try to understand why it means so much to Margaret to find us after all this time. We agree to get our DNA analysed because there is too much at stake, and on opposite sides of the world we spit into our little test tubes. Within three weeks the answer comes back that there is an eighty percent likelihood that we are half-sisters.

*

Meanwhile Margaret is determined to meet me, even though it is not possible for me to travel to Ibiza as part of my already booked and organised research trip. So she comes to Oxford where William and I are staying with an old friend after our visit to Wales, finding an Airbnb close by for two nights. We three meet in the late afternoon outside her Airbnb and begin by taking a long slow walk in the evening sunshine, down through South Park towards St Clements, just to get used to being with each other. We have dinner in a noisy Italian restaurant, and I can see that Margaret is a discerning eater, at ease in Italian as well as English. Where one earth do we begin? We shout at each other over the hubbub, and it seems to feel alright. I think I look like her.

Next day Margaret arrives with a photo album from her childhood. Such a thoughtful idea. I am again relieved to see that it reveals a comfortable upbringing, with warm grandparents in Paris and Auguste's family in Foix. We have a picnic lunch in a nearby park, and then show Margaret something of the most beautiful Oxford colleges, though the sheer number of tourists makes it less agreeable than it might have been. The following day, before Margaret takes her taxi all the way back to Gatwick (the only way to do it in less than five hours) we have breakfast together. She tells us more about her childhood (parents both working and largely leaving her to take care of herself); her realisation that she should take charge of her life at a very young age; her marriage at nineteen to a Swiss man she meets in Spain; her life with young children in Italy; and then a long successful career in Switzerland, followed by retirement to Ibiza. She cannot stay any longer with us because the man she married at nineteen (and later divorced) is dying and she needs to be with him. She speaks French, Italian, Spanish and English fluently. Bill would have been very impressed. Is this genetic? We talk about what kind of siblings we can become at this stage of our lives and living at such distances from each other.

As the apprehension about this meeting fades away, I stop thinking about what my sister is like, and what interests we might have in common, and begin to think of her as just that: my sister. William feels the same way. Colin in San Francisco is not sure that he needs to know more, but after our reports decides to email her. She Skypes with him, and he persuades her to adopt his preference for doing everything with FaceTime.

I go on looking for evidence of Bill's movements after he is parachuted into France, and any possible letters that might have been exchanged with Anne-Marie. I can be certain only that they had a little over a week together. Barbara remembers Anne-Marie telling her, so long ago, that Bill asked her to come back to England with him, saying he had family in Coventry. Anne-Marie could not, it seems, imagine living in the 'north' of England. But she wrote to that address, finally including a photograph of herself with Margaret as a baby on her lap. She heard nothing back. By then Bill was in Rome, on his way to life in Vienna.

*

Margaret is, of course, part of Bill's story, but only the version of his story that I am telling. As Margaret rightly puts it, her relationship is with us, her siblings. From what I can tell her about Bill's life, she can imagine those traits she has perhaps inherited from him. She looks like him too. We don't need to talk much about him now. We just talk to each other like brothers and sisters.

Family research is often tedious, and slow to provide what are—individually—small rewards. It is true that persistence and patience and a credit card can bring a whole family slowly into focus as you count the number of miners, grocers and early deaths and use Google maps in street view to stare at their narrow homes. But there is also serendipity. Who could have imagined that they would find a sister, whom they were not looking for, in a war records depository?

I think Bill would certainly have approved of Margaret. I want to write that he would have approved of the way we found each other. What might he have said about our research into his life? Surely, he would like the fact that his children found reason to respect him more and to like him more. But he would probably have hated our sympathy for his black moods and our attempts to understand him.

*

Of his children, it might seem that Colin most clearly understands Bill, and sympathises with the causes of his drinking and his unpredictable outbursts. He was the least surprised by Denzil's revelations, though he does not know why. And as a successful businessman himself, he always appreciated Bill's achievements at Mitchell Cotts. He was very pleased when I was able to resurrect and flesh out that career from the company magazines, but for Colin it was confirming his perceptions rather than creating new ones. More importantly, as the details of Roy's efforts to become Bill surfaced, Colin's empathy for his father increased. It is almost as though the father who emerges provides powerful reassurance that Colin had understood him correctly, allowing Colin access to his own emotions. He tells me as we finalise the manuscript that, 'Everything I have learned about him is consistent with the warm, respectful, and admiring feelings I had toward him throughout my life. I loved him deeply, especially in his later years when he became increasingly frail and vulnerable. As I write this to you, tears roll down my cheeks.'

Typing this out, I find my eyes are prickling too. But they are prickling for my older brother, to whom I was never close as a child, and who also moved far away from our parents, but in the opposite direction to me. We have seen little of each over the intervening years, but talking to him about this book has been a remarkable revelation. I suspect it has told him little new about me, but it has told me much that I did not know about him. Colin did not develop protective armour like mine but remained vulnerable and open. I think that must have been painful sometimes, but the story of Roy now gives him 'immense pleasure'.

William's responses have been different again. When I asked him to describe his reactions to this project, he wrote back: 'First of all, what is interesting is that up until now I have not really ever thought very much about my relationship with Dad, what exactly it was. I know that when he died I felt a great loss, and sadness.' It was William who spent many years living close to Bill after Colin and I had gone abroad, and I think Bill had more respect for his farming life than he had for my career. This is something I have only recently come to see, but somehow it has never mattered to me. Perhaps it is another illustration of the protective armour I had grown? Or did I find plenty of affirmation from Janet to balance the scales? I also sense that Bill felt very protective of his youngest son, all his life. Despite the difficulties in their relationship, William must have known this because he tells me that 'when Dad died I felt suddenly alone' and that 'while Dad was there I felt safer'. This, too, causes my eyes to prickle.

As for me, it is hard to be sure about the different forces that shaped my response to Bill—temperament, politics, gender? My previous lack of interest in Bill's career probably reflected the fact that as a young adult I had been dismissive of the corporate world—particularly the city of London—as inherently bad. Many of my earliest political ideas were shaped by the intellectual critique of neo-colonialism that dominated left-wing thinking in the early 1970s. When I arrived in Australia in 1976 as a young academic, I even joined a reading group wrestling with Lenin's great work *On Imperialism*. Almost fifty years later, I have a much more nuanced attitude to my father's role at Mitchell Cotts. I am ready to see not only that Bill was a very clever businessman, but that much of what he did was worth doing. I can now appreciate the extraordinary determination and talent that created the comfortable and privileged childhood I had, and with effort I can imagine what it might have been like to grow up at 44 Gynor Place, Ynyshir.

But what I really want to know is whether his father loved him and made that train for him, and how Roy coped with his sudden death. Did his oldest brother Colenso take him under his wing? I want to know what Minna was like. I think I understand Bill better, but I would not say that I *know* him better, nor that I feel differently towards him. Perhaps I feel differently about myself. I wish that Bill's old age and physical vulnerability had made me drop my guard so that I might have felt as close to him as Colin did. But I don't think we choose the relationship we have with our parents. For all of us, it is the product of our life experiences and our temperaments.

Notes

This is not a scholarly book that requires a footnote for every claim or quotation. But I am a former academic who cannot help herself, and the result was 344 footnotes in the final draft. They have been safely archived. The notes I have provided here acknowledge the books and articles and websites on which I have relied in writing about the historical context of my father's life.

Chapter 1. Coal is King: Born in the Rhondda

There are several excellent historical accounts of economic and social life in the Rhondda region of South Wales. The most substantial of these is E. D. Lewis's *The Rhondda Valleys*, University College Cardiff Press, Cardiff, 1963. I appreciated the discovery that E.D. Lewis was himself a Rhondda scholarship boy—another eminent graduate of Porth County Boys (a few years ahead of my father). Stuart Macintyre's *Little Moscows: Communism and Working Class Militancy in Inter-war Britain*, Croom Helm, London, 1980 includes a scholarly account of life and politics in the Rhondda Fach in the 1920s and 30s. Two books by Chris Williams provide a wider context: *Capitalism, Community and Conflict: The South Wales Coalfield 1898–1947*, University of Wales Press, Cardiff, 1988; and *Democratic Rhondda: Politics and Society 1885–1951*, University of Wales Press, Cardiff, 1996.

My descriptions of housing in Ynyshir and the rest of the Rhondda rely heavily on Malcolm Fisk's book, *Housing in the Rhondda 1800–1940*, Merton Priory Press, Cardiff, 1996. For a better understanding of my grandmother's and great-grandmothers' lives in the Rhondda I have relied on Dot Smith's chapter, 'Counting the cost of coal: women's lives in the Rhondda, 1881–1911', in *In Our Mothers Land:*

Chapters in Welsh Women's History 1830-1939, edited by Angela V. John, University of Wales Press, Cardiff, 1991. I only wish I had discovered Rebecca Davies' recent Masters thesis earlier: 'How did gender and poverty impact on the experiences of the mining family in interwar Rhondda, 1918-1939', Open University, January 2023.

Daryl Leeworthy's recent biography of Gwyn Thomas—who attended Porth County Boys just a couple of years ahead of my father—offers another approach to understanding life in the Rhondda in the 1920s and 1930s. I have used Leeworthy's quotation from Dai Smith about the collective culture of the Rhondda, only to discover that Dai Smith also attended—albeit briefly—Porth County Boys. See notes to Chapter 2 for full details of Leeworthy's book.

In trying to bring this historical research to life I was greatly helped by two fine novels about working-class families in the Rhondda. Richard Llewellyn's *How Green Was My Valley*, Penguin Classics 2001, needs no introduction. Jack Jones' less sentimental *Black Parade* (1935) was reprinted by Parthian in 2009 as part of the Library of Wales series and is a confronting and powerful account of family life in Merthyr from the late nineteenth century to the general strike. Also helpful were the old photographs of Rhondda life reproduced in the series of books called 'Images of Wales' (Tempus Publishing, Stroud), particularly *Cwm Rhondda Fach: Trehafod to Maerdy* put together by David Owen (2003), *Porth and Rhondda Fach: The Second Selection*, compiled by Aldo Bacchetta and Glyn Rudd (1998), as well as *Rhondda Collieries*, compiled by David Carpenter (2000).

For information about coal mining, health, non-conformism, boxing and rugby I have relied on several general histories of Wales. These are Gwyn A. Williams' two books, *When Was Wales?* Penguin, Harmondsworth, 1985 and *The Welsh in their History*, Croom Helm, London, 1982. Also *The Land Remembers: A View of Wales*, Faber and Faber, 1977 by the other Gwyn Williams; and Kenneth Morgan's *Rebirth of a Nation: A History of Modern Wales*, Clarendon Press, Oxford, 1981. The New Zealand rugby tour of 1905 is told in the magical novel by Lloyd Jones, *The Book of Fame*, Penguin New Zealand, 2001.

For accounts of the 1905 mining disaster see Rhondda Cynon Taf Library Service, 'Our Past', at https://webapps.rctcbc.gov.uk/heritagetrail/english/rhondda/wattstown.html. The names and addresses of the victims are listed at https://www.welshcoalmines.co.uk/deathrolls/Wattstown.htm. If you look at these addresses on a map of Ynyshir and Wattstown you can begin to feel the devastating impact it must have had on the whole valley.

The quote about Nonconformity and Welsh identity is from Gwyn A. Williams, *The Welsh in their History*, p. 171. He also described the unifying nature of support for rugby in *When Was Wales*, p. 221. The Inspector's report on Ynyshir Boys School is in the 'Diary or Log Book Ynyshir Boys School 1900–1923', UDR/E/58/34, Glamorgan Archives, Cardiff.

The quote about the end of the good times is from Leeworthy's biography of Gwyn Thomas, p. 43. Gwyn A. Williams, in *The Welsh in their History*, tells the story of Borodin and the Red belt of the British working class on p. 266 and p. 185. The account of Wilf Jones' life is from Bachetta and Rudd's photographic history of *Porth and the Rhondda Fach*, pp. 86–7.

Chapter 2. The Education of Roy

Without Vernon Owen Hughes I would never have really understood the significance of Porth County Boys School in Roy's life. His short book *Porth County: The School and its Boys* was self-published in 1991 but survives in various Welsh libraries and archives. I have used several quotations from this book to describe life in the school in the 1920s and 30s. Gwyn Thomas's autobiography, *A Few Selected Exits*, Seren Books, Bridgend, 1968, in which he describes his own experiences at Porth County Boys, just a couple of years ahead of Roy, is both funny and startling. The book was made into a BBC film starring Anthony Hopkins as Gwyn Thomas. Daryl Leeworthy's *Fury of Past Time: A Life of Gwyn Thomas*, Parthian, Cardigan, 2022, is another invaluable background resource for understanding Roy's experiences at the school, as well as broader aspects of Rhondda culture at that time.

Most of what I have learned about the compulsory years of schooling in Ynyshir at the start of the twentieth century I gleaned from the Glamorgan Archives in Cardiff. The records held there provided answers to my questions about how Roy was able to go to Porth County, as well as his ability to attend King's College, London University. My sources were Ynyshir Log Books, (ER 49/1–4); the Ynyshir Boys Log Book, 1922, and the 'Rhondda Education Authority Scholarships records 1917–1936', (UD/RE/56/).

E.D. Lewis in *The Rhondda Valleys* again provided a wealth of detail about life in this area during Roy's school years. For the broader picture of working-class access to university education between the wars, and the importance of teaching scholarships, Carol Dyhouse's research is invaluable. See her 'Family patterns of social mobility through higher education in England in the 1930s', *Journal of Social History*, vol. 34, no. 4 (Summer, 2001), pp. 817–842, and her 'Going to university in England between the wars: access and funding', *History of Education*, 2002, vol. 31, no. 1, pp. 1–14. The data on the social class of university students in the 1930s can be found on p. 822 of 'Family patterns of social mobility'. The quotes about education scholarships for lower status sons are on p. 827.

I have again relied on general histories of Wales for the background to Welsh educational policy and developments. Especially Gwyn Williams, *When Was Wales?*, and *The Welsh in Their History*. A useful University of Cambridge briefing paper on Welsh education is available at https://sesc.hist.cam.ac.uk/wp-content/uploads/2018/08/Briefing-paper-Wales.pdf (no author or date).

The Institute of Education in London kindly sent me a copy of the 'University of London regulations for Four-Year and One-Year Courses of Professional Training 1938' which explained exactly what funding Roy received while an undergraduate. The MPhil on the Miners

Welfare Fund is by Vernon Owen Scrimgeour Jones, 'Improving the social and working conditions of miners 1920–46', MPhil. Thesis, Sheffield University, 2020. https://etheses.whiterose.ac.uk/27852/

The information about co-op wages is from a website called Coalfield Web Materials: http://www.agor.org.uk/cwm/themes/co-op/co-ops. asp. The quote from Jack Jones' novel can be found on pp. 181–2 of *Black Parade*. Gwyn Thomas's description of school caps and rickets is from *A Few Selected Exits*, p. 4, and his comments on the importance of winning scholarships to escape the pits are found in Daryl Leeworthy's biography, p. 60. The quote about a collective sense of altruism and mutual support is from the anonymous Cambridge briefing paper, as is the quotation about the level of scholarship provision in Wales. Gwyn Williams describes the examination obstacle race in *When Was Wales?* p. 246 and provides the quote about wanting to leave suffocating Wales on p. 247.

Benny's account of the commission on unemployment is on p. 411 of *Black Parade*. The description of the Porth Carnival's contests is by Gwyn Thomas, reported in Leeworthy's biography of him, p. 41, where he also describes the fund-raising purposes of the Porth Carnival.

Gwyn Thomas's description of his relationship with his headmaster is from *A Few Selected Exits*, pp. 39–44. His concern about the sheer height of Oxford students is from p. 49. And his feeling at home listening to a Welsh male voice choir is from p. 212.

Chapter 3. Roy's War: Secrets and Bravery

For a personal account of being recruited into the Field Security Police at the start of the war see Malcolm Muggeridge's, *Chronicles of Wasted Time*, vol. 2 of *The Infernal Grove*, Fontana Collins, London, 1973.

Most of what I know about the Intelligence Corps is derived from Anthony Clayton's *Forearmed: A History of the Intelligence Corps*, Brassey's, London, 1993; and Nicholas van de Bijl's *Sharing the Secret: The History of the Intelligence Corps 1940–2010*, Pen and Sword, Barnsley, 2020 (read on Scribd, meaning no page numbers are available). I have also used F. H. Hinsley and C. A. G. Simkins, *British Intelligence in the Second World War*, vol. 4, *Security and Counter-Intelligence*, HMSO, London, 1990. These authors describe all the different kinds of intelligence activities that someone in the FSP might undertake.

Walter Haydn Davies writes about the importance of movies in the life of Rhondda boys in his book *The Right Place, the Right Time: Memories of boyhood days in a Welsh mining community*, Triskel edition, Christopher Davies Publishers, Swansea, 1975, p. 140.

Social and political life in Cairo is brought to life by Artemis Cooper in her *Cairo in the War 1939–1945*, John Murray, 1989. Doreen Hawkins' personal experiences with ENSA in Cairo are described in her *Drury Lane to Dimapur: Wartime adventures of an actress*, Dovecote Press, Stanbridge, 2009.

A very detailed history of the Political Warfare Executive is provided in David Garnett's, *The Secret History of PWE: The Political Warfare Executive 1939–45*, St Ermin's Press, London, 2002. The atmospheric video about PWE training for the Balkans in Cairo can be found at https://www.criticalpast.com/video/65675045520_British-Political-Warfare-Executive-School_men-discussing_training_attend-lectures.

For the Inter-Allied Mission to liberate the Ariège I have relied on the original reports written by my father for SOE, as well as the accounts by Marcel Bigeard in *De la Brousse à la Jungle*, Hachette, Paris, 1994; and *Pour Une Parcelle de Gloire*, Plon, Paris, 1975. I have also used Erwan Bergot's biography, *Bigeard*, France Loisirs, Paris, 1988. Chapter 3 in this book, 'Les Ailes Deployées' provides the fullest and most vivid account of the mission that I have found, but I suspect it is unreliable in parts, depending overwhelmingly on Bigeard's reminiscences.

For a more academic appreciation see Barnett Singer and John Langdon, 'Bigeard: Last of the Line in Vietnam and Algeria', in *Cultured Force: makers and defenders of the French colonial empire*, University of Wisconsin Press, 2004. Translation from the French of quotations from these books is by me. A first-hand account of a similar Allied mission to liberate south-west France is to be found in the chapter 'The Jedburgh Teams: Fred Bailey in France and Burma', in Sean Rayment's *Tales from the Special Forces Club: the untold stories of Britain's elite WWII warriors*, William Collins, London, 2014.

On the question of social class in the British army I have relied heavily on Arthur Marwick, 'World War II and Social Class', in A. C. Duke et al (eds) *Britain and the Netherlands*, Martinus Nijhoff, The Hague, 1977; and Ben Macintyre's *Colditz*, Penguin, 2023.

The description of what Bill and Dicky are wearing in their first photograph together in uniform comes from Muggeridge's book, p. 89, while his description of hostilities between the Red Caps and the FSP at Mytchett can be found on pp. 91-2. The deployment to the Middle East is described in van de Bijl's, *Sharing the Secret*. The role of the FSP is described by Captain Sir Basil Bartlett in *My First War: An Army Officer's Journal for May, 1940: Through Belgium to Dunkirk*, Chatto and Windus, 1940.

Clayton describes Cairo as a city made for espionage and subversion on p. 153 of *Forearmed*. Artemis Cooper's description of Cairo night life is on p. 127; Doreen Hawkins' sympathetic account of soldiers in the desert is on pp. 93-4 of *Drury Lane to Dimapur*.

Marcel Bigeard's description of his training in Algiers is on p. 17 of *De la Brousse à la Jungle*, and his description of Bill is on p. 18. His account of their flight and parachute drop into the Ariège is on pp. 18-19. Singer and Langdon's perspective is to be found on p. 273 of their chapter 'Bigeard'. The description of the team on the plane is by Bigeard's biographer, Bergot, and can be found on p. 114. The account of the use of the Château de Lauquié by the Gestapo is from the regional newspaper, *La Depeche*, 18 September 2022;

https://www.ladepeche.fr/2022/09/18/la-villa-lauquie-entre-petite-et-grande-histoire-ariegeoise-10551361.php. The description of the gala celebration in Foix is from the newspaper *Libération*, 'La mission interalliée reçoit...Une soirée inoubliable', pp. 1–2, 18 September 1944. All translations from the French are mine.

Keith Lowe's description of the emotional outpourings experienced by the liberating armies is from his book *The Fear and the Freedom: Why the Second World War Still Matters*, Penguin, 2018, pp. 28–9. Bigeard's account of dancing with Edith Piaf is in *Une Parcelle de Gloire*, p. 44.

Chapter 4. Never Going Back

The source for the material on class in the British army in this chapter is Geoffrey Field's '"Civilians in Uniform": Class and Politics in the British Armed Forces, 1939–1945', in *International Labor and Working-Class History*, No. 80 (Fall 2011), pp. 121–147. The quotations about class prejudice can be found on p. 125. The stories from Colditz are to be found in Ben Macintyre's *Colditz*, and Douglas Bader is quoted on p. 175.

On the theme of fear and freedom I am referring to Jean-Paul Sartre's *Existentialism is a Humanism*, a lecture given in Paris in October 1945; and Erich Fromm's *Fear of Freedom*, Routledge Classics, originally published in England in 1942. These themes shape Keith Lowe's interesting book *The Fear and the Freedom*. The quotation about clutching at an ideology to avoid the agony of freedom is on p. 149.

The newspaper interview with Denzil Griffiths about his uncle Roy was published as 'Hero who took town back from Nazis single-handed', Catherine Norton, *The Western Mail*, 4 March 1996.

Germaine Greer's book about the search for her father's origins is *Daddy, We Hardly Knew You*, Hamish Hamilton, 1989. Her question about her father modelling himself on the royal family is from p. 55;

the quote about members of the Secret Service leading a quadruple life is on p. 141.

Chapter 5. Love and Spying: From Vienna to Civvy Street

For background information about Vienna at the end of the war I have relied on Nicholas van der Bijl's book *Sharing the Secret*, especially chapter 11, 'Occupied Trieste, Germany and Austria'. I have also used Keith Jeffery's *The Secret History of MI6 1909–1949*, Penguin, 2011. For a more imaginative but well-informed take on post-war Vienna there is John le Carré's *A Perfect Spy*, Penguin, 2018. His description of the Airborne tie is on p. 29, while the quotes about Marcus Pym's experience in Vienna are on pp. 474–476.

I have quoted Hilary Mantel from her essay 'No passport Required', pp. 304–5. It is reproduced in her *A Memoir of My Former Self: A Life in Writing*, John Murray, London, 2023.

Hermione Lee's *Penelope Fitzgerald: A Life*, Chatto and Windus, London, 2013 is the source of my descriptions of Janet Russell and her time at Oxford University before the war. The quotes about Janet and 'Les Girls' can be found on pp. 49–50.

For Sidney Lamert's role in the De La Rue company I have relied on *The Highest Perfection: A History of De La Rue*, by Peter Pugh, Icon Books, 2011.

The quote from Germaine Greer about not doubting her father's story can be found on p. 110 of *Daddy, We Hardly Knew You*.

Chapter 6. Success: International Business and Life in the Stockbroker Belt

For an extraordinarily rich source of information about life in Britain immediately after the war see David Kynaston's *Austerity Britain, 1945–51*, Bloomsbury, 2007. The quote about Britain as a land of hierarchical social assumptions can be found on p. 59. Kynaston also provides the long quote from Correlli Barnett's book about the elite of Britain's industrial system, on p. 446. Kynaston is also the source of the story about Churchill and birdseed, on p. 59.

The quote on the demolition of old country houses is from David Kynaston's second volume *Family Britain 1951–57*. For the background material on class consciousness and British industrial culture in the immediate post-war years, I have relied on all four of Kynaston's volumes (*Tales of a New Jerusalem*), as well as Correlli Barnett's *The Lost Victory: British Dreams, British Realities 1945–1950*, Pan Macmillan, 2001.

The historical framework for understanding large trading companies like Mitchell Cotts comes from an excellent book by Geoffrey Jones, *Merchants to Multinationals: British Trading Companies in the Nineteenth and Twentieth Centuries*, Oxford Scholarship Online, March 2022. This work provided valuable insights not only into the way these companies changed and evolved after the Second World War, but also into the kinds of managers and directors needed for their continued success. The quotations I have used are to be found on pp. 154–5, and pp. 207–8.

For detail about the Mitchell Cotts Group, I am indebted to the material uploaded on his WordPress site by Chris Dick, including a short history of the company written by his father, who was group chairman for most of my father's time with the company. Chris has also uploaded his mother's illuminating diaries written as she travelled the world with her husband, visiting group enterprises. From their visit to Ecuador in 1964 there are several photos of Bill standing around in fields of pyrethrum, or down on the tea plantation in the Amazon basin. https://thedebutantediaries.wordpress.com

For everything else about Bill's career with the Mitchell Cotts Group I have relied on the almost complete set of *The Cottsman* magazines held by the British Library.

The academics describing Bigeard's career and his reunion with Bill are Singer and Langdon, pp. 298-9. The interview with Marcel Bigeard where he again finds tears in his eyes thinking about Bill is printed in *L'Événement du Jeudi*, 13-19 September 1990, as 'Bigeard: les petits gars et l'esprit de corps'. Bigeard's account of Bill staying with him in 1954, and possibly working for MI6, is from *Pour Une Parcelle de Gloire*, p. 44.

St John Philby tells his own extraordinary story in *Arabian Days*, Robert Hale, London 1948, and the material about his relationship with Mitchell Cotts is from the Philby Archive held at St Antony's College Oxford, from boxes 5/3/1; 5/3/5/6; 5/3/15. His love of Westminster School is described on p. 28 of *Arabian Days*. For Kim Philby's love of Westminster School see Ben Macintyre's *A Spy Among Friends*, Bloomsbury, London, 2014, with the scarf story on p. 279. The description of St John's political unreliability is from Keith Jeffery, *The Secret History of MI6*, p. 208.

Fiona Hill tells her remarkable story about the English education system in *There is Nothing For You Here*, Harper Collins, 2021. The information about Elizabeth David is from Artemis Cooper's biography, *Writing at the Kitchen Table*, Faber, 2011. The quotes about dismal meals are on pp. 131-2.

The information about Moss Bros. is from Willa Petschek, 'Fashion: rented clothes fit for a royal event', *New York Times Magazine*, 12 July 1981. The account of the Zephyr Six is from *The Independent* newspaper at https://www.independent.co.uk/life-style/motoring/features/zephyr-the-last-of-the-big-british-fords-2222976.html

Britain's love of doing the pools is analysed in Keith Laybourn's book, *The Football Pools and the British Working Class*, Routledge, 2022, while I have quoted David Kynaston on the checking of scores, from p. 195 in *Family Britain*. Kenneth Morgan's Welsh boxers can be found on p. 133 of his *Rebirth of a Nation*. On the background to my father's enthusiasm for boxing I have used the book edited by Peter Stead and Gareth Williams, *Wales and its Boxers: The*

Fighting Tradition, University of Wales Press, Cardiff, 2008, and Kenneth Morgan's *Rebirth of a Nation*. The description of mountain fighting in the valleys is by Clive Davies, 'Boxing in booths and on mountaintops' in *Glamorgan Family History Society Journal* 150, June 2023. The account of contemporary bare-knuckle boxing is from Wales Online, https://www.walesonline.co.uk/sport/boxing/wales-two-best-bare-knuckle-21324453.

On the Special Forces Club in London see Sean Rayment's *Tales from the Special Forces Club*. The quotation about the Official Secrets Act is on p. 5.

The data on holidaying abroad is from Kynaston, *Family Britain*, p. 212.

Kingsley Amis' reflections on his character Jim Dixon are reproduced in Kynaston, *Family Britain*, p. 360.

Germaine Greer's thoughts about why her father did not come to school speech nights are on pp. 89–90 of *Daddy, We Hardly Knew You*. Kynaston's description of fathers in the 1950s is from *Family Britain*, p. 595.

Chapter 7. Boredom and Frustration: From the City to the River Teifi

Robert Hughes' reflections on fly-fishing are to be found in his book, *A Jerk on One End: Reflections of a Mediocre Fisherman*, Ballantyne, New York, 1999. Ben Macintyre's thoughts about Hughes and fishing are to be found in *The Times*, 10 August 2012, 'How fishing got Robert Hughes hooked on art'.

For the story of my own attempt to avoid boredom see Chapter 1 in my *Imaginative Possession: Learning to Live in the Antipodes*, Upswell, 2021.

Chapter 9. A Family Reconsidered

The quote from Gwyn Williams comparing the Depression in Wales with the Irish famine is on p. 194 of *The Welsh in their History*.

Germaine Greer's thoughts about why a good man cannot live with secrets is from p. 171 of *Daddy, We Hardly Knew You*. The suggestion that Australians are not interested in anyone's background can be found on p. 113; her brother Barry appears on p. 303.

Laura Cumming's book is *On Chapel Sands: My Mother and Other Missing Persons*, Vintage, 2020. The quote about her Australian friend is on p. 241.

Acknowledgements

Without the lifelong dogged determination of Denzil Griffiths I would never have known anything about the first twenty-five years of my father's life and my Probert ancestors. After Denzil's death, his widow Audrey, his son Calvin and his daughter Mitch did their best to help me understand the Proberts of the Rhondda.

As I tried to bring Roy's life in the Rhondda into the light and then into perspective, I struck gold with local historians and librarians. I must thank Deborah Cooke from the Glamorgan Family History Society, housing historian Malcolm Fisk, and both Hywel Matthews and Simon Golding from the Treorchy Library which covers the Rhondda Cynon Taf County Borough. Hywel was bombarded with emails from me and dug up many useful pieces of information about the Proberts and the Knights from Ynyshir with unfailing grace. The Glamorgan Archives in Cardiff provided answers to the puzzle of Roy's schooling and university education. Oliver Snaith kindly dug out Roy's university history from the King's College London archives for me.

It was through Facebook, as I finished writing this book, that I found two living relatives (second cousins) who have memories of visiting their Aunty Minna at 44 Gynor Place before she died in 1954. The group calls itself 'Ynyshir and Wattstown People!' and many members tried to help me with my search for Roy's family. I regret that my dislike of Facebook prevented me from finding this group before I visited Ynyshir in 2023.

In researching Bill's war experiences, I would not have got very far without the generous help of Fred Judge at the British Military Intelligence Museum, and Paul McCue, expert on all things SOE. I must thank Jonathan Rée, whose father also worked for SOE during the war, for introducing me to Paul. Above all I would like to thank Colonel (Ret'd) Nick Fox OBE, who answered innumerable emails from me and even helped me find the family of the Royal Marine who was responsible for bringing my mother and father together in post-war Vienna. Both Paul and Nick are Trustees of the 'Secret WW2 Learning Network' (https://secret-ww2.net), a charity established to educate, commemorate and inspire people about the secret and clandestine aspects of the Second World War. Nick is also a Trustee of 'Libre Resistance' (https://www.libreresistance.com), an organisation created to keep alive the memory of the men and women who engaged in Special Operations Executive actions in France during the Second World War.

Without a lunch with David Torrance, I might never have worked out how to find the children of Bill's closest friend from his pre-war university days at Kings College, Dicky Flynn. Thanks to his research tips I found his daughter Dymphna Flynn who not only helped me work out what Bill was doing during a couple of mysteriously blank years before the war but shared with me the wonderful notes her oldest brother made about Dicky's war experiences – which included a lot of material about Bill. I am only sorry that Patrick Flynn died before we could get together on this hunt for our fathers. Dymphna not only filled in significant holes in the story but had herself been to see a memorial to Bill in the south-west of France. She also found and shared three poignant photographs of the young Bill and Dicky clowning around in Cairo as 'spycatchers', just before the Italian invasion of Egypt.

For many insights into Bill's business career, I am grateful for the wisdom of Chris Dick, son of the Chairman of Mitchell Cotts Group, who donated a complete set of the company magazine, *The Cottsman*, to the British Library where I was able to read them. Chris also kindly shared some of his mother's photographs of Bill taken while they were both touring pyrethrum fields and tea plantations in Ecuador in the 1960s.

On the research trip to England and Wales I was also able to visit the Middle East Centre, St Anthony's College, Oxford which holds the fascinating St John Philby Collection which Debbie Usher helped me navigate. I might not have found either of these invaluable resources had I not been coached by a proper historian, my ex-husband, Richard Gillespie. Not only did Richard help me track down many sources of valuable information in various archives, including The Cottsman, but he also did so many university inter-library orders for me that I could stop buying second hand books from World-of-Books at Goring-By-Sea. Richard has also been one of my most perceptive readers as the drafts developed, having met Bill both here in Melbourne and on several visits to the Béarn.

My ex-husband is not the only family member to have been exploited. I am incredibly lucky to have a son-in-law who knows everything one could possibly need to know about digitizing photographs. Ed Blake has wrought magic with my old photographs, shown me how to crop and edit images, and wrestled with some very difficult digital photographs from various archives. Daryl Leach from the Rhonnda Cynon Taf Library provided me with a perfect tif of the photograph of colliery craftsmen from 1890. I have made every endeavour to acknowledge the source of all photographs (though most are from my mother's old albums).

Many people encouraged me to write this book when I first started talking about my father's secret past, and without them I might never have believed it could interest a wider audience than my family and friends. This kind of encouragement is invaluable if you are attempting something you have never done before. Martha Macintyre read the whole manuscript and was a wise critic, pushing me to think harder about what it was like to have Bill as a father and pointing out clichés and grammatical errors. Old colleagues from my years at RMIT University, Martin Mowbray (who loves Welsh rugby and Male Voice Choirs) and John Murphy (who introduced me to Find My Past and ancestry research), have been consistent supporters, as has Jean Holland.

I asked everyone I knew who might have a significant memory of Bill to give me their honest impressions of him. This produced some quite startling stories, and I am grateful to John Bayley, David Turnbull, my cousin Michael Gush, Mary Bankes and above all, Martin O'Collins – who as a teenager saw the very best side of Bill.

My publisher Terri-ann White encouraged me from the moment I told her what I was up to and kept pushing for the historical context of Bill's life. My editor Nadine Davidoff pressed me to write more about what she called 'the emotional heart of the story' – how my understanding of my father was colliding with the things I began to discover, and how I had to think differently about him. I have been determined to avoid any simplistic psychologising or speculation, but I needed some kind of framework in which to place Bill's extraordinary life. In what I like to think of as a stroke of genius I contacted Phil Barnard, whom I have not seen for forty years – since we were both undergraduates at University College London. With a lifetime's research experience at Cambridge University's Medical Research Council Cognition and Brain Sciences Unit, Phil not only offered to read the whole manuscript but then a few days later spent ninety minutes on Skype talking to me about how to understand Bill's unusual ability to re-invent himself. I am incredibly grateful for Phil's insights, particularly because I have discovered that many people are quick to project onto Bill some theory of their own about his character that tells you more about them than my father.

My brothers Colin and William never flinched once I started on this project, despite my digging up all our youthful follies. They have allowed me to write freely, only challenging me when they wondered if I had the evidence to support my interpretations. As Colin told me, I should write whatever seemed important 'provided it was true'. He then read the whole manuscript line by line, sending me his perspective on key moments of interpretation. My brothers and I have learned a great deal about our father, and something at least about ourselves. I only wish our cousin Denzil were alive to see the result.

About Upswell

Upswell Publishing was established in 2021 by Terri-ann White as a not-for-profit press. A perceived gap in the market for distinctive literary works in fiction, poetry and narrative non-fiction was the motivation. In her years as a bookseller, writer and then publisher, Terri-ann has maintained a watch on literary books and the way they insinuate themselves into a cultural space and are then located within our literary and cultural inheritance. She is interested in making books to last: books with the potential to still be noticed, and noted, after decades and thus be ripe to influence new literary histories.

About this typeface

Book designer Becky Chilcott chose Foundry Origin not only as a strong, carefully considered, and dependable typeface, but also to honour her late friend and mentor, type designer Freda Sack, who oversaw the project. Designed by Freda's long-standing colleague, Stuart de Rozario, much like Upswell Publishing, Foundry Origin was created out of the desire to say something new.

www.ingramcontent.com/pod-product-compliance
Lightning Source LLC
Chambersburg PA
CBHW042141160426
43201CB00022B/2367